BALI

LOMBOK

First Edition
1994

TABLE OF CONTENTS

List of maps 6
Imprint 8

BALI

THE HISTORY AND CULTURE OF BALI 15
- by Bernd F. Gruschwitz
Introduction 15
Balinese society 31
Religion on the "Island of Gods and Demons" 38
The cycle of festivals 46
A guide to etiquette 49

AT THE PARTING OF THE WAYS 57
- by Berthold Schwarz
Denpasar 57
Kuta / Legian 62
Bukit Badung 68
Sanur 71
Lembongan 74

**CULTURE AND KITSCH IN BALI'S
HOLY LAND** 83
- by Berthold Schwarz
Badung 83
Tabanan 88
Gianyar 91
Bangli 106

A WILDLIFE RESERVE IN THE FOREST 113
- by Berthold Schwarz
Jembrana 113
West Buleleng 119
Volcanoes, temples and black sands 125
Singaraja 125
Lake Bratan 132
Around the volcano of Batur 133

UNDER THE VOLCANO 143
- by Berthold Schwarz
Klungkung 143
The south coast 148
Besakih: Mother of all temples 151
Amlapura 155

LOMBOK

THE HISTORY AND CULTURE OF LOMBOK . . . 165
- by Bernd F. Gruschwitz
Lombok society **167**
The religion of Lombok **169**
Festivals and ceremonies **171**
A guide to etiquette **173**

AUSTERE BEAUTY **177**
- by Bernd F. Gruschwitz
Western Lombok **177**
Senggigi and the "Gilis" **185**
Northern Lombok and Gunung Rinjani **189**
Eastern Lombok **194**
Southern Lombok **196**

FEATURES

Balinese cuisine **208**
- by Dorothee Krause
Balinese dances **212**
- by Dorothee Krause
Music and dance of Lombok **218**
- by Bernd F. Gruschwitz
Balinese Gamelan music **220**
- by Dorothee Krause
Wayang Kulit **223**
- by Dorothee Krause
Art and craftsmanship **226**
- by Bernd F. Gruschwitz
Ikat and double-Ikat **230**
- by Dorothee Krause
Encounter with a Batik-artist **233**
- by Barbara Müller
Cock-fighting **235**
- by Bernd F. Gruschwitz
Stick-fighting in Lombok **238**
- by Bernd F. Gruschwitz

GUIDELINES

Practical tips **245**
Language guide **250**
Authors and photographers **251**
Index **252**

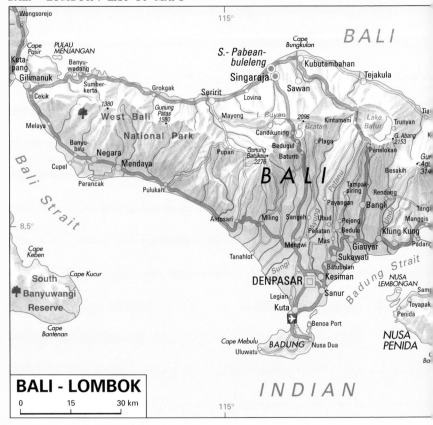

LIST OF MAPS

Bali - Lombok 6/7
Denpasar 58/59
Southern Bali 63
Kuta / Legian 64
Sanur Beach 71
Nusa Penida 74
Western Central Bali 84

Eastern Central Bali	93	Mount Batur	136
Western Bali	114	Eastern Bali	144/145
Northern Bali	126/127	Lombok	178/179
Lovina Beach	129	Ampenan / Mataram / Cakranegara	180

Nelles Guides

... get you going.

AVAILABLE TITLES

Australia
Bali / Lombok
Berlin and Potsdam
Brittany
California
Caribbean:
 Greater Antilles,
 Bermuda, Bahamas
Caribbean:
 Lesser Antilles
Crete
Cyprus
Egypt
Florida
Hawaii
Hungary
India North
India South
Indonesia West
 (Sumatra, Java, Bali, Lombok)
Kenya
Mexico
Morocco

Munich and Surroundings
Nepal
New York and New York State
New Zealand
Paris
Philippines
Provence
Spain North
Spain South
Thailand
Turkey

IN PREPARATION

Cambodia / Laos
Canada East
China
Malaysia
Moscow / St. Petersburg
Rome

BALI - LOMBOK
©Nelles Verlag GmbH, 80935 München
 All rights reserved

First Edition 1994
ISBN 3-88618-392-0
Printed in Slovenia

Publisher:	Günter Nelles	**English Editor**	Angus McGeoch
		Translation:	Jane Baunebridge,
Managing Editor:	Dr. Heinz Vestner		Angus McGeoch
Project Editor:	Bernd F. Gruschwitz	**Color**	
Editorial:	Eva Ambros	**Separation:**	Reproline, München
Cartography:	Nelles Verlag GmbH	**Printer**:	Gorenjski Tisk

- 01 -

INTRODUCTION TO BALI

For travelers from the west there is hardly an island in the world that stimulates such flights of the imagination as does Bali. And this is easy to understand. For nowhere else offers the wonderful prospect of palm-fringed beaches, with black sand as well as white, backed by a paradise of tropical vegetation, and terraced rice-paddies, where the hand of man has picturesquely enhanced the contours of nature. And this landscape is home to a delightful people, bound together by a shared veneration of their gods, whom they worship in colorful and dramatic rituals that have been faithfully observed for hundreds of years. It is true that mass-tourism and the modern infrastructure that goes with it have to some extent reduced this idyll to a more prosaic level, but so much of the old Bali has been preserved in all its richness and variety, that the visitor cannot help but succumb to its charm. And if you are staying more than a few days in this region, you should certainly visit the neighboring, though very dissimilar island of Lombok. There too you will find an incomparable, almost indescribably beautiful tropical landscape.

Geography

Both islands, Bali and Lombok, belong to the Republic of Indonesia, which comprises some 13,700 islands in all, making it the world's largest archipelago. It stretches north and south of the equator and forms a boundary between the Indian

Previous pages: Taking sacrificial gifts to the temple. Before a cock-fight. Traditional procession on a national holiday in Negara. Sunrise in the mountains around Lake Batur. The mythical bird-god Garuda.
Left: Ducks keep down insects and provide valuable fertiliser.

and Pacific Oceans. Indonesia reaches from Sumatra in the west to Irian Jaya (part of New Guinea) in the east, and, in the north, from Kalimantan, which occupies 70% of the island of Borneo, to the most southerly island of Roti, off Timor. If placed over a map of Europe, the archipelago would stretch from Gibraltar to the Urals, and from southern Sweden to Sicily. Indonesia's land area alone amounts to some 770,000 sq. miles (2 million sq.km), or four times the size of France, and the total coastline of all the islands is about 25,000 miles (40,000 km) – which is almost as great as the circumference of the earth.

Bali and Lombok are the most westerly of the Little Sunda Islands, which stretch eastward from Java as far as Timor. Bali lies roughly on latitude 8° S. and longitude 115° E. and with an area of 2147 sq. miles (5561 sq. km) it is more than twice the size of the state of of Luxembourg. From east to west it measures about 90 miles (145 km), and the maximum distance from north to south is around 53 miles (85 km). Bali is only separated from Java by a narrow stretch of water, barely 1 1/4 miles (2 km) wide, which was dry land until the end of the last ice-age. The province of Bali includes three other islands to the south-east, the largest of which is Nusa Penida. Bali's highest peak is the active volcano, Gunung Agung, rising to 10,308 ft (3142 m). To the west of it is a chain of volcanoes, five of which are more than 6500 ft (2000 m) high. On their north side the mountains drop steeply down to the sea, leaving room for only a narrow coastal strip. To the south lies a broad plateau through which rivers flowing southward have cut deep ravines, which have been terraced to create the rice-bowl of the island.

Lombok is separated from Bali by the Lombok Straits, which are nearly 1000 ft (300 m) deep in the middle. The island lies exactly midway between latitudes 8° and 9° S. and on longitude 116° E. It has

15

an area of 1829 sq. miles (4739 sq. km) making it about half the size of Cyprus. With Sumbawa, it forms the province of Nusa Tenggara Barat. The northern part of Lombok is a mountain chain from which the active volcano of Gunung Rinjani rises to 12,225 ft (3726 m).

Volcanic activity

Like the rest of Indonesia, Bali and Lombok owe their existence to the collision of two tectonic plates in the earth's crust, and the resultant volcanic activity. The formation of these islands began some 70 million years ago, when the relatively light Australo-Indian plate (the Sahul plate) drifted into the heavier south-east Asiatic plate (the Sunda plate), and was gradually pushed underneath it. This process, which still continues today, has caused the edge of the Sahul plate to melt at a depth of about 50 km. The mol-

ten magma rises up through cracks and fissures in the brittle fringe of the Sunda plate, and forms the chain of volcanoes which dominate the landscape of both islands. At the same time, part of the sedimentary rock of the Sahul plate has been ground off by the Sunda plate, so that in the southern plateaux you can see limestone hills dotted with rocks from the Sunda plate. Because of this tectonic turmoil, earth-tremors, earthquakes and volcanic eruptions are part of everyday life in Indonesia. In the whole of the archipelago there are some 200 active volcanoes. In this century, two of Bali's 10 active volcanoes have given the island a grim reminder of their presence with several devastating eruptions, while one on Lombok has been more muted.

Flora

Following their volcanic genesis, the islands gradually acquired their cloak of tropical rain-forest over a period of several million years. This unique ecosys-

Above: Extinct volcanoes. Right: The prospects for the rice-harvest look promising.

tem, still not fully explored today, never ceases to astonish with the richness and variety of its plant and animal species, but sadly human settlement is encroaching on it and pushing it back into more inaccessible regions. Today there are only a few areas in the foothills of the central volcanic chain, and in the national park in the west of Bali, which still have a dense cover of evergreen jungle. The true rain-forest now only accounts for about 10% of the island's land area. It has been replaced, in fertile areas, by extensive rice cultivation and other types of plantation. At lower altitudes, where the climate is hot and dry, the land has often turned to steppe-like plains, where nothing will grow but elephant-grass (*alang-alang*) and *lontar* palms.

Amid the great variety of flora one or two species of tree are so widespread as to be easily noticeable. In the middle of a village you will often see an ancient tree with roots spreading out from the trunk several feet *above* ground. This is the remarkable banyan-tree (*waringin*), which

is sacred to the Balinese and may not be cut down. According to legend, it was under just such a tree that the Buddha received his enlightenment. Around temples you will frequently find the shrub-like frangipani, whose propellor-shaped white or pink flowers are sometimes the only adornment left on the bare, silver-gray branches. Like the frangipani, the brilliant red or orange hibiscus flower is used to adorn temple-figures and their worshippers. Another beautiful shrub is the datura, with white or pink, bell-shaped flowers. The poinsettia, which in Europe is only thought of as a pot-plant, grows to the size of a tree in these parts, as do the rubber-plants, ferns and bamboos. The air is often filled with the scent of jasmine, and the eye is ravished by the bougainvillea's sea of color. Lakes and ponds are carpeted with water-lilies and the incomparable Indian lotus. One is struck by the profusion of orchids, which can be seen at any market. Make sure you bring along an identification guide to tropical plants.

17

Fauna

When the British zoologist Sir Alfred Russell Wallace saw the deep and fast-flowing current of the Straits of Lombok, he claimed that this was the boundary between the fauna of Asia and that of Australia. Later scientists have modified this notion, so that both islands have now been identified as forming part of a transitional zone known as *Wallacea*. It is nevertheless a remarkable fact that east of Bali none of the larger land mammals, such as tiger or rhinoceros, are to be found, while on the islands to the west of Lombok, there are none of the marsupials that are typical of Australian wildlife.

Today, however, you will look in vain for the Balinese tiger, a small cousin of the Indian and Asian carnivore. The last reported sighting of this creature was as long ago as 1937. Much the same is true of the rhinoceros.

Above: The only Orang-Utans left on Bali are in the zoo. Right: Banteng at work.

A few of the shapely, doe-eyed, wild red cattle called *banteng* are still said to be roaming the West Bali National Park, but their smaller domesticated relative is a common sight in the countryside. Around many temples and sacred groves you will come across the gray Javanese monkeys, but you should approach them with caution: they can easily snatch glasses or ear-rings from the unwary tourist. On Lombok, in the Rinjani region around Tetebatu, black long-tailed monkeys are still to be seen.

Among the larger animals which add color to village life on both islands are the pot-bellied pig, and two species of water-buffalo, which are used to pull ploughs and carts. The menfolk of the village are very proud of their fighting-cocks, often with brightly dyed feathers, which crow at passers-by from their wicker cages. Every morning and evening you will see crowds of ducks waddling along, driven by a duck-herder with a feather broom, through the meadows to or from the rice-fields. Indoors there are two species of gecko to keep down the swarms of mosquitoes. These shy creatures, though often as much as a foot (30 cm) long, stay hidden during the day, behind pictures or mirrors, and only appear at dusk; and if a Balinese hears the gecko's sharp *to-keh* sound nine times in a row, it means he will have happiness and prosperity.

A particularly remarkable species of bird is the Balinese white starling. It can be seen on Nusa Penida, in the West Bali National Park and often, sad to say, in cages. There are only something between 60 and 200 surviving examples of the species in the wild, and extinction stares them in the face. In Petulu, central Bali, a spectacle not to be missed is that of flocks of white herons returning from the rice-fields every evening to roost.

Another extraordinary phenomenon are the myriad squeaking bats seen in the Goa Lawah caves, on the south coast.

The island economy

In spite of the boom created by the influx of tourists, now in excess of 1 million a year, the backbone of Bali's economy is still its highly developed but traditional agriculture. About one-fifth of the arable land is given over to rice-growing, in water-logged paddy-fields. These are usually built in terraces on the sides of valleys and produce two harvests a year. An even larger proportion of the land, about a quarter, is cultivated in the normal way, and being reliant on natural rainfall, only produces one crop each year. In the highlands there are plantations of coffee, tobacco, fruit, vegetables and cloves. By the sea the main sources of income are fishing, salt-panning and the harvesting of sea-weed.

About 10% of the population are employed in the tourist sector. Tourism has also spawned small businesses, mainly in textile manufacturing and retailing. To date no industries of any great size or significance have developed on the island.

Very sensibly, the Balinese authorities are carefully monitoring tourist growth and restricting development to certain defined areas such as Nusa Dua.

Lombok has remained, apart from a cluster of tourist hotels near Senggigi, a purely agricultural community, and one which is subject to periodic famines – more so than Bali – particularly in the dry belt of the south-east. The main farm products are similar to those of Bali. Remarkably, though, tobacco is the second largest agricultural export after rice. The most important of Lombok's exports, by value, is volcanic pumice-stone. Since 1985 it has been shipped to Hong Kong where it is used, among other things, in the manufacture of fashionable stone-washed jeans.

From humble beginnings, tourism has created a veritable gold-rush in the west of the island. In Senggigi, buildings are going up wherever you look. The figure of 100,000 visitors a year, which once seemed like a distant ambition, had already been reached in 1991.

HISTORY AND CULTURE
OF BALI

Prehistory and early history

Until human remains were unearthed in East Africa, which could be attributed to an even earlier date, the Indonesian archipelago was considered to be the cradle of mankind. In 1891, a skeleton had been discovered near Trinil on the river Solo in Java, which was identified as that of an ape-like man who walked upright - the scientific name is *pithecanthropus erectus*. However, a more precise classification showed it to be a *homo erectus*, whose relatives evolved, as we now know, around 1.6 million years ago. The age of the biped known as Java Man, is put at 700,000 years. From this we can assume that in the early palaeolothic period ancestors of *homo sapiens* walked upright through the Indonesian rainforest looking for food. Their territory would have included Bali, which was at that time still linked to Java by an isthmus. In the late palaeolithic age, around 300,000 years ago, people of negrito and Melanesian race began to settle on the island. They were probably still only hunter-gatherers and fishermen. Palaeolithic axe-heads and other stones, sharpened on one side, have been found near Sembiran in northern Bali.

From about the third millennium B.C. proto-Malay and early-Malay peoples, ethnically akin to the Mongols, arrived from the Asian mainland and mixed with the aboriginal inhabitants, or else drove them into the mountains, the jungle, or on to islands to the east. About 100 gravestones and the remains of a neolithic set-

Left: Gilded statue of a god, in the house of the artist Blanco in Ubud.

tlement from this period were discovered after the Second World War near Cekik in the west of Bali. Earlier some stone axes and potsherds had been found.

The next wave of migration took place from about 300 B.C. when Austronesian Malays came from south China and the area that is now North Vietnam. They brought metal-working skills with them to Bali. It was probably these people who also introduced new agricultural methods, notably that of growing rice in water. The megaliths to be seen in many of the temples date from this pre-Hindu period. The most impressive relic of the time is the Moon Drum, said to be the largest bronze gong in the world to be cast in a single piece. It is in the temple of Penataran Sasih at Pejeng, in a rather inaccessible position. The ornamentation of the gong and the way it has been worked link it to the Bronze Age Dongson culture of North Vietnam. However, it is not clear whether it was actually brought from there, or made in Bali. Once again the incomers drove the indigenous population into the mountain regions, where they live to this day, under the name of Bali-Aga, and pursue their own form of religion, which has scarcely been influenced by Hinduism.

The Indianisation of Bali

Over 2000 years ago Indian traders reached the archipelago, attracted by its wealth of minerals and spices, and Bali became part of a trading network which reached as far west as the Mediterranean and the Roman Empire. At the same time merchants came from China, and with them Buddhist pilgrims seeking the holy places of their religion in western Indonesia. As early as the 2nd century A.D. the existence of states established in Java and Sumatra is attested in Chinese documents, and a little later in Indian texts and in the works of the Greek geographer, Ptolemy. But earlier still, in about 300

B.C., the Indian epic, *Ramayana*, talks of a "Golden Isle" *(Suvarnadvipa)*, which can be identified as Sumatra. The name gives some clue to the kind of goods that were exported from Indonesia at that time: these were products of high value, not only gold, but other precious metals, as well as tortoise-shell, medicinal herbs, aromatic woods and spices. Chronicles concerning relations with China frequently mention Indonesian emissaries at the imperial court, who were no doubt soliciting the emperpor's support as a counterbalance to excessive political influence from the Indian sub-continent.

In the wake of the Indian traders came Hindu priests, scholars and artists who established themselves at the courts of the Indonesian rulers and were soon setting the pattern of religious and cultural life. This is why the earliest inscriptions to be found in Indonesia are written in Sanskrit, the priestly language of the

Brahmans. The script they used, called the *Pallava* script, after a Tamil dynasty, came from India.

The steady stream of pilgrims which is known to have started in the 7th century, favoured the spread of Buddhism. At the same time as Charlemagne, in Europe, was commissioning the building of his modest Palatine Chapel in Aachen, a Buddhist temple on a vast scale, the Borobudur, was being completed in Java. But, as if the strength of Buddhism had been drained away by this great achievement, it began to decline soon afterwards and a renaissance of Hinduism took its place. Hardly more than 50 years later, a huge Hindu temple complex was built as a counterpart to Borobudur, at Prambanan, also in central Java.

Until well into the 10th century, written evidence of events in Bali remains rather vague. Early Chinese sources mention a kingdom called *P'o-Li*, which presumably refers to Bali. Not until the year 930 or thereabouts, when the Javanese king Sindok extended his power to the

Above: The bronze gong of Pejeng – it is the largest in the world cast in a single piece.

east of that island, does Bali make an appearance in history. There were already many family connections between the princely families of Bali, and the dynasty of King Sindok, who ruled the kingdom of Mataram, in Java. The expansionist ambitions of Mataram soon led to rivalry and disputes with the mighty Srivijayan empire of Sumatra, culminating in a battle in which Mataram was heavily defeated, its capital laid waste, and the king put to death. At this point, the high priests, concerned for the future survival of Mataram, sought a new king and their choice fell on the 28-year-old Balinese prince, Airlangga (sometimes spelt: Erlangga), who was living in seclusion in a monastery. His father was a Balinese ruler, Udayana II, and his mother the Javanese princess Mahendradatta, a great-granddaughter of the same King Sindok, who in 930 had made Mataram a center of power in Indonesia.

As the new king, Airlangga ruled both eastern Java and Bali, and his reign is considered the first cultural flowering in the region to have involved Bali. Inscriptions in the ancient Balinese language began to appear from the 9th century, and from the 11th century onwards they rank alongside those in ancient Javanese. It is from this era that we have the most impressive of Bali's archaeological monuments: Goa Gajah, a group of monasteries in Bali's "Holy Land" around Pejeng, and Gunung Kawi, a temple built in a style reminiscent of Indian sacred architecture. Balinese mythology pays particular attention to the mother of Airlangga and assigns her a scarcely flattering role. An outbreak of plague, which cast a shadow over the final years of Airlangga's reign, is attributed to the evil machinations of this embittered widow, whose name is Rangda. Ever since then, she has represented the embodiment of everything that threatens the life of the village community, and spectacular rituals are performed at regular intervals, in

which she is fought off by the good animal spirit of the village, the Barong. Legend has it that she is buried in the temple of Bukit Dharma, near Kutri.

Before Airlangga handed over the reins of power, he divided the kingdom between his two sons. The one who inherited the territory of eastern Java, known as Kediri, after its capital city, achieved dominance by force of arms. Bali went its separate way. However, a Javanese king of the rival Singhasari dynasty, named Kertanagara, seized the throne of Kediri, and in 1284 sent an expeditionary force to reconquer Bali. Until then, the center of political power in Bali lay between the rivers Petanu and Pakerisan, in Bedulu and Pejeng. Only eight years later Kertanagara was himself ousted by political rivals and Bali once again became independent. From the dynastic wranglings in east Java, Kertanagara's stepson, named Raden Vijaya, emerged as the new king. He went on to found the Majapahit empire, whose influence extended throughout south-east Asia, until the arrival of the Europeans.

With the expansion of his power, in 1343 Bali once again fell under the sovereignty of Java. The occupation was led by Gajah Mada, who as the king's chief minister exercised royal authority. Now part of the Majapahit empire, Bali followed Java's example and adopted Indian customs and religion once again. From 1343 the islanders began, slowly and unwillingly at first, to accept the civilisation which still exists in Bali today. Artistic traditions, both indigenous and introduced from abroad, were nurtured in the courts of the vassal kings of Bali, refined and brought to a peak of perfection. Hinduism blended with native beliefs to produce the time-honoured rituals and festivities which are so much part of Balinese life that we cannot imagine the island without them. In the ancient Javanese epic *Nagarakertagama,* Bali is described as "that other island, which in

all its customs and traditions concurs with Java." This refers, of course, to the pre-Islamic Java.

In the 15th century the Islamic colony of Malacca, on the mainland peninsula of Malaya, opposite Sumatra, was already establishing itself as the main trading center of the region, a fact which sounded the death-knell for the Majapahit empire. At the same time, the Islamic faith was spreading rapidly through south-east Asia, not least because it challenged the Hindu caste-system and thus won many converts among the non-aristocratic merchant class. When the Majapahit empire finally collapsed in 1520, and most of the bastions of Hinduism fell to Islam, the elite of the Hindu priests and artists sought refuge on Bali. Under the leadership of Batu Renggong the island became in 1520, for the first time in its history, a united and independent kingdom. It was

Above: A terra-cotta figure from Majapahit.
Right: Dutch sailing-ships at anchor in Batavia harbour, 1657.

now Bali's turn to exercise its power over other islands and indeed Lombok, Sumbawa and parts of eastern Java were obliged to submit to Bali's rule. For two centuries the political and cultural capital of Bali was at Gelgel, near Klungkung, which continued until the 1950s to maintain its claim, at least nominally, to be the intellectual center of the island.

From the arrival of the first Europeans until full colonization

For a long time Bali remained a backwater as far as the Europeans were concerned. For one thing, no-one knew what natural wealth the island held, and for another it was guarded by reefs and thus very inaccessible to ships. Furthermore Bali was densely populated, which made it less suitable than, for example, Sumatra for establishing large-scale plantations.

The first European seafarers to sight Bali were Portuguese, and the island appears as *Java Minor* on charts from the beginning of the 16th century. One of the first to land there looking for treasure was the English privateer, Sir Francis Drake. Five years after Drake, in 1585, some Portuguese attempted to set up a trading-station there, but their ship went aground off Bukit Badung, and only five of the crew survived. Then, in 1597, the little Dutch fleet of Cornelis de Houtman dropped anchor, and he and his exhausted crew were charmed by the island paradise, which they christened *Young Holland*. Two of the Dutchmen stayed ashore, married Balinese girls and learned the language. One of them later looked after Dutch interests, acting as a middle-man. For the time being, however, the Netherlands did not set up a permanent colony. Even when the Dutch East India Company was created in 1602, it was content with an arms-length trading relationship, in which the Rajas of Bali distinguished themselves by selling their subjects as slaves in exchange for

opium for their courtiers and nobles. This trade, in which Chinese merchants tried to challenge the Dutch monopoly, lasted more than 200 years. During this time the Dutch limited themselves to driving off Balinese incursions into east Java and keeping foreign competitors at bay.

During the Napoleonic Wars the Netherlands were briefly incorporated into the French empire, and Britain, in the person of Sir Stamford Raffles, who later founded Singapore, expressed an interest in establishing a base in the Far East. Thus, in 1814, in his capacity as Governor of Java, he paid a visit to Bali. The Congress of Vienna restored to the Netherlands their former colonial possessions, but suspicion of Britain's ambitions drove the Dutch colonial administration to take a firmer grip on Bali.

After long negotiations, which the Balinese rulers cleverly managed time and again to delay, Dutch troops finally landed on northern Bali in 1846. The excuse put forward by the Dutch on later occasions, was that islanders were taking flotsam which had come ashore from wrecked ships, and treating it as their legal property. The Dutch arrived with 58 ships and 3000 men, including 1700 infantrymen, only 400 of whom were Europeans. The expeditionary force, equipped with rifles and mortars, came ashore at Buleleng. They were faced by some 15,000 Balinese, armed mainly with spears and *kris* (large Malay daggers). However, the Dutch succeeded in capturing Singaraja and destroying the royal palace. When they advanced on the secret hiding-place of the Raja's brother, Prince Gusti Ketut Jilantik, in Jagaraga, in order to take complete possession of northern Bali, a Danish merchant named Mads Lange, who ran a private business empire from Kuta in the south of the island, stepped in and offered to act as mediator. With his help the Dutch succeeded in getting the Raja of Buleleng to sign a treaty whereby he acknowledged the supreme authority of the Dutch government in Batavia (now Jakarta). In order to enforce this treaty and to extract a fine of 400,000

guilders, the Dutch established a military garrison on Bali. However, the resistance of the Balinese was by no means broken, and found a charismatic leader in Prince Gusti Ketuk Jilantik, who, as soon as the main Dutch force had left the island, made it his job to see that the treaty was not adhered to. Consequently, when the Raja of Buleleng had apparently broken the treaty, the Dutch returned in 1848 in order to force him into submission by military means, and there was another pitched battle. This time they marched on Jagaraga with 2400 men, 775 of them European, but they were caught in an ambush which Jilantik and his 16,000 warriors had prepared for them. The Balinese now had 1500 rifles and 25 cannon, and killed 264 of the invaders, as well as losing 2000 of their own men. The Dutch fled back to their ships and the Raja of

Above: The ritual suicide of Prince of Badung and his retinue. Right: The family of a Dutch colonial official.

Buleleng had certainly won a battle, but not the war.

Only a year later another, even larger Dutch force appeared on the north coast, and this time they succeeded in capturing Jagaraga. The Raja of Buleleng and his brother Jilantik withdrew to the south. The Dutch crowned their victory by turning their attention to other kingdoms. With the help of 4000 soldiers provided by the Raja of Lombok, a client of the Netherlands, the kingdom of Karangasem was subdued in 1850. Unable to face the hopeless situation, the Raja of Karangasem led his entire entourage in an act of mass suicide *(puputan)*.

Previously, in Jagaraga, the wife of Prince Jilantik had led all the women of the royal court of Bululeng in a similar tragic and terrible *puputan*.

The highest ranking kingdom in Bali, called Klungkung, was initially spared from conquest by the Dutch. Meanwhile 30,000 warriors, led by the Raja of Buleleng and Prince Jilantik, had assembled in the city of Klungkung. The Dutch sol-

diers, already weakened by an epidemic of dysentery, suffered heavy losses in a night battle, and would have retreated, if some of the Raja of Lombok's guerillas had not succeeded in getting into Klungkung, where they killed the Raja of Buleleng and poisoned Jilantik.

The Dutch were making their dispositions for a final attack on Klungkung, when the Dane, Mads Lange, intervened once again, because he could see that his mercantile empire would be threatened if the Dutch took over the island. He persuaded another Balinese ruler, the Raja of Tabanan, to step in with his troops and tip the scales against the invaders. The Dutch, faced with the prospect of having to fight on two fronts, negotiated a truce with the Dewa Agung (ruler) of Klungkung and his ally. This was Mads Lange's finest hour.

The Dutch now briskly set about consolidating their power in the territories which they had been able to occupy. In "their" principalities, they installed regents who were, in the main, members of old princely families, well-disposed towards the Dutch, and supervised by local colonial administrators known as *controleurs*. Dutch troops continued to play a role, whenever the struggle for power between different Balinese states threatened to undermine colonial security and authority. In 1882 the Dutch established their capital in the port of Buleleng, also known as Singaraja. In their sphere of influence they banned the Hindu ritual of burning widows on their dead husbands' pyres; and they decreed that Balinese women should always keep their breasts covered in public – something which hitherto had, surprisingly enough, only been required of prostitutes. Notwithstanding, the burning of widows continued, as did the plundering of wrecked ships, which had also been forbidden by the Dutch.

In 1906 an outbreak of plundering prompted the Dutch finally to subject the southern part of the island to their authority. They dispatched a disproportionately large force against the Prince of Ba-

27

dung, who had refused to make any reparations for goods stolen from a Chinese merchant-ship. The prince had no alternative but to seek death with honor, and he and 600 members of his court committed *puputan*, either at their own hand, or by walking into a hail of Dutch bullets.

The Raja of Tabanan, who had cherished the hope of being appointed regent, received the devastating news that his palace had been burnt down and that he was to be exiled to Lombok, whereupon he also took his own life.Two years later, in 1908, Klungkung fell to the colonial troops. Again there was scarcely any resistance, and the Dewa Agung entreated his gods in vain to make the earth open and swallow up the enemy "long-noses" and their native lackeys. Helpless, he and 200 of his courtiers were forced to choose ceremonial suicide. Bali now belonged indisputably to the Netherlands.

Left: Gusti Bagus, Raja of Karangasem (in about 1920). Right: The German painter and musician, Walter Spies.

The road to independence and beyond

In the decades that followed, the Dutch extended their administrative system over the whole of Bali. This is the period when the myth of Bali was born. In 1920, a German doctor, Gregor Krause, who had been working in Bali in the years up to the First World War, published an illustrated book about the island, which for the first time gave Europeans an evocative and alluring glimpse of this last paradise on earth. From now on Bali was visited by an ill-assorted procession of artists, anthropologists, drop-outs, jet-setters...in fact anyone who was curious to discover the legendary island for themselves. Foremost among them was the German painter and musician, Walter Spies, whose home at Campuan (Ubud) became a place of pilgrimage for eminent and not-so-eminent visitors. To the outside world it seemed that every Balinese, be he artist or peasant, was somehow living in perfect harmony with the cosmos. In fact, these years saw the beginning of a new wave of Balinese artistic activity which showed clear traces of assimilated European influences, without denying its ancient cultural heritage.

The outbreak of the Second World War brought all this to an end. In February 1942 Japanese troops invaded the island without encountering any resistance. The Dutch forces, together with most of the civilian European population had already been evacuated to Australia.

In 1945, following the capitulation of Japan, an Indonesian independence movement was launched under the leadership of Ahmed Sukarno and Mohammed Hatta, who later became Sukarno's vice-president. During the war years, these two men had, in collaboration with the Japanese, set up an armed militia to take the place of the Dutch authorities.

The Dutch now tried to reclaim their former colony, but found themselves up against determined resistance both from an ill-assorted liberation movement comprising right-wing nationalists and communists, and from the anti-colonial nation which had defeated Japan in the Pacific war – the United States.

However, in Bali at least, the Dutch overcame this resistance without much difficulty. In November 1946 a detachment of less than 100 Indonesian soldiers were cornered near Marga and fought to the very last man under their commander, Ngurah Rai. However, in Java, it was the nationalists who finally prevailed, not without the help of the USA. In 1949 the independence of Indonesia was declared, though the republic continued to owe formal allegiance to the Queen of the Netherlands until 1954.

Even after independence, the right and left-wing factions continued to wage a bloody and treacherous civil war, from which Sukarno eventually emerged victorious. This charismatic leader, whose mother was Balinese, contrived to stay in power by playing off conservatives against communists in a series of cleverly managed coalitions. On the international stage, Sukarno stood alongside Tito, Nasser and Nehru at the head of the group of non-aligned nations, who held an importance conference at Bandung in 1955 and proclaimed a "third way" between the two dominant power-blocks of East and West.

Internally, after a brief honeymoon with democratic elections, Sukarno ushered in a dictatorship under the name of "Guided Democracy." However, political tensions remained as acute as ever, between the still rather feudal local rulers, and the communists, who had won many supporters in the impoverished and over-populated islands, Bali among them. Nevertheless, Sukarno personally enjoyed making frequent visits to Bali with his large retinue. These vistits were much resented, since the local population were expected to provide large amounts of free food, gifts and even, it was rumoured, their daughters. To make matters worse, in 1962 there was a plague of unusually large rats which ravaged the crops. Then, in March 1963, the sacred Mount Agung erupted with tremendous force, blanketing eastern Bali with ash and lava.

There was an attempted military coup in Jakarta in 1965, which provoked massive retaliation against suspected communists throughout Indonesia. Bali, being a Hindu society in a predominantly Moslem nation, and known to have separatist ambitions, was singled out for particularly vicious retribution, in which tens of thousands of civilians lost their lives. At the end of it all, Sukarno's position was permanently weakened, and the reins of power were taken over by the army strong-man, General Suharto. With his policy of a "New Order," which still prevails today, he assumed dictatorial powers, at the same time opening up Indonesia to foreign investment, much of which, ironically, comes from Japan.

BALINESE SOCIETY

Balinese society is still based on the virtually self-sufficient agricultural village community, and yet this traditional culture has achieved a remarkable aesthetic sophistication in its artistic expression. Amazingly, this culture has survived untarnished by the influences of the outside world, modern entertainment media, urban and commercial pressures, and the relentless expansion of tourism. The rhythm of Balinese life is still determined by rice-growing. The planting, irrigating and harvesting of the crop twice a year requires organisation on a scale that goes beyond individual families and involves the whole community. Thus the majority of the population play their part in this agrarian cycle, and in the rituals which accompany it. In fact, everyone is obliged to make his or her specific contribution to the communal organisation of food production. The success of the harvest depends on each villager doing a spell in the fields and helping on the administrative side, as well as observing the time-honoured religious ceremonies.

The Balinese universe

Generally speaking, the horizon of the traditional country villages is a narrow one. Their world is limited to contacts with the surrounding villages, the nearest market-town, and those temples which have an importance for all the islanders, and to which they occasionally make pilgrimages. Before the advent of radio and TV, the Balinese knew virtually nothing of the outside world. Though brought up on the Indian epics, like the *Ramayana*, acted out in shadow-theater and dance, they believe these to be ancient Indonesian, or even Balinese legends.

Left: Important religious festivals are always attended by a Pedanda, or high priest.

The sea which surrounds the island is strange and rather frightening to the Balinese, and so one often finds people from other races, such as the Bugis, settling on the coast and making a living from seafaring and fishing. Although water in general is sacred to the Balinese, in their tripartite physical and spiritual cosmos, the sea represents the home of demons and spirits unfriendly to man.

At the opposite pole, so to speak, are the soaring volcanic mountains, first and foremost Gunung Agung, which is to Bali what Fujiyama is to Japan. This is the dwelling-place of the gods, deifications of the forces of nature and of ancestral spirits. Between the mountains and the sea lies the world of man, the bone of contention over which the forces of Good and Evil are in continuous strife.

This cosmology determines the whole attitude of the Balinese, even down to the details of everyday life. They do not orientate themselves by the abstract concepts of north, south, east and west, but rather by sunrise and sunset, mountains and sea. The mountain-sea relationship is critical: anything which is in the direction of the mountains from where the observer is standing, is considered closer to the gods and therefore holy; while anything that lies in the direction of the sea is thought to be closer to the underworld and hence impure. (Remember that the mountain range stretches right across Bali from east to west, and the greater part of the island lies to their south.) Not only is every village laid out according to these co-ordinates, but the same priciples apply to individuals. Thus the holiest part of the body is the head – and for this reason it is generally thought bad manners to touch a Balinese on the head; but the feet are the most impure part of the body, since they touch the earth, which in turn is close to the underworld. For this reason new-born babies are for several weeks kept away from the ground, or are only allowed to touch it lightly.

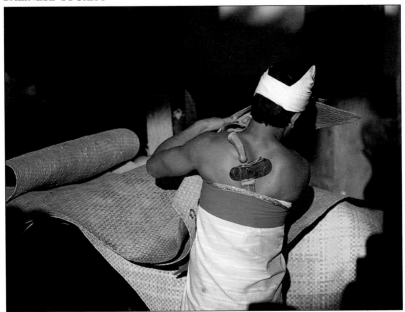

The caste system

One fact above all others governs the social hierarchy of Bali, and that is the adoption of the very rigid social structure which the the invading Aryan people brought with them from the Indian sub-continent. This Indian influence reached its height when the Hindu ruling class of the Majapahit empire of Java fled to Bali before the onslaught of Islam in the early 16th century. From that time onward, Balinese society was, and still is, divided into two. The great mass of the population, probably more than 90%, belongs to the lowest caste, the *Sudra* or *Jaba,* which consists in the main of peasants and manual laborers. Above it is an upper stratum, which itself is divided into three castes, collectively known as the *Triwangsa.* In theory, the supreme caste is the *Brahmana,* comprising the priests

Above: The kris embodies the authority of the male. Right: Women of the lowest caste often have to do the hardest work.

and learned scribes, whose names always include the title *Ida Bagus* for men and *Ida Ayu* or *Ida Dayu* for women. Their knowledge of the hallowed rituals of their religion and the exclusive right to bless the holy water, gives them a permanently privileged position in society. In political terms, however, the highest caste is the *Ksatriya* or *Satriya.* This is made up of the senior members of the princely families of Klungkung, Gianyar, Bangli, Badung and Tabanan, who at various times in history have in fact been equal or superior to the Brahmanas. The titles borne by the male members of the caste are *Anak Agung, Cokorda, Cokorda Gede, Dewa, Dewa Agung* or *Ratu,* while the women are called *Anak Agung Istri* or *Dewa Ayu.* The lowest of the three noble castes is the *Wesya,* to which high-ranking warriors and rich merchants once belonged. Membership of all three noble castes is only possible through inheritance. The *Wesya* are distinguishable by the names *I Gusti* (male) and *I Gusti Ayu* (female).

Bali differs from India in that this hereditary class division has never been regarded as absolutely immutable, and today, under pressure from political and economic change, especially in the towns, the system is gradually breaking down. Nevertheless, one encounters traces of its influence again and again. For example, at ceremonies a Sudra will always avoid sitting higher than a member of a noble caste. But the relationship between the castes is shown most noticeably in the highly complicated modes of address used in conversation.

Each caste has its own special language, which the caste member abandons as soon as he starts talking to a member of another caste. This results in the odd, but apparently accepted phenomenon whereby a noble will address a Sudra in the latter's idiom, while the Sudra in turn has to speak to the noble in *his* own eductated form of language, of which the Sudra has only a very limited mastery. However, use of the official language of all Indonesia, *Bahasa Indonesia*, has

become compulsory and serves as a neutral means of communication between castes, thus having a levelling effect on Balinese society.

Alongside the caste divisions, certain professions have achieved a special status. It is worth mentioning in particular the blacksmiths, whose ability to work with fire and molten metal was once cloaked in secrecy. The *Pande*, as they are called, have their own temples and graveyards. Another sign of their social recognition is that when members of the noble Triwangsa talk to them they use the High Balinese language.

The village

The arrangement of houses and streets in a village follows the same principles all over the island and is based on the east-west and mountain-sea axes. The main street always runs from the seaward side *(kelod)* towards the mountains *(kaja)* and is crossed by side-streets running east to west *(kangin-kauh)*. Along the

33

tower which houses the *kulkul*, a deep-toned drum that is beaten with different rhythms, depending on whether it is announcing a village assembly or a temple festival, warning of an accident or disaster, summoning help or mourning the death of a villager. Sometimes the *kulkul* hangs over a platform in the spreading branches of a *waringin* tree, towering above the village square. In the shade of this tree, also known as the banyan, a market is held every three days. This is where the womenfolk come into their own. Any money they earn from selling at the market, they can keep for their own personal use.

Towards the sea, at a distance from the village, stands the temple of the dead, the *pura dalem*, which is dedicated to the underworld and usually has an unfenced burial-ground and cremation area. This is where Durga, the goddess of death, is worshipped.

main street are rows of identical farm-steads, enclosed by rectangular walls, which mark out the territory of the individual family from that of the village community as a whole.

The village is divided into three zones, corresponding to the Balinese cosmos, and each zone has its own temple. These zones symbolize, in an abstract way, the three stages of human existence: birth, life and death. Nearest the mountains, and also usually to the east of the village, is the temple of birth or beginning, *pura puseh*. It is dedicated to the god Brahma, creator of the world. In the middle of the village, which embraces the daily life of mankind, not just symbolically but in a very practical sense, stands the village temple of *pura desa*, and beside it the meeting-hall or *bale agung*. Very often there is also a *wantilan*, the place where cock-fights are held. Then there is a

Above: The Banyan tree in the middle of a village is sacred to the Balinese. Right: Tidying up the village before a festival.

The Banjar

The inhabitants of a village belong to various associations of a functional kind, the largest of which is called the *banjar*. Larger villages are made up of several banjars, each of which include about 70 families. The banjar is a kind of self-governing committee, to which any adult villager can belong, regardless of trade or occupation. In this context "adult" means that the person must be married and in most cases should also have a first child. When a man joins a banjar, his wife automatically becomes a member as well. Interestingly, the younger generation form the bulk of the banjar, and parents step down when their son becomes a member. The group meets roughly once a month to discuss and reach decisions on village affairs. It is a duty to belong to a banjar and to take part in its meetings. Decisions can only be reached by a unanimous vote. Consequently meetings can be very protracted and there is a lengthy search for a

compromise that everyone is happy with. This of course means that in any given village major changes can only take place very gradually.

The principal task of the banjar is to see to the building and maintenace of the village infrastructure. Every member is obliged to help with the physical work, if for example the meeting-hall has to be repaired, a new bathing-place constructed, a religious festival held or the village cleaned and tidied up. Celebrations within a particular family are shared by the whole banjar, whether it be the filing of teeth, a wedding, the first birthday of a new member of the family, or the burning of the dead. On such days as these the festivities are accompanied by the village *gamelan* orchestra playing instruments owned by the banjar. When the time comes round for certain regular religious ceremonies, the banjar's masks and costumes are produced from an ancient and much-weathered shrine, dusted off and put to use in the dramatic re-creation of, for example, the conflict between Barong and Rangda, the opposing spirits between whom the world is held in equilibrium. In this way the village recovers its own inner tranquility, for a while at least.

The Subak

There is a specific association of rice-growers, called the *subak*. Each one includes all the farmers whose fields have been assigned to one irrigation system. On average a subak has about 200 members, which means they are larger than a banjar. They meet every 35 days under the leadership of an honorary chairman and discuss all matters relevant to rice cultivation. In the subak, as in the banjar, the priciple of unanimity prevails, and the decisions relate to problems of irrigation, fertilisation, the use of insecticides, and the labor required for the harvest. The observation of traditional ceremonies is also on the agenda. The most important and costly measures concern the building and regular repair of the irrigation canals and retaining-dykes.

Every subak traditionally maintains its own temple dedicated to the rice-goddess Dewi Sri. She who is said to reign over the rice itself is worshipped with a very special reverence, so that the harvest may prosper. Being so imbued with divinity, rice is sacred to the Balinese and is therefore considered as a most suitable food to be used as an offering to other gods.

The family and the farmstead

The Balinese villagers live in extended families in their own farmsteads, shielded by walls from demons and from the rest of the village. The extended family includes the paternal grandparents, parents, children and daughters-in-law, since adult sons remain at home until they have acquired a farmstead of their own. In addition, there are often widowed or destitute relatives. Once their basic livelihood is assured, the principal aim of any couple is to produce children. Childless bachelors are regarded as failures. There is a strong tradition of having large families, though recently the state has been trying to bring down the birth-rate with a family planning campaign, which is endeavoring to restrict couples to two children each.

Although every new baby is greatly cherished and protected in the first months of its life, there is almost no individuality when it comes to name-giving. The principle is to name the child according to its position in the family. The first-born, whether boy or girl, is nearly always called *Wayan*, or more rarely, *Gede* or *Putu*. The second child is called *Made* or occasionally *Kadek* or *Nengah*, the third is *Nyoman* or *Komang* and the fourth is called *Ketut*. For subsequent children, the naming cycle starts again with Wayan, or else they are all simply called Ketut. To differentiate between boys and girls, an *I* or *Ni* is put in front of the name.

Above: Rural peace away from the main highway. Right: The women of Bali have to combine many different roles.

The more prosperous the family, the more pets and farm-animals they will have, sharing their homestead. Yapping dogs and loudly crowing fighting-cocks mingle with free-ranging hens and pot-bellied pigs. A well-off rice-farmer will usually have a team of water-buffalo and a few of the antelope-like *banteng* cattle. The way the farmstead is divided up once again reflects the Balinese concept of the universe. In the *kangin* corner, facing the mountains, stands the family temple in which reverence is paid to the gods and ancestral spirits. Beside it, also facing the mountains, but on the *kauh* (west) side, are the sleeping-quarters of the head of the family and his wife. These are built on a stone foundation and can be locked. The bed is so arranged that the sleeper's head is nearest the mountains, the seat of the gods, or the sunrise, which is the second most favorable position. The center of the yard is where communal family life takes place. Here, the rest of the family occupy bungalows, called *bales,* which are more or less open and where they live and sleep. Some *bales* are ceremonial pavilions, reserved for such occasions as wedding-nights, or family meetings. On the side furthest from the mountains are the hen-coops, pigsties, rice-stores and the kitchen. From the height and size of the storage-loft, an outsider can get a good idea of the wealth of the family. The entrance to the farmstead is a narrow gateway, reached by steps, and behind which stands the *Aling-Aling,* a wall intended to keep out evil spirits. It seems that these demons, though dangerous, are not very bright and can only move in straight lines. Thus they invariably bump into this obstacle, and this teaches them that the farmstead is a place to be avoided in future.

In constructing the buildings of the farmstead, the body-measurements of the head of the family provide the basis for all the dimensions. Before building starts, an expert who is well versed in the

ancient *lontar* writings, takes the head of the family's measurements in the prescribed manner, and then, depending on the caste to which he belongs, the size of his fortune, the local conditions and the contents of the relevant document, the expert will determine the length of the outer wall, for example, or how large certain *bales* are permitted to be. Thus the height of the enclosing wall, for instance, must always be calculated as four times the length of both arms extended (from middle finger to middle finger), plus one cubit (arm-length, about 45 inches), plus one hand's breadth, with thumb and little finger outstretched. In calculating the proportions of the *bales*, other smaller units of measurements from the head of the household are used.

In this way, harmony is guaranteed between the owner of the new house and his immediate environment – a notion which has also played a part in western architectural theory since the Renaissance, if not earlier, but which is all too often forgotten in this day and age.

RELIGION ON THE "ISLAND OF GODS AND DEMONS"

Bali has often been called the "Island of Gods and Demons" or "Island of a Thousand Temples." And with good reason, since the life of the Balinese, right down to the most routine detail, is governed by religious beliefs and accompanied by religious observances. Perhaps one of the most striking examples of this are the innumerable wicker baskets one sees, filled with blossom or rice, and presented as offerings to the gods or demons in return for spiritual refreshment or comfort. You will find them outside a boutique in Kuta or on the edge of the crater of Gunung Agung; at a dangerous crossroads or on a stone altar in the middle of the garden of your hotel. As you travel through the countryside, you will often come across women on their

Above: Decorations woven from palm-leaves hang in the main street. Right: A religious procession going to a sacred well.

way to a temple with sacrificial offerings piled artistically on their heads. Religion is usually the basis of any spectacle you see, even though it may seem to be pure entertainment. Although westerners may find this profound intertwining of the sacred with the profane very unfamiliar, we should remember that it is not so many generations ago that our forefathers' lives were governed, from the cradle to the grave, by the bells of the parish church – it is only the tune that is a little different.

Agama Hindu Dharma

Balinese religion draws upon different sources, and, even within the relatively narrow confines of the island, has always taken a variety of forms. It can happen that a Balinese from one village will be completely at a loss to understand the significance of rituals that are celebrated in the next village. It also seems to be the case that he cannot follow the incantations muttered by the priest at his own village ceremonies and is certainly not very interested in their meaning. Followers of this religion are therefore not greatly concerned with intellectual debate about the one true and universal path to truth. It seems more a matter of welding many different beliefs into a common and rather abstract concept of salvation. Achieving harmony through diversity could well be their watchword. But in spite of the many and various outward forms taken by this religion, it is possible for the outsider to grasp a number of clear and definite principles.

In very broad terms, it can be said that the religion of the Balinese is a form of Hinduism, with a character very much its own, which exists only in Bali and in a few neighboring islands influenced by Bali. This Hinduism, which arrived in Bali from eastern Java, recognises the trinity of the gods Brahma, Vishnu and Shiva, but of the three it venerates Shiva

in particular. Furthermore, this form of Hinduism had, in Java, absorbed certain characteristics of Buddhism, so that even today some ceremonies are unthinkable without the participation of a Buddhist priest. However, the most striking way in which Balinese Hinduism differs from other forms of the religion, is the presence of many ancient Malayan animistic beliefs, which are a particularly important element of popular religion in Bali. From this deep-rooted source comes the widespread belief that the whole of nature is inhabited by spirits. According to this concept, even a solid rock possesses a soul. The forces of nature are subordinated to an all-powerful godhead, over whom man can only have a very limited influence. This probably explains why the Balinese are anxious to preserve a contact with their ancestors, since according to their belief-system, they are dependent on their ancestors for protection against these natural forces. Ancestor-worship is a way of warding off the angry outbursts of the elements.

On top of these animistic foundations is constructed a Hindu pantheon into which a number of additional Balinese deities have been installed.

This religious view of the universe assumes a well-ordered cosmos in a constant state of evolution. The force which holds it together is called *Dharma,* and this is opposed by the de-stabilizing force which is *Adharma*. This interaction accounts for the continuous creation, existence and dissolution of things. Beyond the reach of human imagination rules the Supreme being, the bringer of order, Sanghyang Widhi Wasa. He is the Absolute, beyond comprehension, the unification of all divine powers. Therefore he stands above and outside the cosmos, over which the lesser gods struggle with one another. This embodiment of the divine principle incidentally provides the Balinese with a useful argument to prove that their form of Hinduism is perfectly compatible with the tenets of the Indonesian state ideology. For one of the five basic rules of the Indonesian constitution requires that every citizen should be a follower of a monotheistic religion.

More familiar to the ordinary people than Sanghyang Widhi Wasa is his embodiment in the form of a trinity: the *Trishakti* or *Trimurti*, comprising Brahma, Vishnu and Shiva. Brahma is held to be the Creator of the world, Vishnu its Preserver and Shiva, the Destroyer. Shiva shows clearly to what extent Hinduism thinks in terms of mutually compatible opposites. Thus destruction is not merely seen as something negative, but as a precondition for renewal, for the regeneration of the world. To the Balinese, Shiva is often no more than another name for the ancient sun-god Surya, or the mighty god Mahadewa who inhabits the volcano of Gunung Agung. But in Hinduism such transformations are not uncommon. Each of the three divinities is quite capable of manifesting himself in various different forms, or else, according to scripture, has been through different incarnations. Traditional beliefs ascribe frequent incarnations to Vishnu, in particular. So it is that Rama, the hero of the *Ramayana* epic, is also considered to be an earthly representation of Vishnu. At other times, Vishnu is thought to be Krishna, the flute-playing cow-herd and seducer of women, who is usually portrayed with a greenish-blue face.

So that the gods should not be alone, and indeed to prevent them from growing weary and pining away, they are provided with divine consorts, who embody their *Shakti*, their godly energy and creative power. This shows that in this cosmology, it is the female deities who maintain its dynamism and creativity.

Brahma is linked with Saraswati, the goddess of wisdom. Vishnu has as many female partners as he has earthly incarnations. The most important are Dewi Lakshmi, the goddess of fortune and prosperity, Dewi Sri, the goddess of fertility or of rice, and the especially popular Sita, Rama's steadfast wife.

Shiva's partners represent the most flamboyant and violent aspects of life among the gods. Dewi Uma, the goddess of love and beauty, is one of them, as are Durga, goddess of death, and Kali, the bloodthirsty goddess of destruction.

The world of the gods is completed by a whole army of demons and spirits, which have attributes of night, the underworld and the realm of shadows. Like the gods, they make frequent appearances in the middle world of men, where they do their evil work. Man's endeavors are directed not only towards ridding the world of evil, but also neutralising its effect, so that a harmonious co-existence of opposites can be achieved on earth.

Mankind possesses an immortal soul, called *Atman*, which according to its *Karma Pala* is incarnated again and again in an endless series of rebirths (*samsara*). The Karma Pala is a kind of destiny which is derived from one's behavior in earlier lives. Unlike the Hindus of India, the Balinese believe that the soul of an ancestor enters the body of a new-born baby and thus returns to his own clan. This cycle is so important to the Balinese that they consider the fate of being reborn in an alien and unknown body more terrible and painful even than death itself.

The highest goal of human existence is to break out of the cycle of reincarnation so that the soul can be reunited with the Supreme Being, in perfect harmony. This release from the Samsara is called *Moksa*; and there are three ways, or *marga*, by which Moksa can be achieved. The direct way, which is, however, the most difficult and worthy of admiration, is that of complete renunciation. Through mystic contemplation and meditation man rids himself of his earthly fetters and prepares the way for his soul to find eternal harmony.

Right: From a raised seat the Pedanda seeks contact with the gods.

The second path is that of knowledge and exemplary behavior. He who decides to follow this path is introduced to the scriptures by teachers, deepens his knowledge, and with the inner strength which this gives him, endeavors for the rest of his life to abide by the ten commandments, which are not very different from those of the Christian tradition.

The third path, which is the one taken by the majority of Balinese, is that of ritual devotion to the gods. This consists of observing the prescribed rites and sacrifices and thus, step by step, getting ever closer to Moksa.

Priests: Pedanda and Pemangku

For the ordinary Balinese, ideas of religion and morality are presented in the dramatic performances of the Indian epics *Ramayana* and *Mahabharata,* in dance, on stage and in shadow-theater. However, the priests draw their wisdom from the oldest sacred writings of Hinduism, the ancient Indian *Vedas* and *Up-*

anishads. These are hermetic texts of great lyrical power, and contain many mysterious allusions. The priests who devote themselves to these scriptures are known as *Pedanda* and belong to the Brahmana caste. Keeping themselves remote from the daily distractions of earthly life, they spend their days meditating in their private temples and seeking union with Surya, the Balinese form of Shiva. Their one practical connection with the people consists of providing holy water, since they are normally the only ones who know the required method of preparation and incantations. At the same time the sale of this water is a source of income for them.They are only to be seen at important national temple festivals or ceremonies. On these occasions, as if they were already existing on some higher plane, they sit enthroned like saints on specially constructed seats, above the heads of the masses, and summon the gods to their presence with ritual gestures and murmured mantras.The shivaitic priests can be recognized by their

knotted hair, while the Buddhist clergy have hair of shoulder-length.

Closer to the common people are the ordinary temple priests, or *Pemangku,* who generally belong to the lowest caste. They are charged with carrying out all the daily duties connected with the temple. These include receiving gift-offerings, supervising temple festivals and organizing processions. While the Pedanda, as High Priest, is responsible for the spiritual quality of a ceremony, the Pemangku is busy seeing that everything goes according to plan. He may give the signal for the next phase of the ritual, or take the holy water from the Penanda and sprinkle it over the congregation.

Someone who stands in a key position between the people and their gods is the *Dalang,* or shadow-player. He is considered to be a priest, or at least has an

Above: Colored rice-cakes are the main element in these beautifully constructed sacrificial pillars. Right: The mighty gates of the new Pura Ulun Danu temple in Batur.

elevated social position, comparable to the priests. His art brings the myths of India and Indonesia alive for the people. The characters which he conjures up perform on various social, linguistic and dramatic levels. His noble heroes speak a language of which the common people only have a rudimentary understanding. For this reason, and to add to the entertainment-value, there is an almost Shakespearian gallery of servants, fools and yokels, who provide a running commentary on the action in a simplified, demotic language, thus enabling the audience to appreciate the epic drama and get some laughs into the bargain.

Balinese temples: Pura

In addition to the hundreds of thousands of family temples, there are a large number – no-one has ever counted them, but it must be at least 20,000 – of village, association, tribal, clan and state temples in public places. These *Pura* differ from family temples only in their size and fur-

nishings. Unlike Hindu temples in India, the ones in Bali generally do not have any closed rooms. Even in the innermost parts of the temple the view to the mountains, held to be the throne of the gods, must remain unrestricted, so that the gods, whose presence is desired at temple festivals, have no difficulty in making their way there.

A temple will comprise two or three rectangular unwalled courts, which either lie on the same level, or (in mountainous areas) are built in terraces, one above the other. The forecourt (*jaba sisi*) lies nearest the sea, and the innermost court, the Holy of Holies, (*jeroan*) is nearest the mountains. Between these two, larger Pura often have another interior court (*jaba tengah*). The temple is entered through a tall, divided gateway (*candi bentar*). This looks like a tapering tower, split in two, and symbolizes a mountain of the gods, rent asunder by supernatural forces. The Holy of Holies is reached through a second gateway (*kori agung* or *padu raksa*), of which the upper part is

usually closed. This entrance is generally guarded by the terrifying mask of *Kala-Boma*. In addition to this, to the left and right of the entrance stand two figures of demons (*raksasa*) armed with clubs, to keep out others of their kind. An *Aling-Aling* wall behind the Kori-Agung gate finally makes the interior of the temple demon-proof.

The outer and central courts contain various buildings which are used in the preparation of temple festivals. Then, in the innermost area of the Jeroan there is a raised chair for the Pedanda (*bale pawe-daan*), the pagoda-shaped *merus* with as many as eleven roofs (*tumpang*), which are chiefly dedicated to the triple gods of the Trishakti, several shrines (*pasimpan-gan*), which are dedicated to other gods, and finally the most important throne for a god, the *Padmasana*, decorated with lotus-blossom, and intended to tempt the Supreme Being to linger in the temple. Appropriately, this throne is located in the propitious Kaja-Kangin corner of the Holy of Holies.

Worship, festivals and ceremonies

Apart from modern holidays, such as Indonesian Independence Day on 17th August, all festive occasions in Bali have a religious background and look back on long traditions, often 1000 years old, or more. The first historically attested holy man to have brought the Javanese-Hindu philosophy and religion to Bali, was named Danghyang Markandeya. In the 8th century he established himself in an old hermitage on the slopes of Gunung Agung, in order to bring to the Balinese a belief in the Absolute Being, Sanghyang Widhi Wasa. This holy place is still, to this day, the site of the most important temple on the island, the mother temple of Besakih.

The son of Markandeya, Empu Sang Kulputih, was responsible for introduc-

Above: The gate of the Puri Saren in Ubud.
Right: After the festival the consecrated gift-offerings are brought home again.

ing the colorful sacrificial ceremonies and regular temple festivals, of which the most important is the festival of *Odalan.* Then, in the 11th century, Empu Kuturan drew up the outlines of the Balinese cosmos, with its significant alignments, by which, even today, the Balinese orientate themselves, and which have a profound influence on everything, right down to ornamentation and the smallest architectural measurements. The basic framework of Balinese ceremonial can also be traced in these alignments. What followed were simply refinements, usually introduced by one of the rajas or his court. These customs and beliefs were soon firmly rooted in the Balinese mentality, and not even the arrival of the Europeans changed them, since the Dutch, for quite a long period, were anxious to protect the islanders from foreign influences. This is certainly one of the reasons why the number of native Christians remained so small, and the only Moslem communities of any size are in the north and west of the island, and in the capital.

Odalan and Galungan/Kuningan

From the rich variety of festivities, let us take only the *Odalan* festival and the week of celebrations from *Galungan* to *Kuningan. Odalan* takes place once a year, and is the time when every temple is brought out of obscurity, and for one, two, or as many as ten days, depending on its importance, is transformed into a the scene of a religious celebration for gods and men.

Every villager or member of a Subak has a particular responsibility in the preparations. The women's task is to prepare the gift-offerings. They weave little baskets and symbolic figures, bake and color the little rice-cakes, and at the climax of the festival carry these to the temple, piled high on their heads. Later the consecrated gifts are brought home again and eaten by the family.

In the temple forecourt, the menfolk enthusiastically stage cock-fights, which are expressly permitted by the authorities during the festival. The blood of the defeated bird flows into the earth and is supposed to propitiate evil spirits. The *gamelan* orchestra plays late into the night in honor of the gods who, drawn by the meditation and ritual incantations of the priests, have come to take their places on the decorated thrones of stone. Shadow-plays and dramatic spectacles are presented for the entertainment both of the gods and of the worshippers, who are dressed in festive sarongs, temple sashes and blouses or shirts. The most elaborate dancing takes place on the last evening of the *Odalan* in the Holy of Holies, as a fitting farewell to the gods. After that the temple and its spirits sink back once again into a holy slumber. Whereas the *Odalan* festival is especially dedicated to one temple, the purification of the whole village is the chief purpose of the ten-day festival from *Galungan* to *Kuningan* (in the pre-islamic *Wuku* calendar).

Before the festival the men erect tall bamboo poles, from which dangle attractively woven figures, mostly representing the rice-goddess Dewi Sri. The whole village is swept, public buildings are decorated, little domestic altars are set up in front of each homestead, and here and there faded paintwork is touched up. On the feast-day of *Galungan* itself a rich array of gift-offerings are brought to the Temple of Birth, to celebrate the creation of the world and the provisional victory of Good over Evil. After the temple ceremonies everyone gets together for big family parties, for which even the grown-up children make a special journey home from the towns.

On the day of *Kuningan* (the word means "yellow"), yellow-colored rice is brought to the temple. On this, the second most important feast after *Galungan*, the Balinese remember their ancestors and the holy men, and go on joyful pilgrimages to the national temples, in which the holy men practised. The day after *Kuningan*, the festival ends with games.

45

THE CYCLE OF FESTIVALS

The Balinese consider life as no more than a transitional stage for their souls on the way to Moksa, that redemption which for the Hindu believer represents complete harmony with God. The particular emphasis on transition – in the literal as well as the metaphorical sense – is reflected not only in the way temples are constructed but also in the ceremonies which mark the stages in a person's earthly life. Not surprisingly, no part of the temple is given more attention than the gates, which symbolize the passing from one world into the next. Similar importance is laid on the occasions marking the beginning of a new stage of life.

Birth and first birthday

Even before a birth takes place, in the third and sixth months of pregnancy, a

Above: Participants at a tooth-filing ceremony are sprinkled with holy water.

purification ceremony is held in the farmstead. From now on the parents must refrain from swearing. The expectant mother is considered impure, in a religious sense, and must therefore stay away from temples and rice-fields.

After the birth, the ceremonies are directed towards the by-products of the birth, known as the "Four Sisters," namely placenta, umbilical cord, amniotic fluid and blood. These have to be buried in a yellow-painted coconut-shell near the entrance to the parents' sleeping quarters. This spot is felt by every Balinese to be his immediate spiritual home, and for the rest of his life he will always lay offerings here on special days.

For a long period the new-born baby may not touch the ground (considered impure), and for 42 days mother and baby are themselves held to be impure, though the father only for three days. On the 12th day after birth the infant is given a provisional name and the cradle is watched over by the winged god Rare Kumara, protector of children.

At the end of 42 days, a purification ceremony is held in a special bathing-place, after which the mother may once again enter the temple. The child is now also freed from the impurity of its birth. After 105 days, which is half the period of the Wuku calendar, a festival is held in which the child receives a new name. It is usual on this occasion for a life-size dummy of the child to be made and thrown outside the farmstead, to distract the evil spirits who are lurking there. The next festival takes place 210 days after the birth, when the baby may be put on the ground for the first time. It has now left its divine existence and entered the earthly world. But it is not allowed to crawl – it is not an animal, after all. The baby's head is now shaved, except for one lock over its forehead, and the hair is presented to the god of children, Rare Kumara, as a final offering.

Less attention is paid to the child's first birthday, and further ceremonies do not take place until the toddler loses its milk-teeth, a girl has her first menstrual flow or a boy's voice breaks.

The filing of teeth

Another indispensable ceremony for evey Balinese who wishes his life-cycle to follow the prescribed form, is the filing of teeth. Normally this should take place in late adolescence, and certainly before marriage. In this ceremony, which is attended by large numbers of the family and its clan, six teeth in the upper jaw, in other words the jaw nearest to the realm of the gods, are filed down to an even, straight line. The symbolic value of this is that, by having the animal-like canine teeth filed down, a person is freed from animal desires. Each of the six teeth stands for one of the undesirable vices of lust, anger, greed, mental confusion, drunkenness and envy. It is to be expected that anyone who has his or her teeth trimmed in this way, will behave as a mature adult from then on. Furthermore, pointed canine teeth are considered unattractive as well as unseemly.

Marriage

Even today it is still the custom in Bali for marriages to be arranged by negotiation between the parents of the couple. Such marriages are dictated by social convention and economic necessity, and are the occasion for costly rituals and celebrations. Alongside this there always used to be a less expensive way of starting a marriage: stealing a bride. This was in fact closer to the western conception of marriage for love, since the bride-to-be was always warned in advance that she was to be "stolen" and would be only too happy to co-operate. The bride's parents were expected to pursue the abductor, and make an elaborate show of objecting, before finally coming to terms with their daughter's "fate" and reaching an amicable arrangement over it.

Nowadays, abduction has a more symbolic character and is a joke which the whole village can share. After the abduction and the obligatory honeymoon, spent away from the village with friends of the bridegroom, the two families get together for the proper wedding ceremony. This varies in form from village to village, but the end result is the same in all cases: the woman leaves her family and moves into her husband's homestead. Through the marriage the couple both become full members of their banjar.

Cremation

Without doubt the most important event in the ceremonial cycle of earthly existence is the one celebrating the cremation of the dead. In this way, those left behind can assure that the soul of the dead relative, freed from its physical vestiges, will ascend to heaven. Depending on the wealth of the family, the corpse is

47

either first buried until enough money is available for a ceremonial cremation, or it is placed in a *bale* in the farmstead until the precribed period of 42 days has elapsed and the body can be consigned to the flames. Often several families, or the whole village, will club together and organize a mass-cremation of all the bodies which in recent years have been laid to rest in temporary graves. Sometimes it is possible to join in the celebrations of rich families and thus save some of the costs.

It often takes weeks of work to prepare two gaudily decorated coffins for each body: one to transport the body, the other to be used in the cremation itself. On the day of the cremation, once the domestic ceremonies are ended, the corpse is taken in the first coffin to the place of cremation. On the way through the village, the coffin is carried at the double, being violently shaken and turned round in circles.

All this makes for a cheerful spectacle, during which the pall-bearers frequently have water poured over them. The purpose of this is to confuse the soul of the dead person, so that it will not find its way back to the farmstead and haunt the living occupants. Having reached the funeral-pyre they place the body carefully in the cremation coffin they have brought with them, and what follows is rather an anti-climax. The result of weeks of work, with the corpse in it, is set alight with the aid of gas-jets. When everything is reduced to ashes, the white ash from the bones is separated from the rest and at a later date is taken in a ceremonial procession to the sea, or to a river, where it is scattered over the waters. Thus is the soul of the departed finally set free.

When a Brahman, or other leading figure is cremated, the ceremony is immensely elaborate and draws visitors from far and wide. Every ten years, at Besakih, there is a ceremony of purification, before which all the island's graveyards have to be emptied and the bodies burnt.

Above: A cremation in Ubud. Right: Who is dancing, and who is calling the tune?

A GUIDE TO ETIQUETTE

A westerner in Bali can make many mistakes. But the Balinese are very forgiving – provided the visitor shows a willingness to treat the country and its people with consideration. However, if in your wanderings you carelessly trample down the dyke-like boundary walls between the rice-fields, thus threatening the laboriously maintained basis of life, you will make yourself very unpopular. If you find yourself in dispute with a Balinese, and do not give him the opportunity to save face, you must be prepared for him to become more entrenched in his position, since, according to his concept of honor, he has no other choice. Even when shopping in Kuta you should always maintain your own dignity, while respecting that of the man desperately trying to sell you a watch. Behavior which may just seem tiresome to you, is often the other person's fight for survival. You may not be able to make their life any easier, but equally you should not burden them with further hardships. If you are not interested, do not raise false expectations. A quiet but firm refusal is more appreciated than any amount of nervous dithering.

Incidentally, not everyone will be trying to sell you something. Often they just want to have a chat, and try out their latest English words on you. You have to learn to tell the difference. At all events, if you can master a few words or phrases in the national language, Bahasa Indonesia, this will make for better understanding and will endear you to your island hosts. On the other hand, most shopkeepers will be prepared to accept defeat in the face of a firmly pronounced: *"(saya) tidak mau "*– " I don't want it."

At temple festivals

Foreigners are usually allowed to enter a temple and to take part in a temple fes-

tival. However, since the Balinese are communicating with their gods in these ceremonies, visitors are expected to abide strictly by certain rules.

The greatest reticence is required in all behavior. This begins with your clothing, which must be modest and decent. Shorts, T-shirts and the like are completely unacceptable. Men are required to wear a long-sleeved shirt, a sarong and a temple-sash (*selendang*), and sometimes also a cloth tied round the head (called a *destar* or *udeng*). Women should wear a long-sleeved blouse, or a *kebaya* like the Balinese women. You should not arrive at a religious occasion, sweating. Walls and other parts of the temple structure are sacred to the Balinese, and it is sacrilege to touch them with the foot, since this is regarded as impure. You should also take care never to place yourself between people praying and the shrine or throne of a god. It is more appropriate to sit than to stand. In this way you avoid any insult to the gods or their priests, by appearing to stand above them physically.

If you want to leave your seat before the end of a ceremony, you should follow the Balinese custom and walk with the body slightly bowed.

You should never take photographs without the permission of someone in authority. A friendly approach will usually secure this permission. However, flash-bulbs should not be used at temple festivals, and in fact it is positively dangerous to use them on occasions when dancers go into a trance.

Even if there is no festival in progress, you should not enter a temple unless you are decently dressed and preferably wearing a temple-sash, tied round your waist like a belt.

People who have recently suffered a bereavement in the family, those with open wounds, and women during their menstrual period, are considered impure (*sebel*) and may not enter a temple. If any human blood were to "defile" the floor of a temple, an elaborate (and costly) purification ceremony would then have to be carried out.

Invitations

If you are invited by a Balinese family to their home, you should always arrive properly dressed, though not necessarily wearing a sarong. Westerners tend, anyway, to look rather less than elegant in one of these garments. It is quite usual to take a little gift with you, as a kindness to your hosts or their children. But you will find that it is accepted rather discreetly and put to one side, since the host does not wish you to get the impression that he is at all acquisitive. Except for business meetings, and sometimes even then, it is customary to arrive about half an hour later than invited. You should leave your shoes at the front-door and enter the house in your stockinged feet.

Right: "Wanna take a photo? OK, any time, Mister!"

When greeting your hosts, you will find the handshake, rather in the European manner, is perfunctory and not too firm. It is important to observe the correct order of precedence among those present, according to age and title. One does not sit down until invited to do so. If people are sitting in the traditional style on cushions and mats, be careful not to point the soles of your feet in anyone's direction, since this is considered an insult. Nor should you point at anyone or anything with your foot.

If you are invited to a meal, do not start eating or drinking until your host has indicated in a friendly way that you should do so. When the first dish is put in front of you, it is advisable not to eat too heartily, since you will always be served a second helping which you must not refuse, unless you are actually feeling ill. Your host will also deem it an honor if you try at least a small helping from every dish that you are offered. If bowls or dishes are handed round, be sure always to take them with the right hand and pass them on with the same hand. This is because the left hand is reckoned to be impure on account of its function in cleaning intimate parts of the body, and at most should be used only to support the right elbow, when one is passing things round. At the end of the meal, always leave a little food on your plate, "for Mr Manners," as we used to say. Only, in Bali it is intended for the gods, and shows both that your host has provided more than enough and that you have not indulged in the vice of gluttony.

Dealing with officials

Should you have any matters that you want to have dealt with swiftly by government authorities or any other official body, you should, perverse as it may sound, have some time to spare, or should at least look as if you have. A calm and friendly demeanor, showing re-

spect to the person you are talking to, without being obsequious, is the surest way to success. Impatience seldom does any good; on the contrary, it just means that the offcial has to control his anger at the disgraceful behavior of his customer, and this can take quite a while. What does help, however, is to dress your best, despite the tropical temperature. For men this means: polished slippers, long trousers, and a long-sleeved shirt; for women, a decent dress, or knee-length skirt and modest blouse, always with a bra underneath. Whatever you wear, you should always try to look clean and well turned-out.

Behavior in public

Although it is not unusual for Balinese of the same sex to go around hand in hand, an open show of affection *between* the sexes in public is not customary. Something which seems very uninhibited to Europeans – such as bathing naked or washing in a river – is not without its own restrictions. Men and women have separate bathing-places or different times for bathing. It is extremely impolite to stare at someone, still worse to photograph them, while they are washing. A Balinese who is relieving him- or herself, is simply "invisible" to the others.

When talking to a Balinese, you should neither fold your arms in front of you, nor put your hands on your hips. Both gestures give the impression of arrogance and are therefore very impolite. Although you may be touched frequently by Balinese, without any disrespect being intended, you as a foreigner should be very reticent about touching others. The Balinese code of behavior forbids the touching of someone on the head, even if this is meant in a friendly way. For the Balinese, the head is the most sacred part of the body, and one should not even stroke children on the head. As in the west, it is impolite to point at people. If you want to beckon someone, you do it by stretching out your arm and waving your hand with the palm facing downward.

AT THE PARTING OF THE WAYS

DENPASAR
KUTA / LEGIAN
BUKIT BADUNG
SANUR
LEMBONGAN
NUSA PENIDA

Where is the "real" Bali? It is surely that triangle of luxuriant tropical landscape which fans out from the limestone knob of the Bukit Badung peninsula. Here in the south of the island, proverbially at the feet of the gods who sit up in the volcanic mountains, is where the heart of Bali beats. The fertile river valleys and plains provide ideal conditions for rice-growing. The shimmering paddy-fields and elegantly constructed terraces of emerald green are the emblems of Balinese civilisation. Not surprisingly, this rich store-house is the most densely populated part of the island, where every aspect of its varied and colorful life unfolds before you.

The main center of population is the southern tip, with the rapidly expanding capital, Denpasar, its high-rise tourist hotels and the coast of alluring, sandy, palm-fringed beaches. Since the 1960s, ever-growing hordes of tourists have descended on this part of Bali, and the number of foreign visitors expected in 1993 is a staggering 1.3 million.

Gone for ever are the days when Denpasar was just a small town, presided

Previous pages: On the beach. Young Legong dancers take a break. Left: A temple monkey enjoying the view from the Pura Luhur Ulu Watu.

over by a local raja, and Kuta, the inexpensive tropical paradise on the coast, south-west of Denpasar, was no more than a fishing-village. In a higher price-range, but equally booked up, are the luxurious beach resorts of Sanur and Nusa Dua, the former once occupied by the old-guard Brahman caste, and the latter a deserted beach on the bone-dry peninsula of Bukit Badung.

DENPASAR

Since being named as Bali's capital in 1958, Denpasar has grown into a bustling and rather unromantic city of 300,000 inhabitants. All day long the streets are crammed with hooting, three-wheeled taxi-buses called *bemos,* on the look-out for passengers, swarms of mopeds and large buses belching fumes. Thanks to the considerable foreign earnings from tourism, the little market town which had grown up around the raja's palace of Permecutan, has become one of the most affluent cities in Indonesia. Denpasar means "east of the market," but the local people usually cally it Badung, a name which refers not only to the former seat of the raja, but the whole principality and the modern adminstrative district which stretches from the Bukit Badung peninsular up to the volcanic Catur massif.

57

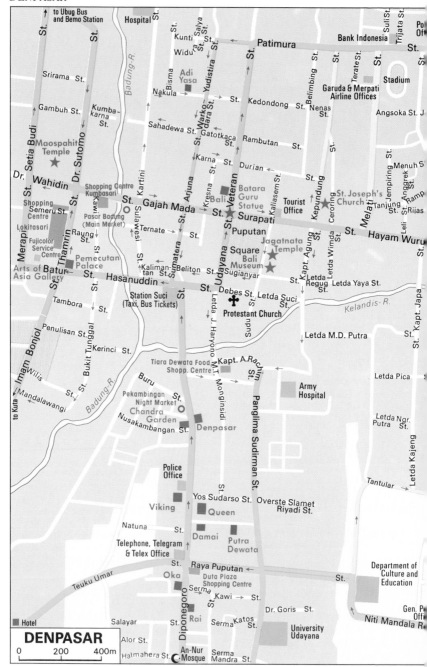

DENPASAR

0   200   400m

■ Hotel

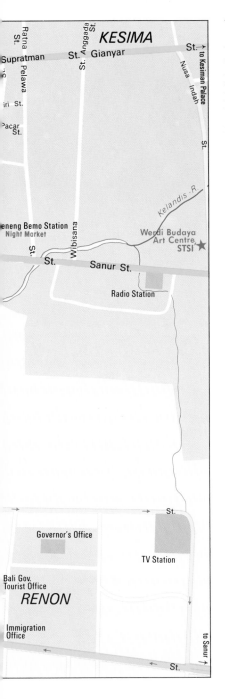

The rajas and nobility of Badung traditionally came from the Ksatriya caste, which even today forms the elite of Denpasar – from administrative officials to hotel-owners. However, the mass of the population is ethnically very mixed. The insatiable city is swallowing up the surrounding rice-fields and village communities. It has already reached the Bay of Benoa to the south and the artists' village of Batubulan to the north, and acts as a magnet, drawing people in from the countryside and villages. The immigrants are not only from Bali. Even in the 1930s, in the wake of the Dutch colonial masters, Denpasar saw an influx of Moslem traders of Buginese, Indian and Arab origin. In recent decades, large numbers of Moslems have arrived from Java and Madura, and they daily answer the Muezzin's call to prayer at the mosques of Raya Masjid and An-Nur Masjid, on the Jalan Diponegoro.The Javanese can often be seen peddling their wares in the streets or running makeshift eateries called *warungs*. The businesslike Chinese, both Buddhist and Christian, belong to the commercial elite of Denpasar. On the flat roofs of their tall office buildings you can see not only satellite-dishes, but also spendid gilded pagoda-like shrines to their ancestors. It would be very risky to believe in no god at all, since atheists get lumped together with communists.

The younger generation, estranged from traditional village life, seek a new cultural orientation in the westernized lifestyle of Kuta on the one hand, and on the other – perhaps in a more lasting way – from the Indonesian metropolis, Jakarta. The *lingua franca* of the whole Indonesian archipelago, the offical language, Bahasa Indonesia, is derived from the Malay spoken by traders all over South-East Asia. From Denpasar, through university, school, cinema and television, it is gaining supremacy over the native tongues of the island. The national ideology of Indonesia, "Unity in

59

Diversity" (*bhinneka tunggal ika*) is beginning to take root in Bali's young capital. The different caste-based languages, which in rural Bali separate princes from rice-farmers the moment they open their mouths, no longer have any place in modern city life. Here, videos are more popular than shadow-plays; and the individual can escape from the all-powerful, all-embracing, divine order of the Hindu cosmos. Yet, at the same time, the deeply traditional countryside is receiving a new injection of energy and ideas from Denpasar – in art and religion, in dance, music and painting. Following the Indian example, the Brahman theologians are attempting to convert the Hindus of Bali from their polytheistic pantheon, and to focus their faith on the one Supreme Being, the Sanghyang Widhi Wasa, at the same time relegating the pre-Hindu animistic beliefs to the level of superstition.

Above: The four-faced Batara Guru stands in Puputan Square. Right: The Art Center seen at dusk.

In the State College of Dance, STSI (*Sekolah Tinggi Seni Indonesia* in Jalan Nusa Indah) and the SMKI (*Sekolah Menengah Karawitan Indonesia* in Batubulan, also known as KOKAR), new choreography for the old temple dances is developed, as well as completely new dances which are performed all year round on stage at the Werdi Budaya Art Center (formerly Abiankapas). However, the most impressive shows are during the *Bali Arts Festival* in June and July. The programs also include performances of the *Ramayana* ballet in the classical Javanese style, and competitions between *gamelan* orchestras.

A walk round the city

City life in Denpasar centers round **Puputan Square.** The name recalls the *Puputan*, or mass ritual suicide of the entire royal court of Pemecutan on 20th September 1906. This was an example of the heroic self-sacrifice of the ruling class of Bali faced with the superior arms of the

Dutch soldiers, who had been sent on a punitive expedition against the Raja of Badung, for having ordered the looting of a Chinese merchant-ship which had recently gone aground on the coast. In the center of the square stands a **bronze memorial** to those who lost their lives in the fight for liberation from the Dutch at the end of the Second World War.

In the north-west corner of Puputan Square, at the major crossing of Jalan Gajah Mada and Jalan Udayana, the four-faced **Batara Guru** looks out from his pedestal over the swirling city traffic, to the four points of the compass. The 15-foot (5m) high stone statue is dedicated to Shiva, the "Great Teacher." The face pointing east is that of Iswara (Indra), while Brahma looks southwards, Mahadewa to the west and Vishnu to the north. The last-named is easy to recognize by his insignia, the shell horn and the Wheel of Life (*cakra*).

On the east side of the square rises the modern **Pura Jagatnata**, the "Temple of the Lord of the World." Inside there is a seven-tiered throne of stone, standing in the middle of a lotus-pond and holding a gilded statue of Sanghyang Widhi Wasa, the Supreme God.

Adjoining the Jagatnata temple to the south is the **Bali Museum.** This was established by the Dutch colonial government in 1932 as an ethnographic museum, and displays archaeological finds, native handicrafts, dance-masks and paintings, as well as illustrating the main architectural styles of Balinese temples and palaces. It is well worth a visit, especially before starting a tour of the island.

The central building of the museum is a replica of a palace in the East Balinese Karangasem style. In front of it stands a row of original stone sculptures from the 16th century, representing musicians. Inside, finds from the neolithic period are on display, as well as models showing various initiation rites such as tooth-filing. The nextdoor building (opposite the

Kulkul Tower, with its huge drum) is a replica of the palace of Buleleng in northern Bali. It contains, among other things, valuable figures of the dragon-like Barong, carved dance-masks, old shadow-puppets (*wayang kulit*), traditonal *ikat* woven fabrics and an excellent collection of *kris* knives. The third museum pavilion shows the palace architecture of the Rajas of Tabanan (West Bali). It houses a collection of ivory carvings and Bronze Age finds from Gilimanuk.

One of the busiest shopping-streets of Denpasar is **Jalan Dr. Wahidin/Jalan Gajah Mada,** with the bustling vegetable- and textile-markets of **Pasar Badung** and the large **Kumbasari Shopping Center** on the river Badung. Right beside the Kumbasari complex, the **Pasar Malam** (night market) opens in the late afternoon and is a favorite spot for anyone wanting to have a good and cheap evening meal. Other night markets worth visiting for their cheerful local atmosphere and the complete range of Javanese and Balinese dishes that they offer, can be found on the east side of city, in the **Kereneng Bemo Terminal**, and in the **Pekambingan Market** in **Jalan Diponegoro**, a major commercial thoroughfare.

Near the junction of Jalan Dr. Wahidin and Jalan Dr. Sutomo you come to the oldest Hindu temple in the city, the 14th century **Pura Maospahit**, dating from the beginning of the Javanese colonisation period. Its entrance in the traditional *Candi Bentar* (split gate) form, is guarded by statues of the mythical bird Garuda and the wind-god Batara Bayu.

Another paradise for shoppers is the continuation of Jalan Dr. Sutomo, called **Jalan Thamrin** and dominated by the **Lokitari Shopping Center**. Not far from here, on Jalan Hasanuddin, stood the palace of the aristocratic Pemecutan family, which was destroyed during the Dutch invasion of 1906. It was later rebuilt and became the **Pemecutan Palace Hotel**, where today guests are welcomed in the lobby by a *gamelan* orchestra. Adjoining the hotel garden, the former palace temple, the **Pura Pemecutan**, has been reconstructed in appropriate style.

If you leave Puputan Square and walk eastwards along Jalan Surapati, you soon come to a side-turning called Jalan Kepundung. There you will find, not a temple but a Catholic church, the **Gereja Katolik St Joseph,** whose interior decoration combines Christian iconography with Balinese art forms in a very unusual way. Apart from Catholics, Denpasar has the whole gamut of Christian congregations, including Protestants (Jalan Debes), Seventh Day Adventists (Jalan Surapati) and the joyfully singing adherents of the Pentecostal Church (Jalan Karna).

Returning to the main street, keep heading east and you will finally reach Jalan Nusa Indah (formerly Jalan Bayusuta) and the **Werdi Budaya Art Center**, Denpasar's venue for festivals and exhibitions. People looking for souvenirs of the best quality, will find what they want in the exhibition and sales center next door, with its paintings, woodcarvings, and a representative cross-section of Balinese arts and crafts. A whole room is given over to mementos of Walter Spies, the German-born artist who made his home in Bali, and contains examples of his photography as well as reproductions of his paintings. North of the Art Center stretches the district of **Kesiman**, the one place left which still gives an idea of the old village atmosphere of Denpasar, before the advent of reinforced concrete. Look for the old, brick-built **Raja's Palace** with its handsomely ornamented ancestral temple, the **Pura Kesiman**.

The best of modern Balinese architecture is to be seen in the new government district in the south-eastern suburb of **Renon,** which is bordered by Jalan Tantular and Jalan Niti Mandala. This is where the official residence of the Governor is located, together with various ministries, the Head Post Office, the Immigration Office and the Tourist Office.

KUTA AND LEGIAN

People who predict the impending destruction of Balinese culture and blame it on the tourist invasion, have only one good things to say about Kuta: it has a guaranteed genuine and phenomenal blood-red sunset. And since there are no seasons in the tropics, this wonderful free show takes place punctually every evening at six o'clock. But on Kuta's wide, 3-mile (5 km) long beach, civilisation has already come to the parting of the ways: if you come here looking to spend your day in peace, you are out of luck – you will face a never-ending stream of mobile souvenir-shops, boys selling cool drinks, girls selling sarongs and women offering you a massage. (Don't worry, Kuta is not like Thailand's Pattaya. You really do get a massage – nothing more!). The women

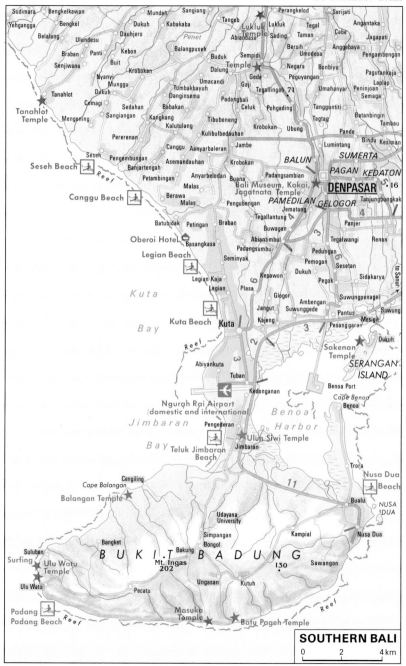

Sudimara Bengkelkawan Mundeh Sangiang Perangkelod Serijati
Yehgangga Bengkel Dukuh Kabakaba Tangeb Lukluk Lukluk Tegal Antangka
Belalang Dauhjero Luklu Sading Taman Cabe Jagapati
Ulundesu *Penet* Abianbase Bersih Umodesa Anggebaya
Braban Panti Kebon Balangpuseh Buduk Sempidi Negara Bonbiyu Pengambengan
Senjiwana Buit Dalung Temple Gede Peguyangan Pagutankaja
Nyanyi Krobokan Umacandi Gaji Tegallingah 71 Umahanyar Peninjoan Laplap
Munggu Tumbakbayuh Padangbali Semaga
Tanahlot Dukuh Danginsema Celuk Pohgading Tangguntiti Batanbingin
Cemagi Sedahan Babakan Tagtag Tambau
Tanahlot Mengening Sangiangan Kangkang Tibubeneng Krobokan Ubung Pande Bindu Kesiman
Temple Kalutulang Kulibulbedauhan Lumintang
Pererenan Canggu Aanyarbaleran Jambe SUMERTA
Seseh Pengembungan Asemandauhan Krobokan BALUN
Seseh Beach *Reef* Banjartengah Anyarbelodan Buana Padangsambian PAGAN KEDATON
Petambingan Malas Bali Museum, Kokai, DENPASAR •16
Canggu Beach Berawa Pengubengan Jagatnata Temple Tanjungbungkak
Malas Buwagan PAMEDILAN GELOGOR 4
Batubidak Petingan Braban Tegallantung Jematang
Oberoi Hotel Basangkasa Padangsumbu Abiantimbul Tegalwangi Renon
Legian Beach Seminyak Pedungan Panjer
Pemogan Dukuh Sesetan
Kuta Legian Kaja Kepawon Pegok Sidakarya
Legian Plasa Suwungpenagel
Bay Kuta Beach Kuta Glogor Ambengan Pantus Suwung
Jangut Suwunggede Mesigit Dukuh
Kajeng Pesanggaran
Reef Abiyankuta Sakenan SERANGAN
Tuban Temple ISLAND
Kedonganan Benoa Port
Ngurah Rai Airport Cape Benoa
(domestic and international) *Benoa* Benoa
Jimbaran Pengederan *Harbor*
Bay Teluk Jimbaran Ulun Siwi Temple Trora
Beach Jimbaran Nusa Dua
Cengiling Beach
Cape Balangan Bualu NUSA
Balangan Temple DUA
Udayana Nusa Dua
University
Bangket Simpangan Kampial
Suluban Bongol Sawangon
Surfing Ulu Watu BUKIT BADUNG 130
Temple Mt. Ingas Bakung
202 Ungasan Kutuh
Ulu Watu Pecatu
Padang Masuka
Padang Beach *Reef* Temple Batu Pageh Temple

SOUTHERN BALI

0   2   4 km

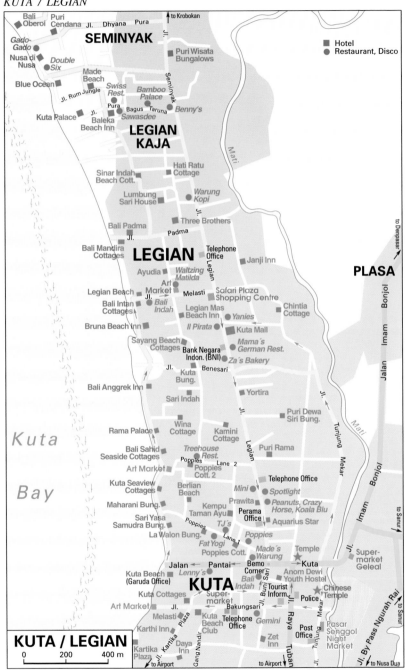

KUTA / LEGIAN

- ■ Hotel
- ● Restaurant, Disco

SEMINYAK

LEGIAN KAJA

LEGIAN

PLASA

Kuta

Bay

KUTA

Bali Oberoi
Puri Cendana
Jl. Dhyana
Pura
Jl.
to Krobokan
Seminyak

Gado-Gado
Nusa di Nusa
Double Six
Blue Ocean
Made Beach
Swiss Rest.
Jl. Rum Jungle
Pura
Bamboo Palace
Bagus
Taruna
Sawasdee
Benny's
Kuta Palace
Jl. Baleka Beach Inn

Puri Wisata Bungalows

Mati

Sinar Indah Beach Cott.
Hati Ratu Cottage
Lumbung Sari House
Warung Kopi
Jl.
Bali Padma
Three Brothers
Jl.
Padma
Bali Mandira Cottages
Legian
Telephone Office
Janji Inn

Ayudia
Waltzing Matilda
Art Market
Jl.
Melasti
Safari Plaza Shopping Centre
Legian Beach
Bali Intan Cottages
Bali Indah
Legian Mas Beach Inn
Yanies
Chintia Cottage
Bruna Beach Inn
Il Pirata
Kuta Mall
Mama's German Rest.
Sayang Beach Cottages
Bank Negara Indon. (BNI)
Za's Bakery
Jl. Kuta Bung.
Benesari
Bali Anggrek Inn
Sari Indah
Yortira
Jl.
Legian
Puri Dewa Siri Bung.
Rama Palace
Wina Cottage
Kamini Cottage
Puri Rama
Bali Sahid Seaside Cottages
Treehouse Rest.
Poppies Lane 2
Art Market
Poppies Cott. 2
Kuta Seaview Cottages
Berlian Beach
Telephone Office
Maharani Bung.
Mini
Spotlight
Kempu Taman Ayu
Prawita
Peanuts, Crazy Horse, Koala Blu
Sari Yasa Samudra Bung.
Poppies
Perama Office
Aquarius Star
La Walon Bung.
TJ's
Lane 1
Fat Yogi
Poppies
Poppies Cott.
Made's Warung
Temple
Jalan
Pantai
Bemo Corner
Kuta
Supermarket Geleal
Lenny's
Bali Indah
Anom Dewi Youth Hostel
Kuta Beach (Garuda Office)
KUTA
Tourist Inform.
Chinese Temple
Kuta Cottages
Supermarket
Bakungsari
Police
Art Market
Melasti
Plaza
Kuta Beach Club
Telephone Office
Gemini
Post Office
Rasar Senggol Night Market
Karthi Inn
Daya Inn
Zet Inn
Kartika Plaza
Gang Nandir
to Airport
to Airport

Imam
Bonjol
Jalan
to Denpasar
Tunjung
Mekar
Bonjol
Imam
to Sanur
to Sanur
Jl. Raya
Tuban
Jl. By Pass Ngurah Rai
to Nusa Dua

KUTA / LEGIAN

0   200   400 m

who pummel you with strong hands became so numerous in the 1980s, that they were issued with a kind of licence-plate – their registration-numbers painted in bright red on their straw hats. You either hate the whole beach business – or you find ways to enjoy it: for example, every morning you get "your" *Ibu Massage* to knead you from head to toe for a discount price. Then, while grilling yourself on the sand, you find that deliciously fresh pieces of pineapple miraculously appear in your mouth, or an ice-cold beer is brought to you on a tray. You don't even have to move. Fancy a pair of those trendy flared pants that are all the rage in Legian? Sure. They will bring the whole boutique to you. Wood-carvings from Ubud, silver jewelry from Celuk – whatever you want you can buy on the beach. The only thing in short supply is shade, but at least you have a big selection of straw hats. If you are blessed with a sense of humor, you can have a lot of fun with the boys and girls who come to sell you things, and learn a few words of Bahasa Indonesia along the way.

The stars of Kuta Beach are the surfers – and no longer just the Australians: the local village kids have now mastered the art of riding the waves and are just as good, if not better. The best waves are to be encountered from March to July, on a coral reef lying offshore. If you are new to surfing but are willing to take your chance, you can rent a second-hand board from one of the watersport shops in Kuta – but whether you actually make it to one of the breakers is another matter, because there are always a lot of crafty old hands just waiting to get up on a really good wave.

And when you are in the sea, do not underestimate the strength of the undertow, which every year claims more victims than the sharks. That is why lifeguard stations have been set up on the beach. So when you are swimming, stay near the beach, inside the reefs. Once you

are out beyond the third wave, it gets pretty dangerous.

If you are looking for quiet and solitude on the beach, you only have to walk a little way further along the coast in a north-westerly direction. Beyond Legian you virtually leave the hurly-burly behind you, and once you have passed the Oberoi Hotel you are alone with the roar of the surf. The beaches by the villages of Canggu and Seseh are still untouched by tourism. In theory it would be possible to walk as far as the sea-temple of Tanahlot, a good 8 miles (13 km); but in practice you would have to cross several estuaries, which are fairly deep at high water, and not everyone may want to try.

Travelers who visited Kuta in the early 1960s – usually backpackers on a low budget – found nothing there but a handfull of fishermen's huts and farmsteads, which looked idyllic enough under the cocnut palms, but were pretty poverty-stricken. Just a few simple hotels, nothing like the legendary Kuta Beach Hotel of the 1930s, catered for beach-holidays. Otherwise the nearest overnight accommodation was 6 miles (10 km) away in Denpasar. But the inhabitants of Kuta reacted quickly to the increase in demand and built simple *losmens* (basic but clean appartments, from the French: *logement*), for the long-stay travelers who appeared in their thousands in the 1970s – on the overland quest for paradise, which in those days was reckoned to lie somewhere between Afghanistan and the South Pacific. Today there are over 300 simple *losmens* for people who want to stay on a limited budget. In addition there are something like 60 bungalow establishments in the middle price-range, and a good dozen luxury hotels such as the Pertamina Cottages near the airport, and the Oberoi Hotel north of Legian.

If you take an afternoon stroll down **Jalan Legian**, you may well get the feeling that the tourism boom carries the

seeds of its own destruction.The 2-mile (3 km) long main street linking the once separate villages of Kuta and Legian, is jammed with smelly, hooting *bemos,* taxis, hire-cars and mopeds, through which death-defying cyclists weave their way. The fact that this is a one-way street does not make it any better. On the other hand, Jalan Legian offers everything the holidaymaker's heart could desire: money-changers, car and motor-cycle hire-firms, travel agents offering "cremation tours," video shops, fashion boutiques, hand-woven ceremonial cloths from Sumbawa, batik bikinis from Denpasar, transparency-film kept cool in the fridge, "Australian Bars," "Swiss Restaurants," open-air discos and, last but not least, call-boys for the lonely. Along the back streets leading down to the beach are row upon row of *losmens.*

Crazy as this gold-rush mentality may seem, there is no getting away from the

Above: On the beach at Kuta. Right: One of the great variety of beach peddlers.

fact that it has made the citizens of Kuta a great deal more prosperous than the rest of the island. A large part of the capital invested comes from Kuta itself, and profits are immediately re-invested – which is far from the case with the luxury hotels which have been dumped in the landscape at Sanur and Nusa Dua. On the debit side of this boom are theft, prostitution and drug-trafficking; however, the police have got things reasonably under control – at least during the day. After dark the "Anglers" get to work, sophisticated thieves whose speciality is silently fishing your valuables out from behind barred windows.

The direct route to the beach takes you along **Jalan Pantai Kuta**, which gets hopelessly jammed around sunset.This is where those who have discovered the secret of life, or are still looking for it, meet at any time of day or night in **Made's Warung.** While other trendy spots in Kuta come and go almost weekly, Made's has remained for 20 years simply *the* place, an institution sacred to the interna-

tional banana-pancake brigade. Sitting down with Australian jaffles, Javanese gado-gado, Italian capuccino, German apple-strudel, or English gin-and-tonic, and watching the world go by along Jalan Pantai – this is how one starts or ends the day. When Made's closes around midnight, "Kuta society" switches over to the Indian **New Goa** in Legian.

If you want to eat American-style in Kuta, do not despair: you can satisfy your craving at the Kentucky Fried Chicken outlet in the Gelael Supermarket on Jalan Imam Bonjol. For everyone else there is a broad spectrum of Asian and international cuisine on offer; and you should not miss the fresh fish and seafood, from tuna to lobster.

The culinary arts of Indonesia are revealed to you every evening in the **Pasar Senggol Night Market** (near the Post Office) – and at prices that do not make a big hole in your budget! This is the right atmosphere in which to try Balinese *babi goreng*, Javanese *sate ayam* or Chinese *cap cay.* In Poppies Lane, the "old estab-

lished" **Poppies** restaurant serves you in style with Balinese and Mexican dishes and Australian fish 'n chips. A restaurant famous throughout the island for its excelent Mexican tacos and enchiladas is **TJ's**, a little further down the same street, towards the beach. You can get a pizza right next door at **Fat Yogi**, and - 24 hours a day – at **Il Pirata.** Japanese secretaries on a few days' holiday buy their take-away snacks at **Takitate Bento** in Jalan Legian. An amazing variety of coffee is offered at **Benny's** – popular for brunch and at other times – you should try *Kopi Bali,* a native product from the highland interior of the island. You should beware of omelettes with ingredients described as "special" or "magic": they contain hallucinogenic mushrooms which have an effect that is similar to LSD.

From 10 pm onwards disco-fever takes over in Kuta and Legian. Old Bali hands then foregather in the **Gado-Gado** or the **Double Six** in Jalan Legian. A younger crowd can be found in the **Crazy Horse**

BUKIT BADUNG

The peninsula of Bukit Badung is connected to the mainland of Bali by a narrow isthmus edged with mangrove swamps. In contrast to the well-watered and fertile rice-growing country around Denpasar, it is a dry, porous, riverless plateau; a lump of limestone rising 600 ft (200 m) out of the sea – the name Bukit simply means "hill." Only between October and April is it possible to catch rain-water in paddy-fields; during the dry season the inhabitants have to draw water from cisterns. The soil is poor; bushes and cactus are the main vegetation, and the roads are bordered by acacias and kapok-trees. Until the last century the thinly populated peninsula, riddled with limestone caves, was reserved for hunting by the Rajas of Mengwi and Badung. On the west and south coasts there are high cliffs dropping dramatically to a rocky shore on which the great, long rollers of the Indian Ocean break continuously, attracting surfers from all over the world. At the south-west corner, perched spectacularly above a sheer, white chalk cliff is the sea-temple of Ulu Watu, which is well worth visiting. The east coast has magnificent sandy beaches, and it is here that the ambitious Nusa Dua hotel project took shape in the 1980s, almost seeming to grow out of the bare earth. This backward region, whose people once lived from fishing, salt-panning and plundering wrecked ships, has recently experienced a rapid transformation into a dream destination for international package tourists. Even some departments of Udayana University have been moved here as part of a long-term plan to urbanise what used to be the poorest area of Bali.

(which has live music) and the **Koala Blu**. The nearby discos, **Peanuts** and **Spotlight** attract their surf-shattered clientele every evening with strobe-lights and giant video projections.

A considerable number of up-market drop-outs from Europe and America have settled in and around Kuta. Many of them are involved in fashion design and provide inspiration for the astonishing variety of designs and fabrics on sale in innumerable textile shops – from the open-air stalls in Jalan Pantai, where you have to haggle with skill and persistence, up to the yuppie boutiques in Jalan Legian with their fixed price-tags. The most popular souvenirs include leather goods, bags and baskets woven in rattan, jewelry, paintings, wood-carvings, and ceramics which can be bought at the Art Market (Pasar Seni).

Above: Cliffs on the south coast of the Bukit Badung peninsula. Right: The entire south-west coast, including the Bukit Badung peninsula is a paradise for surfers.

In the neck of the peninsula lies the fishing village of **Jimbaran**. The impressive catches which are landed every morning from large seagoing boats on Jimbaran's western shore, go straight to

the kitchens of the big hotels in Sanur and Nusa Dua. The fine sandy beach of **Teluk Jimbaran** (Jimbaran Bay) is nearly 3 miles (5 km) long and, with new hotels under construction here, is being opened up for tourism. Because of a long offshore coral reef, only small outriggers or *prahus* are to be seen, with their brightly colored sails, skimming across the calm waters of the broad, crescent-shaped bay. The fishermen are happy to take paying passengers aboard.

Towards sunset, you should pay a visit to the attractive old village temple of **Pura Ulun Siwi,** which was built in the 17th century, under the Mengwi dynasty. It is maintained by rice-farmers and is the most important of the Subak shrines in Bali, dedicated to the rice-goddess Dewi Sri. Inside, sacred Barong and Rangda dance-masks can be seen, as well as a soaring, eleven-tiered *tumpang meru,* dedicated to Shiva.

The roads across the peninsula are still narrow, winding and full of potholes. Going south towards Ulu Watu, after the

turning off to the Udayan campus, motor-cyclists can head north-west, at the village of **Bakung**, along a rough road to the fishing-village of **Cengiling**. From here, a short walk brings you to the cave-temple of **Pura Balangan**, on the shore of an isolated sandy bay. At the northern end of this bay there is also a small Chinese temple, the **Pura Konco**.

From Bakung a rutted path takes you southward to a little sea-temple called **Pura Masuka,** standing high up on a breathtaking cliff. A little to the east of Bakung, in the village of **Ungasan**, another equally rutted path leads off to the cave-temple of **Pura Batu Pageh**, in a cave at the foot of a high cliff.

Continuing on the road to Ulu Watu, one passes **Gunung Ingas** which, at 663 ft (202 m), is the highest point of land in the peninsula. The winding road runs westward through Pecatu and arrives finally at the **Pura Luhur Ulu Watu**, the "temple atop the high cliffs." The name Luhur comes from *ngeluhur*, the Balinese word for "attainment of *moksa*,"

"enlightenment ;" for it is here that the 16th century Hindu religious teacher and reformer, Pedanda Bau Rauh, is said to have achieved the highest state of bliss through years of meditation. The temple is dedicated to the Goddess of the Sea, Dewi Danu, and the best time to visit it is when the sun is sinking into the sea and the stone of the temple is bathed in a coral-pink glow. The whole cliff, which drops a dizzying 660 ft (200 m) vertically into the Indian Ocean, is worshipped as the goddess's ship of stone, and the temple, which is one of the most important in Bali, is said to have been built in the 11th century by a Brahman named Kuturan, on the site of a pre-Hindu sacrificial altar. It is one of the nine "directional" temples which protect Bali from all sides; Ulu Watu guards the southwestern extremity of the island.

A flight of 70 steps leads up to a split *candi bentar* gate, decorated with the

heads of demons. Its curved shape is thought to represent the wings of the sacred bird, Garuda, which bore the god Vishnu. Behind it lies the temple forecourt (*jaba sisi*). Beyond, a covered doorway leads to the central courtyard. The Kori-Agung gate, through which one enters the Holy of Holies (*jeroan*), is unusual for Bali in being arched. It is flanked by two stone statues of the elephant-headed god Ganesha, in the same dancing pose that his divine father, Shiva, adopts as *Nataraja* (King of the Dance). Above the archway a much-weathered mask of Kala-Boma can be seen. In the inner courtyard stands a three-tiered *tumpang-meru* dedicated to Shiva, flanked by two limestone figures of watchmen armed with cudgels.

The simple, straw-roofed shrines are in themselves not particularly impressive, but the view over the cliffs and the sea is spectacular. On a clear day you can see as far as Cape Bantenan on Java, some 37 miles (60 km) distant. And not far away are some of the best surf beaches in the

Above: The temple of Pura Luhur Ulu Watu perches high above the waves.

world: **Suluban** is 1 1/4 miles (2 km) away, with restaurants and *losmens* on the beach, and northward lie **Padang-Padang** and **Balangan**.

At the north-east corner of Bukit Badung peninsula a long, flat spit of land thrusts out into the Bay of Benoa. Its landward side is fringed with mangroves, but the ocean side has a magnificent sandy beach. Up until ten years ago the local people lived mainly from fishing and harvesting coconuts. The little port of **Tanjung Benoa**, at the end of the spit, was inhabited mainly by Chinese merchants – a Buddhist temple still bears witness to this – and by Buginese sailors, whose descendants still gather every Friday in a small mosque.

Then in 1970, tourism experts from the World Bank homed in on the Hindu village of Buala and its deserted 2-mile (3 km) beach; in due course a multinational investment group developed a luxury-standard hotel complex here, called **Nusa Dua** (Two Islands). Only 8 miles (13 km) from Ngurah Rai airport, the first of these glitzy establishments, the **Buala Club Hotel**, opened its doors in 1979, also serving as a practical training-school for the neighboring college of hotel management. By 1992, seven more luxury hotels had been put up, providing 3000 beds for sun-seekers from all over the world, who must come prepared to spend freely during the most expensive weeks of the year, at Christmastime and in July and August. Cynics describe Nusa Dua as a "beach ghetto:" for this artificial paradise, with its elegantly landscaped gardens laid out beneath coconut palms, is fenced and guarded. Peddlers and massage-ladies are not admitted, and one is insulated from all the noise , bustle and smells that are so typical of Balinese life. By buying up large areas of land and fencing them off, the developers have carefully avoided the unsightly spread of *losmen*s such as one sees in Kuta, Ubud, Lovina Beach and Candi Dasa. The more sports-

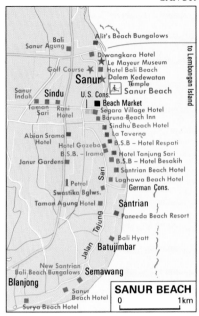

minded vistor will find a wide range of activities on offer at Nusa Dua, including tennis, riding, scuba-diving and snorkeling, parasailing, sail-boarding and, of course, surfing.

SANUR

The blue lagoon of Sanur is protected from the ocean rollers by a coral reef. Its waters are therefore delightfully calm most of the time, and ideal for sailboarding or snorkelling – the vivid colors of the little fish that swim among the coral are quite breathtaking. However, at low tide the sharp edges of the coral can be a problem if you want to bathe. There are enjoyable trips to be made out to the reef in boats called *jukungs*. These are outriggers, with brightly colored sails, in which the fisherman go out at night, equipped with kerosine lamps, to catch prawns. During the day you will find them at the landing-stage at the end of Jalan Hangtuah, near the Alit Beach bungalows. There are also boat-trips to Serangan,

71

Lembongan and Nusa Penida.The more courageous can try parasailing, and get a birds-eye view of the 3-mile (5 km) long Sanur beach.

In contrast to the bustling life of Kuta, Sanur has a reputation for being quieter and more civilized (as well as more expensive), and is popular with older visitors. Early risers are treated to a picturesque sight when the sun rises at about 6 a.m. over the island of Nusa Penida.

Back in the 1930s, this palm-fringed beach paradise was discovered by western artists and became a popular refuge for well-to-do lotus-eaters. Among these trend-setters were the German painter, Walter Spies, and the novelist Vicki Baum, who wrote *Life and Death in Bali.* Then there was the American ethnologist Jane Belo (author of *Trance in Bali*), and Margaret Mead, the anthropologist who made a close study of the Brahmans of Sanur. This traditional Pedanda community was once held by the Balinese to be the home of "Black Barong," whose dangerous magic power required constant appeasing. Nowadays the hearts and minds of the local tradespeople respond more readily to the magic of the credit-card produced from the pocket of a pair of batik bermuda shorts. Notwithstanding, the temple of **Pura Dalem Kedewatan** in Sanur (near the remains of the Bali beach Hotel, which was destroyed by fire in 1993), is frequently the scene of religious processions. The resident Brahmans, known beyond the island as being learned in the *vedas* and experts in sacrificing, receive many visits from devout Hindus seeking spiritual solace. A temple dance featuring the *kris,* unique to this village, is performed only by women – and then only on rare occasions.

Before the Second World War the Belgian artist, Adrien Jean Le Mayeur, set up a studio in Sanur, and as well as painting

Right: Outriggers waiting for the next trip out from the beach at Sanur.

in the post-impressionist style, he collected antique sculpture from all over Bali. After his death his house was converted into the **Museum Le Mayeur**. It can be found near the beach, south of the Diwangkara Hotel. The artist appears to have been more than a little fascinated by bare-breasted Balinese girls, and must have been happy to escape from the inhibitions of Europe: he married his favorite model, the talented native dancer, Ni Polok, who lived on until 1985.

In the 1960s the then president of Indonesia, Sukarno, who was himself half-Balinese, decided to open up the island to tourism, as a means of bringing in much-needed foreign currency. The necessary capital investment was provided by the Japanese – as reparations for their occupation of the island during World War Two. Thus it was that in 1966 Sanur saw the opening of the 10-storey **Bali Beach Hotel**, the first modern hotel on the island to meet international luxury standards. It had tennis-courts, a bowling-alley and a 6-hole golf-course, and catered predominantly for Japanese visitors. However, it was ill-starred from the outset and suffered from ghosts and apparitions in the early years until a temple was built in its grounds. But even this does not appear to have appeased the gods, since in January 1993 it burned down.

Newer, pricier and more exclusive is the **Bali Hyatt,** one of the famous American chain, situated further down the beach to the south. Its design is strongly influenced by Balinese architecture, even down to the swimming pool which features a replica of the grotto of Goa Gajah. This efficiently run hotel also has the most fashionable disco in Sanur, with an international clientele.

Another luxury establishment is the **Sanur Beach Hotel**, with well-tended gardens, several restaurants, an open-air stage on which traditional dancing is performed every evening, and a first-class buffet beside the pool. Owned by the In-

donesian state airline, Garuda, it has more than 400 rooms and is located at the southern end of the beach.

Most of the hotels, restaurants and souvenir-shops are stretched out along **Jalan Tanjung Sari,** which runs parallel to the coast. As you might expect in a high-class beach resort, both quality and prices are noticeably higher than in Kuta. On the beach, at the end of Jalan Segara Ayu, the villagers of Sanur run the **Beach Market,** a co-operative venture selling handicrafts, batik clothes and beautifully painted paper kites – since kite-flying is a favorite pastime among the boys of the village.

Expedition to Serangan

The little island of Serangan lies just 1 1/4 miles (2 km) off the southern end of Sanur beach. The shortest crossings are from **Mesigit** or **Suwung,** from where motorized *jukungs* take passengers over to the island. About 2000 people live there, most of whom are Moslems. The main village is **Dukuh**, in the north. The islanders' chief source of income is breeding sea-turtles (*penyu*). Off the beach at Dukuh, bamboo cages lie in the water in which the turtles are fattened up. The meat from these creatures is appreciated both by the native Balinese and by the tourists, and is eaten either grilled on a skewer as *Sate*, or minced up as *Lawar*. Unfortunately, the turtle-farms of Serangan are unable to produce enough to meet the growing demand of the restaurant trade, and the sea-turtles are threatened with extinction. This is because they are now brought in by fisherman who catch them in the wild, round the islands of eastern Indonesia. So if you eat sea-turtle in Bali you are contributing to the disappearance of yet another species from our planet! Worse still, the islanders regard turtle eggs as a delicacy, so ever fewer of these armour-plated reptiles come out of the water to lay their eggs in the sand, and if they do, the eggs are immediately dug up and taken to market in Denpasar to be sold along with the turtles themselves.

73

to Sanur

LEMBONGAN
ISLAND

to Kusamba   to Kusamba

Reef
Cape Biasmenfik Prapat Ped Dalem
Jungutbatu   Penataran Kutampi Mentigi
              Toyapakeh   Ped Temple   Telaga Sampalan Batumalapan
Lembongan   Sentalkangin
                    Biyaung Sentalkawan   Reef
              Sebunibus   289   Karangsari Cave
                          Jurangpait Glagah   Karangsari
          Sakti
CENINGAN   139   Celagilandan
ISLAND   Klumpu   Suwana
              Pundukakaja Mt.Mundi   Pulagan Batu Medau
        P E N I D A 529 I S L A N D   Temple
          Penangkidan   Semaya
        Karangjawa Batumadeg   Pejukutan
Cape Sari   Sebuluh   Karang
                        Batukandik 439
          228   Antapan
                    Dungkap   Tanglad
                  Debuloh   Cape Abah
                          422
                        Pamuhan
            Cape Moling   Sekartaji

NUSA PENIDA
0   4km   Cape Bakung

Another important economic activity on the island involves mussels, which divers bring up from the sea bottom. The shells are polished to a high gloss and touted by peddlers who will sell anything in the eternal pursuit of a quick rupiah.

Every year at the festival of *Manis Kuningan* thousands of visitors come to the **Sakenan Temple** at the north-west point of the island, to make a sacrifice to the rice-goddess Dewi Sri and pray for the fertility and prosperity of their family, fields and livestock. In a ceremonial procession of boats, tall figures of Barong-Landung are carried over the waves in order to appease the sea-demons – for the Balinese have a deep-rooted fear of the sea and its unpredictable moods.

NUSA LEMBONGAN

Hardly more than 12 miles (20 km) from Sanur lies a group of three islands, Nusa Lembongan, Nusa Ceningan and Nusa Penida. ("Nusa" means island). Ceningan is the smallest, and Penida is by far the largest. But of the three, Lembongan is the most interesting for tourists. If you are going from Sanur, the most comfortable (and safest) trip is in the passenger launch operated by Bali International Yacht Club. However, the islands can also be reached from Nusa Dua (by charter boat), and by fishing-boat from Kusamba and Padangbai, further up the coast near Klungkung.

If you charter a motorized *jukung* in Sanur – the larger the better – it will take about an hour and a half to reach Lembongan, across the Straits of Badung (Selat Badung), and you will be put ashore at **Jungut Batu.**

The island is only 2 1/2 miles long and 1 1/2 wide (4 km by 2.5 km) and can easily be explored in half a day. But few people do: the white coral sand of the beach near the landing-stage is much too inviting. Divers and snorkellers can spend many happy hours in the crystal-clear waters round the coral reef a little way offshore; and the channel between Lembongan and Ceningan is also known to be a first-class area for snorkelling. All equipment can be hired, including surf-boards. A good tip for surfers: try the breakers over the coral-covered hulk of a wrecked ship.

There are already more then a dozen simple *losmens* in Jungut Batu, as well as some *warungs* and basic restaurants. Fish-dishes are particularly good value, whereas meat has to be brought in from the mainland.

The fact that jaffles feature on the menu indicates that hungry Australian surfers make up the bulk of the guests. A more important source of income than tourism, for the 5000 predominantly Hindu islanders is the cultivation of sea-grass (*siwi*), which is grown in planta-tions near the main village of the island, in exceptionally clear water. It is chiefly supplied to the cosmetic industry. How-ever, the state tourism planners fear that the rather unpleasant smell will put off potential package-holidaymakers, and are earnestly entreating the sea-grass growers to move to Sulawesi!

The interior of the low-lying island is dry and rocky, overgrown with cacti and scrub, in which lizards scuttle about. Anyone seeking peace and quite will cer-tainly find it on this island: there are neither mopeds nor *bemos* – it is one big pedestrian zone, and no-one will try to sell you wood-carvings, paintings or sa-rongs on the beach. One can only hope that the assembled demons of Bali will haunt the investors who propose to turn the place into another Kuta!

Offerings to the sea-gods are made in a **sea temple**, hidden among the man-groves on the coast north of Jungut Batu.

It is only half-an-hour's walk to the old Hindu village of **Lembongan**, the is-land's "capital." Apart from a few little temples built from bright coral stone, and some small shops, this unspoilt village has one curiosity to offer: a subterranean labyrinth, which a villager built beneath his house, presumably to keep away de-mons. Called **Rumah Goa**, which means "House of Caves," it is open to visitors.

NUSA PENIDA

The island of Nusa Penida –12 miles long and 7 1/2 miles wide (20 km by 12 km) and known simply as Nusa to the lo-cals – is believed by the mainland Ba-linese to be the home of a malevolent and dangerous demon called Ratu Gede Ma-caling. Under the name of Jero Gede he appears in the *Barong-Landung* dance as a towering black figure, who, in the dual-istic Balinese world order, functions as the opponent of all that is light, good and creative. The Rajas of Klungkung (the adminstrative region which includes Penida) used at one time to banish mis-creants to this island.

With its dry limestone landscape, where lack of water makes rice-growing impossible, Nusa Penida has none of the charm one associates with Bali. The highest point on the island is **Bukit Mundi,** (1736 ft / 529 m)**.**

There are easily accessible beaches in the north and north-east of the island, whereas the south coast is made up of sheer cliffs, rising to 650 ft (200 m). In the 1920s, Walter Spies discovered a rare species of greenish-colored bat here; and the bird-life of the island includes the white cockatoo and Rothschild's mynah.

The fishing-boats which run from Ku-samba in eastern Bali, will land you on the flat north coast near the little market-town of **Toyapakeh**. There you will find a beautiful white, sandy beach, fringed with palms and looking across to the is-land of Lembongan; but the few tourists who stray there cause such a sensation among the village children that a quiet, undisturbed swim is out of the question. Fishing and seaweed-growing are the main sources of income for the predomi-nantly Moslem inhabitants of Nusa Peni-da's north coast. In the morning, *bemos* run along the "main road", eastwards,

parallel with the beach. On this road lies the inhospitable dwelling of the monster Jero Gede, the **Pura Dalem Penataran Ped**. The island is too poor to afford a temple of any great splendor; the shrine to the dreaded black demon Mecaling stands in the middle of a slimy, green pond. Every three years pilgrims from all over Bali come to sacrifice at the festival of *Usaba*.

So far, the only accommodation on Nusa Penida is to be found in the main town of the island, **Sampalan,** in the form of the simple, government-owned Pemda Bungalows. You will find them near the little harbor of **Mentigi**, which is always crowded with outriggers from Kusamba and Padangbai. In the market of Sampalan, you can buy the local speciality, grilled tuna-fish.

If you want to explore the interior of the island, you need to be able to speak a little Indonesian, since tourists are practi-

Above: Using a rope sling is the only way to climb up and harvest the coconuts.

cally unknown here. The condition of the roads is almost beyond belief to a Westerner. A few rickety *bemos* manage to struggle along them, but they are ideal for mountain-biking. If you have rented a motor-cycle in Bali, you can bring it with you on the *jukung*. You won't regret it. Occasionally motor-cyclists will offer to taxi you about as a pillion passenger, but you are taking your life in your hands!

About 2 1/2 miles (4 km) south-east of Sampalan, a path branches off to the sacred cave of **Goa Karangsari**, where, needless to say, a demon is believed to live. To look at this gigantic stalactite cave, you have to be guided by one of the local children – but negotiate a fee in advance! They will also provide the powerful kerosene lamps, without which you will not be able to see the innumerable bats which flit about above you. In one branch of the extensive network of limestone caverns there is supposed to be a subterranean lake. Emerging into the sunlight again, you will find a beautiful beach of pale sand near the fishing village of **Suwana**. There is another at **Karang**, further to the south-east, but this is rather inaccessible. You approach it through Pejukutan. Near Suwana stands a sea-temple: the **Pura Batu Medau.**

In the middle of the island, at **Batukandik,** there is a religious site, presumed to be pre-Hindu, with a primitive stone sculpture of a mother-goddess with enormous breasts. This is 4 1/2 miles (7 km) east of the village of **Batumadeg,** which is occasionally served by *bemos*. From the village you can also take the road through **Sebuluh** to the wild and romantic south-west coast, with its impressive 650 ft (200 m) high chalk cliffs. Fishermen have established lofty platforms, built into the sheer cliff-face, from where they put out their lines. The villagers living up on the limestone plateau have no immediate water-supply and have to make their way down hair-raising paths to collect fresh water from springs.

DENPASAR

If you can avoid Denpasar, you should do so. It is only worth visiting for the museums, or if you have official dealings with the authorities (for example, if you need to get a motor-cycle license).

Accommodation

LUXURY CLASS: **Bali Hotel**, Jl. Veteran 3, Tel: 25681, attractively furnished, from US$ 48.
MID-PRICE: **Pemecutan Palace**, Jl. Thamrin 2, Tel: 23491, historic setting, near terminus for bemos to Kuta; higher-priced accommodation available, from Rps. 15,000.
BUDGET: **Adi Yasa**, Jl. Nakula 11, Tel: 22679, once popular with backpackers, from Rps. 8.000; **Losmen Marhaen**, Jl. Diponegoro, Gang VII/4, Tel: 23781, from Rps. 7,000.

Restaurants

The Restaurant in the **Bali Hotel** has a good Rijsta-fel. Otherwise you can find good-value Chinese restaurants on Jl. Gajah Mada: **Hongkong**, self-service; Indonesian *warungs* on Jl. Teuku Umar: **Simpang Enam**, Balinese, Indonesian, Chinese; the same on Jl. Diponegoro: **Melati**, Javanese food. The **Café Amsterdam,** on Jl. Diponegoro, serves various specialities, ice-cream and steaks.

Museum

Bali Museum, Puputan Square, open daily except Monday from 8 am until 5 pm, Friday until 3.30 pm; (200 Rps.)

Shopping

Shops selling everything that Bali has to offer – and at rather lower prices than in Kuta – can be found on Jl. Gajah Mada and Jl. Kartini. Opening hours are usually from 9 am until 1 pm and 5 pm until 8 pm.

Important addresses

The Post Office is a little way from the center in Renon, on Jl. Raja Puputan. Just round the corner in Jl. Panjaitan is the Immigration Office. One block to the north, on Jl. Raja Puputan, is the Balinese **Tourist Bureau**.
There is a **telephone office** next to the Post Office in Renon, and another on Jl. Diponegoro south of Jl. Yos Sudarso.
There is no British Consulate but British matters are handled by the Australian Consulate, Jl. Raya Sanur 146, Tel: 35092, Fax: 31990. This consulate also looks after New Zealand and Canadian citizens. The nearest US Consulate is in the resort town of Sanur, Jl. Segara Ayu 5, Tel: (0361) 88478.
The hospital (**RSUP**) which has emergency and intensive-care departments, is in the south-west of the town on Jl. Aru.

KUTA / LEGIAN
Accommodation

In Kuta and Legian, there are over 300 losmens and other basic accommodation from Rps. 10,000 (about £3.60 or US $ 5.90) upwards – as well as a number of attractive medium and luxury-class hotels. The rapid boom has admittedly also produced some rather charmless establishments. Anyone travelling on a limited budget should carefully check the hygiene (get them to show you the *mandi* or shower !) and the location (close to beach and restaurants, but not to building-sites or the noisy main streets). With care, even a little money will get you comfortable and attractive lodgings.
Legian is a bit quieter than Kuta. The hotels in the center between Kuta Beach Hotel and Legian Beach Hotel often have a view of the sea, but are separated from the beach by a road. Prices quoted are always for a double room.
LUXURY CLASS: **Bali Intan Cottages**, Jl. Melasti 1, Legian, P.O. Box 1002 Tuban 80361, Tel: 51770, Fax: 35200, near beach, from US$ 70;
Bali Oberoi, Jl. Kaya Ayu, Legian, P.O. Box 351 Denpasar, Tel: 51061, Fax: 52791, on a quiet beach north of Legian, from US$ 150;
Kartika Plaza, Jl. Kartika, Kuta, P.O. Box 84 Denpasar, Tel: 51067, on the beach, from US$ 80;
Kuta Palace, Jl. Pura Bagus Taruna, Legian, P.O. Box 244 Denpasar, Tel: 51433, Fax: 52074, on the beach, from US$ 75;
Pertamina Cottages, Kuta Beach, P.O. Box 121 Denpasar, Tel: 51161 Fax: 52030, on the beach, close to the airport, from US$ 110.
MID-PRICE: **Bruna Beach Inn**, P.O. Box 116 Denpasar, Tel: 51565, Fax: 53201, near the beach, central location, from US$ 17;
Kuta Cottages, Jl. Bakungsari, P.O. Box 300 Denpasar, Tel: 51101, near the beach, from US$ 22;
Legian Beach, Jl. Melasti, Legian, P.O. Box 308 Denpasar, Tel: 51365, on the beach, from US$ 40;
Nusa di Nusa, Seminyak, P.O. Box 191 Denpasar, Tel: 51414, Fax: 51746, north of Legian near the beach, very quiet location, from US$ 30;
Poppies Cottages, Poppies Lane, P.O. Box 378 Denpasar, Tel: 51059, in the middle of Kuta, with garden and swimming-pool, from US$ 55.
BUDGET: **Anom Dewi Youth Hostel**, in a side-street in the middle of Kuta, from Rps. 10,000 for bed only; **Baleka Beach Inn**, Legian Kaja, Tel: 51931, north of Legian, with swimming-pool, from Rps. 12.000; **Berlian Inn**, Poppies Lane, Kuta, Tel: 51501, central location, from Rps. 15.000; **Kempu Taman Ayu**, near Poppies Lane, Kuta, central, but fairly quiet, from Rps. 9.000; **La Walon Bungalows**, Poppies Lane, Kuta, central, from Rps. 20.000; **Three Brothers Bungalows**, Legian, Tel:

51566, spaciously laid out, accommodation in various price-categories, quiet, has long been a well-kept secret, from US$ 10.

Restaurants

New places are springing up all the time. The choice ranges from good, simple Asian dishes from the wok, to Swiss *röschti*, French *nouvelle* cuisine and American fast food. Here are just a few examples in addition to those already mentioned in the section on Kuta:

If you are not breakfasting in your hotel, try **Za's Bakery** in Jl. Legian or the **Treehouse Restaurant** in Poppies Lane, both in Kuta.

The **Warung Kopi**, in Legian, serves Indian vegetarian food.

For a modest sum you can eat **Nasi Campur** in the restaurant of the same name, on Jl. Raya Kuta.

The beer and pepper steaks are reasonably priced at the **Blue Pub** on Jl.Legian, while **Yannies** is better known for the tame owl which flaps around than for its hamburgers.

The fish and sea-food are good at both branches of **Bali Indah.**

If you are not put off by the Australian atmosphere, **Waltzing Matilda** serves excellent crab dishes. Also excellent is the Thai restaurant **Sawasdee**, in Jl.Pura Bagus Taruna. Their fish soup spiced with lemon-grass has brought tears to the eyes of many a strong man.

In fact, the whole of Jl. Pura Bagus Taruna has become a happy hunting-ground for gourmets looking for meals with a difference, while homesick Europeans can can enjoy solid fare at the **Swiss Restaurant**.

Very popular for its ambience as well as for its food, is the **Bamboo Palace Restaurant** in the same street.

Entertainment and nightlife

Faced with the weekly changing "in" scene, and the incredible number of bars and dives, the general advice can only be: if you like noise, head for the loud discos and bars on Jl. Buni Sari and Jl. Legian. Those who prefer something quieter and more civilised should look in the side-streets or down near the beach.

Anyone who keeps their eyes open will notice that in Legian particularly, the cultural and religious life of the Balinese goes on despite the tourist hurly-burly. In the banjar center, near the Warung Kopi, they practise loudly and enthusiastically on the gamelan for festivals and ceremonies. There they will tell you when the Barong is next going to attend to the spiritual purification of the town.

Shopping

In Kuta and Legian, you can find an incredible variety of goods on sale, from mass-produced items for the tourist market to individual pieces of beautiful craftsmanship. On the spot, it is mainly textiles that are produced. In Kuta, there are several shops which only sell clothes in black and white. Increasingly, the really smart shops are moving to Legian. And their European designer-owners insist on the full prices. Elsewhere bargaining is the rule.

If you want to have something made to order, it is essential to take a pattern or a piece of clothing to be copied. You should look carefully at how well the seams are done. Leather clothes can also be bought off the peg or made to measure. If you are having something made, you should order it at the beginning of the holiday because alterations are often necessary. As you travel round the rest of Bali, it is a good idea to use Kuta prices for comparison purposes. In other places everything should be rather cheaper, especially the average tourist souvenirs.

Important addresses

The **Post Office** is located in a little side-street called Jl. Tujung Mekar, near the night-market, in the south-east of Kuta.

Public **Telephone offices** in Kuta: on Jl. Bakung Sari, right beside the supermarket, or on Jl. Legian near Peanuts; in Legian: Jl. Legian between Jl. Melasti and Jl. Padma.

The **Tourist office** is on Jl. Bakung Sari, east of Jl. Buni Sari, Tel: 51419.

The office of **Garuda Airlines** is in the gounds of the Kuta Beach Hotel at the western end of Jl. Pantai Kuta, Tel: 51179. There is a waiting list which you must put your name on so that you can be called to the desk in turn.

The **Swiss Consulate** is on Jl. Legian Kelod in Kuta, Tel: and Fax: 51735

Transport

To get around Kuta/Legian or go elsewhere, you can hire a bemo or a taxi at any time of day at any junction of Jl. Legian or on the beach road. (Negotiate the price in advance). Sample price for a taxi-ride from the airport to the Oberoi Hotel: Rps. 10.000. Bemos operate regularly from the Bemo station at the little roundabout in Jl. Pantai Kuta to Denpasar (Rps. 400) and to the airport. For other destinations, one must change at Denpasar.

Denpasar is also the starting point for long-distance bus journeys, e.g. to Jakarta. From Jl. Legian in Kuta, the *Perama* bus company runs regular services to other destinations of interest to tourists. Examples: Airport Rps. 3,500; Ubud Rps. 4,000; Lovina Beach Rps. 10,000; Candi Dasa Rps. 7,500;

Senggigi, on Lombok Rps. 13,000; Bangsal on Lombok, the harbor for Gili Air island, Rps. 15,000.

Vehicle hire

Because there is so much competition between hire-firms, Kuta/Legian is the best place to rent Jeeps, motor-cycles, mopeds or pedal-bikes. The general rule is: if you hire for a longer period, you can get a reduction on the daily rate.

Sample prices: Jeep for one day, Rps. 42,000; for one week, Rps. 38,000 per day; for longer, Rps. 35,000 or less per day; equivalent prices for motorbike Rps. 12,000, Rps. 10,000 and Rps. 8,000. Push-bikes are around Rps. 3,000 per day. If you are hiring a motor-bike for a longish period, you should allow a few days to try it out, in order to sort out any mechanical problems. If you want to ride to Lombok on a motor-bike, make sure that your permit is valid for Lombok as well as Bali. If it is not, you will be relentlessly turned back at the ferry.

Petrol (gas) stations can be found on the road north out of Legian and on the road out of Kuta, heading for Sanur.

NUSA DUA
Accommodation

With one exception, all the hotels within the enclosed area of Nusa Dua are in the *LUXURY CLASS:* **Bali Sol**, P.O. Box 1048 Tuban, Tel: 71510, from US$ 78;

Club Bualu, P.O. Box 6 Nusa Dua, Tel: 71310, from US$ 70;

Club Méditerranée, P.O. Box 1 Nusa Dua, Tel: 71520, from US$ 100;

Nusa Dua Beach, P.O. Box 1028 Tuban, Tel: 71210, Fax: 71229, from US$ 120.

MID-PRICE: **Lancun Guesthouse**, Tel: 71983, from US$ 25.

Outside the area, in Tanjung Benoa, there are a few losmens. The cheapest is **Homestay Asa,** from Rps. 17,000.

Restaurants

Every hotel has its own restaurant. The outstanding one is the **Benoa Harbour Restaurant** in the Club Bualu. If you want something simpler and cheaper, you have to go to Tanjung Benoa. Even the restaurants outside the hotel-zone are relatively expensive by Balinese standards.

SANUR
Accommodation

LUXURY CLASS: **Bali Hyatt**, Jl. Tanjung Sari, P.O. Box 392 Denpasar, Tel: 88271, very big hotel complex, but beautifully integrated in the landscape, double rooms from US$ 100;

Diwangkara Beach, Jl. Raya Sanur, P.O. Box 120 Denpasar, Tel: 88577, somewhat hidden beside the sea, from US$ 45;

New Santrian Bali Beach Bungalows, Jl. Semawang, P.O. Box 55 Denpasar, Tel: 88009, Fax: 88185, two swimming-pools, from US$ 60;

Sanur Beach, Jl. Semawang, P.O. Box 279 Denpasar, Tel: 88011, Fax: 87566, from US$ 100.

MID-PRICE: **Alit's Beach Bungalows**, Jl. Hang Tuah Pantai Sanur, P.O. Box 102 Denpasar, Tel: 88567, close to the beach, from US$ 40; **Gazebo Cottages**, Jl. Tanjung Sari, P.O. Box 134 Denpasar, Tel: 88300, has a somewhat faded charm, on the sea, from US$ 35; **Sindhu Beach**, Jl. Pantai Sindhu, P.O. Box 181 Denpasar, Tel: 88441, on the sea, from US$ 40; **Swastika Bungalows**, Jl. Batujimbar, Tel: 88693, beautiful garden, two pools, but not right on the sea, from US$ 30.

BUDGET: **Abian Srama**, Jl. Bypass, Tel: 88792, from US$ 15; three hotels on the far side of the main through road, inland on Jl. Segara offer the cheapest accommodation: **Rani** (from Rps. 15,000), **Taman Sari** (from Rps. 15,000) and **Sanur Indah** (from Rps. 12,000).

Restaurants

All the big hotels have restaurants with correspondingly high prices. For homesick Europeans, there is Italian cuisine in the **Trattoria da Marco** and Swiss food (what else?) in the **Swiss Restaurant**. If you like fish, we can recommend **Lenny's** and the **Kulkul Restaurant**. There are two East Asian restaurants on Jl. Danau Tamblingan: the **New Seoul Korean Restaurant** and the **Japanese Restaurant**. If your stomach has got used to local food, the best and also the cheapest meals can be had at a food-stall on the jetty where the boats leave for Lembongan, or in the inconspicuous little **Wayan's Warung** at the junction of Jl. Tanjung Sari and Jl. Pantai Karang.

Important addresses

Post Office, Jl. Segara, inland. In the Bali Beach hotel complex, you will find offices of the following **airlines** : Cathay Pacific, Continental Airlines, Garuda, KLM, Malaysian Airlines, Qantas, Singapore Airlines and Thai Airways.

The **United States Consulate** is at Jl. Segara Ayu 5, Tel: 80228, Fax: 87760.

Museum

North of the Bali Beach Hotel, the **Museum Le Mayeur** is open daily except Mondays from 8 am until 2 pm, on Fridays only until 11 am, and on Saturdays only until 12 noon. Entrance: Rps. 200. Most of the pictures on display are by the museum's founder, the Belgian artist Adrien Jean Le Mayeur.

CULTURE AND KITSCH
IN BALI'S HOLY LAND

BADUNG

TABANAN

GIANYAR

BANGLI

Central Bali is the cultural heartland of this devoutly Hindu island. Here, away from the main roads, you will find ancient temples, picturesque rice-terraces and a peasant way of life in the villages. The rice-goddess Dewi Sri has looked kindly on the people of central Bali, where it is possible to gather three harvests a year. Water for irrigation is plentiful; numberless streams run down from the volcanic massifs of Batur, Catur and Batukau, cutting deep valleys in the rich red loam, as they flow onward to the sea. The course of these rivers also dictates the pattern of the roads; it is expensive to build bridges and so cross-country connecting routes are rare. Administratively speaking, central Bali is made up of the districts or "regencies" of Badung and Tabanan in the west, and Gianyar and Bangli in the eastern part.

BADUNG

About 12 miles (20 km) north of Denpasar, on the road to Singaraja, stands the residence of the once mighty Raja of Mengwi, whose empire declined at the end of the 19th century. On the way to

Previous pages: At work in the terraced rice-paddies. Left: Returning from the temple.

Mengwi one first passes through the village of **Ubung**, famous for its potters. The busy main road, which, as far as Kapal, also carries heavy truck traffic heading for Java, soon reaches **Sempidi**, a village with three beautifully decorated temples, Pura Desa, Pura Dalem and Pura Puseh. **Lukluk,** the next village on this stretch, is proud of its Pura Dalem temple, which has brightly painted reliefs depicting scenes from the world of farmers and craftsmen.

After a further 10 miles (16 km), one reaches the village of **Kapal,** which is in fact famous for producing clay figures and stone sculpture – but on request they will swiftly cast a Hindu god in cement and paint it with gaudy acrylic lacquer: the Balinese equivalent of a garden-gnome. There is a big demand for new religious statuary, since the damp, warm tropical atmosphere has eaten away many ancient figures almost beyond recognition. All over the island, temples are being restored and their courtyards and gardens beautified: with Garudas, Rangdas and demons from Kapal. Alongside this, there is good business in manufacturing more worldly ceramic products such as drainpipes and lavatory-bowls.

The **Pura Puseh** at Kapal does have some interesting reliefs with scenes from the *Ramyana*, but the real architectural

83

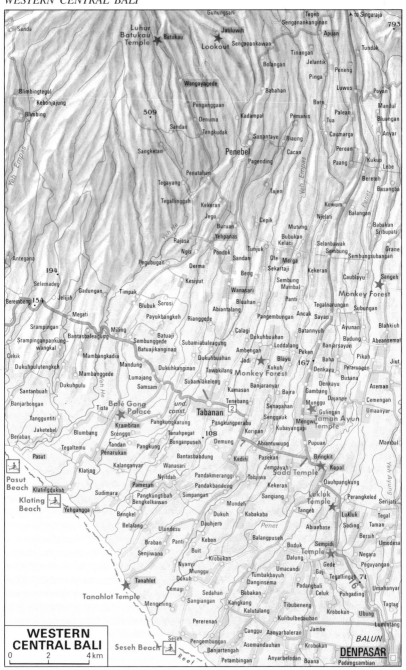

jewel is to be found a few hundred yards (0.5 km) south of the village's main street (about 15 minutes on foot): this is the splendid **Pura Sada,** the ancestral and royal temple of the Rajas of Mengwi. Probably built in the 14th century, its entrance is guarded by an ancient, spreading banyan-tree, whose thick aerial roots conceal a stone throne for the demons of the underworld. In the walled forecourt there are two *bales* for the preparation of sacrificial offerings and for meetings. A covered gateway leads to the *jeroan* or inner temple courtyard. This is dominated by an eleven-tiered, brick-built *candi* (also called a *prasada*), which was restored in 1949 and is reminiscent of the East Javanese Majapahit style. It represents the mountain of the gods, which is held to be the seat of Shiva and was the ritual center of the Mengwi rajadom – its phallic shape was meant to represent the vitality and procreative force of the deified raja. The first of the roofs (the *tumpang*) is decorated with Kala-Boma heads, and on all four sides and corners of the vast base of the temple tower sit the directional gods or *Nawa Sanga*, which the Hindus of Bali adopted from Indian Mahayana Buddhism.

There are a remarkable number of stone thrones in the *jeroan*, 57 of them in all. The **Mekel Masatia,** a group of three larger thrones (on the right as you enter), appear to be a reminder of the Hindu custom of widow-burning (*sati*), which as recently as the beginning of this century was finally banned by the Dutch. According to another legend the three large thrones are dedicated to the leaders of 54 servants who are said to have accompanied the ashes of an East Javanese raja to Bali, in the distant past.

Mengwi

The village of Mengwi, once the center of power in this region, can still be proud to have within its boundaries one of the

most beautiful temples in Bali, the **Pura Taman Ayun**. If you want to enjoy it in tranquility, you must get up early; from 10 am onwards it is overrun with coachloads of tourists. *Taman ayun* means "floating garden," which describes the place very accurately: the royal temple was built around 1740 by the Mengwi rajas, who were members of the Ksatriya caste, and stands on an island surrounded by still, lotus-covered water, that is more like a small lake than a moat. On its banks stand flowering frangipani trees and fruit-trees such as mangosteen, rambutan and durian. The inner courtyard of the temple is enclosed by another, smaller moat.

The buildings and their setting reflect the 18th century Hindu concept of the world as seen by the powerful Mengwi rulers of the time: the orientation is northwards, in the *kaja* direction of the mountains, the volcanoes and the sacred lake of Bratan, whose water feeds the rivers Sungi and Petan. The corresponding seatemple, in the south of Bali, is the Ulun Siwi, which wards off sea demons. It stands on the isthmus leading to the peninsula of Bukit Badung, south of Denpasar. And in the center, in the Pura Taman Ayun, the rajas of Mengwi, supported by the *pedandas* with their vedic wisdom, held the cosmic powers of creation and destruction in harmonious equilibrium through sacrificial ceremonies. But this fine balance was disturbed when, in 1891, the rival rajadoms of Klungkung, Badung, Tabanan and Bangli launched an attack on Mengwi. They were victorious and proceeded to divide up the territory which they had coveted for its fertile rice-fields, the rich coffee-plantations in the north-west and not least for its lucrative trade in opium. Yet the inhabitants of this region still preserve an identity which harks back to the great days of the Mengwi raj.

Fruit and lemonade are sold by businesslike ladies in *warungs* at the entrance

to the causeway over the water to the temple island. In the first courtyard there is a large open-sided hall with a tiered roof, which is used for meetings and dance performances. A flight of seven steps leads up to a *candi bentar* gate through which one reaches the second courtyard. In it stands a tall *kulkul* (bell tower) which you are allowed to climb in order to get a view of the attractive, terraced temple grounds.

A further staircase brings you to the slightly raised *jeroan*, or holy of holies. But first you pass through a gateway reminiscent of south Indian temple towers and then over a small bridge across the inner moat. On the west (left) side of the courtyard are several *bales*, in the middle a stone lotus-throne for the triple gods Brahma, Vishnu and Shiva, and on the east side a row of pagoda-like *merus*. Three of these *merus*, of different

Above: A pause near the Pura Taman Ayun in Mengwi. Right: Plinth decoration in the holy of holies of the Pura Taman Ayun.

heights, standing diagonally behind the *padmasana* (lotus-throne) are said to be dedicated to the mountain deities; a nine-tiered *meru* for the "Lord of Lake Bratan," an eleven-tiered one for the "Lord of Agung" and next to it another nine-tiered one for the "Lord of Batur." Finally, by the end wall of the *jeroan* stands a *meru* with eleven straw-thatched roofs, dedicated to the "Lord of Mount Batakau." In the north-east corner the rice-goddess Dewi Sri – here called Ulun Siwi – has her own eleven-tiered *meru*.

The wooden wall of the **Bale Murdha**, the meeting hall of the village elders to the right of the gate, has recently been decorated with a colourful painting. But much older are the reliefs on the base of the **Bale Pawedaan** (the priests' pavilion) in the center of the west wall: these portray a scene from the *Ramayana*, in which nymphs attempt to distract Prince Arjuna from his meditation.

After visiting the temple you can be taken on a little ferry, pulled by ropes, across the river to the delightful **Man-**

dala **Wisata garden restaurant,** which
stands on the west bank. The Indonesian
and Chinese specialities on the menu are
not cheap but they are good.

Sangeh

Seven and a half miles (12 km) north-
east of Mengwi lies the famous, not to
say notorious, **Monkey Forest of Sangeh.** A visit to the **Bukit Sari temple,**
founded in the 17th century by a raja of
the Mengwi dynasty, can be an unforget-
table experience: it is surrounded by a
hedge of nutmeg trees (*pala*), which are
very rare on Bali, and provide a home for
three tribes of monkeys. These descendants of Hanuman, the monkey-god who,
in the *Ramayana* epic, defeated the
demon Ravan in Sri Lanka, are lacking in
all sense of propriety. They have no inhibitions about attacking unsuspecting
tourists, grabbing their hats or glasses,
even handbags and cameras, and scam-
pering up into the highest branches with
their loot. It is pointless trying to fight
back, but do not despair: just as a mouse
is tempted by cheese, these sacred monkeys can be lured down with peanuts and
bananas. When these greedy sons of Hanuman grab for the food with both hands,
they drop their booty – the numerous locals who sell you the nuts obviously do
pretty well from their partnership with
the monkeys.

Once you are through this "Thieves'
Alley," nothing more stands between you
and the temple. Its pride is a large stone
statue of Garuda. This creature, half-bird,
half-man, is the steed of Vishnu; in
Hindu mythology he is the opponent of
the *Nagas*, the serpent-gods who represent the element of water.

Marga

In Marga, just 6 miles (10 km) north
of Mengwi, there is a **memorial to the
freedom-fighters** who, in November

1946, met a martyr's death when hopelessly outnumbered in a final battle
against Dutch colonial troops. The 94
small *stupas*, looked after by a Buddhist
monk, recall the sacrifice made by these
Balinese, among whom were Christians
and Moslems as well as Hindus.

One might say that it was a strange
double standard which possessed the
Dutch, whose own country had suffered
so terribly under Nazi occupation, to resort to force in reoccupying their former
Indonesian colonies, once the Japanese
had abandoned them. It was not until the
USA threatened to withhold economic
aid from the war-ravaged Netherlands,
that the Dutch brought their colonial
campaign in Indonesia to an end. The airport at Denpasar is named after Gusti
Ngurah Rai, who commanded the Balinese guerillas, and was among those
who died at Marga.

Three miles (5 km) south of Marga is
the village of **Belayu,** where you can
watch women weaving the precious ceremonial cloths (*songket*).

TABANAN

Tabanan may only be a small town, but it is the capital of the regency, or administrative district, of the same name. The last raja of the prosperous state of Tabanan, which was abolished by the Dutch in 1906, had his residence in the **Puri Tabanan**. This was built in the 17th century by descendants of the East Javanese nobility, who had come to Bali in the 14th century with the army of Gajah Mada. Hence the long tradition of art and craftsmanship in the town. Classical literature is held in respect; groups come together to recite from its texts, and competitions are held in the writing of verse.

The famous dancer I Ketut Marya ("Mario," who died in 1968), received his education in dance in Tabanan around the beginning of this century and later went on to create new dances such as the

Above: Chinese porcelain plates adorn the Raja's Palace in Krambitan. Right: The sea-temple at Tanahlot.

Kebyar Duduk and the *Trompong*. Marya was photographed in the 1930s by Walter Spies, and immortalized in the book *Dance and Drama in Bali,* which Spies wrote with the Dutch authoress Beryl de Zoete, and which was published in England in 1938. The town hall is named **Gedong Marya** in honour of this gifted dancer and teacher.

In the painter and ceramic designer, Kay It (died 1977), Tabanan produced the most important impressionist artist in Indonesia. His paintings are exhibited at the museum in Ubud, and the gardens of the Bali Hyatt hotel in Sanur are adorned with his sculptures.

But even artists have to eat: in the **Subak Museum** on the west side of Tabanan you can see a graphic display of the complex organisation of the irrigation associations of the Balinese rice-growers, as well as the different stages of growing the crop in water, and the implements used. There is even a model kitchen with the traditional Balinese utensils of the pre-microwave era.

Krambitan

West of Tabanan lies the artists' village of Krambitan, whose name is thought to be derived from *karawitan,* meaning "beautiful coast." Painting and woodcarving as well as music and dance, are all carried on here; and the neighbouring village of **Penarukan** is well known for its carving in the soft volcanic stone. The painters of Krambitan follow the time-honoured *Wayang* style, in which the famous shadow-drama figures are portrayed in profile, in natural colours of red, black and ochre.

The particular dance style of Krambitan is called *Tektekan,* a kind of processional dance of exorcism, in which the performers carry large cow-bells, rattles and bamboo drums through the village. By arrangement, the dance is performed in the **Bale Gong,** the hall of the old royal

palace of **Puri Anyar**, richly decorated with gilt wood-carvings and Chinese ceramics. This former feudal seat, dating from the 17th century, belongs to the seventh generation of a branch of the Tabanan dynasty, and these descendants of the rajas now run it as a hotel. You can spend the night in one of its elegant rooms, and pretend you are a Balinese aristocrat, surrounded by valuable paintings, sculpture and porcelain.

Less than 4 miles (6 km) south-west of Krambitan, the black sand of **Pasut beach** beckons you to swim in the powerful surf. And **Klating beach** is also within reach, 3 miles (5 km) to the south.

Tanahlot

One of the most famous buildings in the Tabanan regency, if not in the whole of Bali, is the **sea-temple of Tanahlot.** For photographers, a visit at sunset is essential, when the silhouette of the temple is etched in sharp detail against the glowing red of the evening sky. Japanese manufacturers of cameras and film must offer up a daily prayer of thanks to the gods of the sea, whose shrine this is – scarcely any other monument in southeast Asia has so often been committed to celluloid. Alas, it is not a place to come for quiet meditation; endless soft-drink and souvenir-shops line the 300-yard path from the car-park to the sea; enterprising street-traders form a guard of honor – one is ignored only by the black-and-yellow striped snakes, apparently harmless, which doze in holes in the cliffs above the high-water mark.

When the tide ebbs, enabling tourists to walk across to the island of Tanahlot (meaning "land in the water"), the snakes also wriggle over to the temple, where they are worshipped as virtually sacred messengers of the serpent- and water-god Basuki, who is "Lord of the Temple" of Tanahlot. It is to him that the Hindus of Bali make sacrifice in the tall, five-tiered pagoda shrine, which is officially dedicated to the supreme trinity of Shiva, Brahma and Vishnu. There is also a

89

three-tiered *meru* is dedicated to the Javanese yogi and religious reformer Nirartha, (also called Pendanda Bau Rauh), who may have been the founder of Tanahlot in the 16th century. Next to it a sacrificial column (*paibon*) and two *bales*, for the preparation of sacrifices, vie for space on this small, rocky island, pounded by surf.

On the way back to the Tabanan-Denpasar road, one can make a little side-trip to **Pamesan** (Pejaten), near Nyitdah, and admire the skilled potters of the village, whose work includes remarkable glazed ceramics in the Chinese style.

A little further north, in **Kediri**, the big livestock market (*pasar hewan*) is worth a visit: there are black pot-bellied pigs, cattle, ducks and hens galore – the latter often tied together by the legs in handy bundles of a dozen at a time, much to the horror of western animal-lovers.

Above: Moss-covered temple figures in the Pura Luhur Batukau. Right: When carrying loads, a strong head is needed.

Pura Luhur and Gunung Batukau

If you hear the call of the mountains, it is not far to Gunung Batukau, the "Coconut-shell Mountain," an extinct volcano which rises to 7465 feet (2276 m). At its foot lies the Pura Luhur, the ancestral temple of the Tabanan dynasty. This is one of the nine directional temples of Bali, and faces west. From Tabanan you drive northwards through lush green ricefields, as far as **Wanasari** and then branch off in a north-westerly direction to **Yehpanas**. The place-name means "hot water" and with good reason: the sulphur springs are extremely hot, and anyone who immerses themselves for more than ten minutes runs the risk of collapsing.

The road continues northward through thickly wooded volcanic uplands, dotted with fruit-plantations. In **Wangayagede**, the last village before the asphalt road gives out, ambitious climbers can hire an expert local guide to accompany them to the summit of Gunung Batakau.

For mere sightseers the objective of the expedition is easily reached: the **Pura Luhur Batakau** stands at a height of 2300 ft (700 m) in a clearing on the edge of the seemingly impenetrable tropical rain-forest. The site is not particularly large; the largest shrine is a seven-tiered pagoda and is dedicated to Di Made, a raja who ruled over Bali from Gelgel, in the south of the island, in the second half of the 17th century. The rajas of Tabanan worshipped their ancestors in a three-tiered *meru*. On a miniature island in a small pond nearby, there are two shrines, one dedicated to the water deity of Lake Tamblingan, and the other to the "Lord of Batukau."

The route up to the summit of Batukau is steep and slippery; you should allow six hours for the climb and descent. Those interested in botany will find tree-ferns and thorn-palms in their primeval forest setting, a sight all too rare in densely populated Bali. You would not expect to find a cross on the overgrown summit, but there is an ancient, moss-covered stone throne for Shiva in his guise as Mahadewa, great god and ruler of the world. The descent is pretty rapid – sometimes too rapid when it starts to rain and the earth path becomes a slide.

One of the finest panoramic views in Bali can be enjoyed from **Jatiluwih**, a little rice-growing village at an altitude of 2300 ft (700 m). There are already plans to build *losmens* here. Jatiluwih is situated on a small, winding road, which starts in Wangayagede and ends at Apuan, on the road from Tabanan to Bedugul (Lake Bratan).

GIANYAR

The Gianyar regency, which stretches from Batubulan in the west to Tegalbesar in the east, and Punggang in the north, is where you will find the most famous of Balis artists' and craftsmen's villages. The fertile agricultural land yields rich crops of rice, sweet potatoes (*ubi*), soya beans, coconuts (*kelapa*), tobacco and vanilla, as well as fresh-water fish in

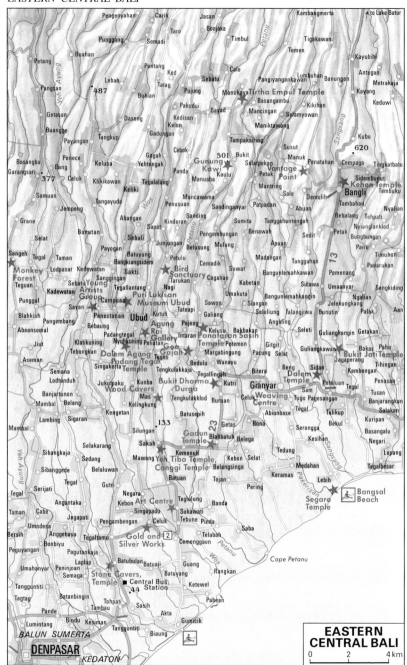

EASTERN
CENTRAL BALI

0   2   4 km

breeding-ponds. At higher altitudes, in the area around Taro, Bali's best coffee (*kopi*) is harvested.

Gianyar offers so many attractions that the selection of destinations must be left to individual preference. However, you must not fail to visit the district around Ubud, the cultural and artistic focal point of the island, where hundreds of painters, wood-carvers dancers and musicians live and work.

Batubulan

Every morning at 10 a.m. there is a rush-hour in Batubulan, a few miles north of Denpasar: it's *Barong* time! Three dance groups make a living in Batubulan by performing traditional trance dances. Audiences are always fascinated by these dance-dramas, performed in front of a temple backdrop, and representing the eternal struggle between Good and Evil. Good is represented by the Barong, half-serpent, half-dragon, and Evil by the wicked witch Rangda, with her sharp fangs and overlong fingernails. The cast of characters also includes charming pricesses with flowers in their hair and dressed in magnificent brocade gowns; bold princes and wild boars; mischievous monkeys and priests versed in magic; and finally some courageous warriors in black-and-white chequered sarongs, who fall under the curse of the Evil One and then – in the climax of the drama – turn their bewitched *krises* against themselves, all to the accompaniment of melodious *gamelan* music. In the end the Barong intervenes and drives away the evil sorceress Rangda, thus restoring equilibrium to the cosmos.

In addition to this, Batubulan is known – as is the neighbouring village of **Tegaltamu** – for carvings made from the volcanic tufa stone, which are on sale in souvenir shops all along the main street. There is even a lovely sandy beach only 2 1/2 miles (4 km) away, at **Gumicik**.

Celuk

Have you got your credit-card at the ready and your pockets full of dollars? If so, then there is nothing to stop you paying a visit to the gold and silver-smiths' center at Celuk. Only hard currencies are accepted; price-tickets on the expensive items lead one to believe that the prices are fixed – and evidence of the fact that many customers pay them without bargaining, can be seen in the stately villas of the shop-owners along the well-made tarmac road. It is more interesting to wander round the back streets and watch the smiths at work with their precious metals in little workshops. And here you can buy rings, necklaces, brooches and ear-rings more cheaply. A walk of just 50 yards can mean a difference in price of 300 per cent! The silversmiths work not only on traditional models, in the so-called "Raja style," but also from drawings by western designers – quite a number of ex-hippies are now active in the international jewelry trade.

The neighboring village of **Singapadu** (which means "twin lions") is the home not only of famous dance troupes who appear at Bali's big beach hotels, but also of talented wood-carvers who specialize in making the wooden *Topeng* masks.

Sukawati

The name of the busy market-town of Sukawati, east of Celuk, is said to be derived from *sukahati,* which means something like "my heart likes it" – apparently a recollection of the magnificent temples and palaces, that were built here in the East Javanese Majapahit style, by a powerful raja named Agung Anom. Sadly, the earthquake of 1917 removed every trace of them.

The **Pura Penataran Agung** in the center of the town was rebuilt; and is still today a place of pilgrimage for the noble clans of the district.

There are two rather curious stone statues of Dutchmen in tropical helmets, sitting on elephants and guarding the *candi bentar* gate of the temple of **Pura Pelinggih Sunya Loka.**

Famous throughout Bali are the Dalangs of Sukawati, who for generations have cultivated the art of puppet-making. They use cow-hide to make the figures for shadow-plays, or Wayang Kulit, and often perform the plays as well. The products of the umbrella-makers (*tukang prada*) are still much in demand – less to keep off the rain than for processions and temple decorations.

Almost opposite the big fruit- and vegetable-market which is held every morning, stands the **Art Center** (*pasar seni*). Here you can buy every imaginable kind of Balinese art and handicraft, from wood-carving to textiles and paintings. Many of the customers are wholesalers who resell the goods in beach resorts.

Above: Wood-carvers at work. Right: Garuda figures in the Pura Luhur Batukan.

Batuan

Over the years, Sukawati has grown together with its neighboring village to the north, Batuan, which has produced many important painters. An inscription dating from 1022 AD was found in Batuan's **Pura Desa** temple. This, and the fact that many village families belong to the legendary Buddhist clan of Griya Agung, are strong indications that Batuan may be one of the oldest centers of culture in Bali. It is the only place where the *Gambuh* is danced. Local wood-carvers make intricate masks for the *Wayang Topeng* (mask-dance) and the *Wayang Wong* (dance-theater), both of which are performed in the village.

In the 1930s, the native artists I Ngendon and I Patera were the first to start drawing with ink on paper, to which they only added white and yellow, to give a muted effect. Around that time, under the influence of Walter Spies and Rudolf Bonnet, another new style emerged from the very traditional Batuan school of painting: alongside the classical religious themes, artists began drawing very detailed scenes from everyday life, and in place of the old *Wayang* style of portraying people in profile, they were drawn in anatomically correct perspective. The portrayal of Balinese life is nowadays taken as far as showing bikini-clad girls on surf-boards and tourists stalking through the village, camera at the ready. A good example of this is the work of I Made Budi, which is on view in the museums of Ubud and Denpasar. You can find copies of the museum exhibits in the numerous picture-galleries along the main street.

About 1 1/4 miles (2 km) further north, near **Sakah**, you can go on walks through the rice-fields and come upon beautifully situated temples that are seldom visited: the **Pura Canggi** and the **Pura Yeh Tiba**, both dating from the 14th century. (Ask the way!).

Mas

Before leaving Sakah and heading eastwards to Blahbatu, it is worth making a little trip 1 1/4 miles (2 km) north the wood-carvers' village of Mas (meaning "Gold"), where the upper crust can trace their line back to one of the holiest clans of Bali: it was founded in the 15th century by no less a personage than the important priest of Shiva from eastern Java, Nirartha (Pedanda Bau Rauh). The marriage of the Sanskrit scholar to a princess from Mas produced the founders of the four most important Brahman clans of Bali. That is why there is scarcely another village whose inhabitants include so many *Ida Bagus* (members of the highest caste).

The temple of **Pura Taman Pule**, with its elaborately carved gates, is said to have been built on the site of Nirartha's dwelling. Its name means : "Temple with a magnificent garden." The senior priest of the place is the keeper of the tantric

flintstone (*vajra*) belonging to the famous Javanese yogi.

Mas has produced some gifted woodcarvers, including such important artists as Ida Bagus Nyana, Ida Bagus Tilem and Ida Bagus Taman. Among the excellent mask-carvers are Ida Bagus Ambara and Ida Bagus Gelodog. Many of these master craftsmen draw their inspiration from the natural shapes of tree-roots, from which they create people, animals and demons.

Whereas earlier Brahman artists devoted themselves exclusively to carving sacred works of art for temples and palaces, the enormous demand from tourists and exporters has called for new motifs, such as, for example, the brightly painted "wooden fruit." These are worked in tropical hardwoods like teak, ebony and jack-fruit; the most costly items are those carved in sandal-wood, since this material has to be imported from other islands. The shops lining the main street are often very stylishly designed and stocked with high-priced

Less than a mile (1 km) from Blahbatu is a favorite picnic spot for Balinese to go at weekends: the waterfall (*air terjun*) of **Tegenungan** near the village of **Belangsinga**. South-east of Blahbatu is **Keramas** (famous for its *Arja* dance-troupe) and near **Medahan** there is a beach of black sand. There stands the **sea-temple of Masceti**, one of the nine ritually significant directional temples of Bali. It is also worth making a trip eastwards to the nearby beaches of **Lebih** with the **sea-temple of Pura Segara**, and **Tegalbesar,** formerly known as Siyut.

On the road from Blahbatu to Gianyar lies the village of **Belega**, whose carpenters have specialized in making bamboo furniture. In the neighboring village of **Bona** the leaves of the lontar-palm are woven into mats, baskets and sun-hats. The dramatic fire-dance, *Sanghyang*, and the *Kecak* are performed there regularly in the evening.

wood-carvings (Topeng-masks, statues of gods, animals, flowers, fruit etc.) If you have enough time, you can even learn the art of Balinese wood-carving from one of the old craftsmen for a modest fee. Another center of wood sculpture is the village of **Kemenuh** on the road to Blahbatu.

Blahbatu

Formerly, one of the many princes of the Gianyar dynasty lived in Blahbatuh. His little palace is today occupied by the **Mantarai Budaya Orchid Farm**, near an important temple called the **Pura Gadun.** In it stands a terrifying head, which represents that of the demon Kebon Iwa, of whom it is said that, using only his long finger-nails, he created the cliff temple of Gunung Kawi, among other things.

Above: Relief showing a scene from the Ramayana. Right: Materials for ceremonial occasions.

Gianyar

The regency capital of Gianyar is a traffic-filled market town without much attraction for tourists, but is nevertheless an important center of Balinese weaving. While here, it is worth looking out for the silk material known as *ikat.* The big stores also sell chic, Kuta-style tee-shirts and batik shirts, which are a good substitute for a jacket, in this damp, hot climate, if one is invited out in the evening. In the factories on the western edge of the town, nimble-fingered but underpaid girls make sarongs from silk and cotton.

At the end of the 18th century, the Raja of Klungkung was weakened by attacks from Karangasem, and Gianyar was able to emerge as an independent rajadom. In 1900, the Dewa Anak Agung Manggis of Gianyar placed himself under the protection of the Netherlands and therefore was spared when the Dutch invaded Bali in 1906; the **Puri**, his palace in the center of the town was destroyed in 1885 by a rival

raja, rebuilt, then destroyed again by the earthquake of 1917. The building you see today is still the seat of the ruling family which has influence at a national level. (The palace can only be visited with special permission). Pagoda roofs in the Chinese style on some of the buildings are evidence of the contribution of the numerous Chinese merchants who lived in Gianyar when it was in its heyday. Their descendants still maintain one of the few **Buddhist temples** in Bali, on the road to Lebih, south of the main square called Alun-Alun.

About 3 3/4 miles (6 km) north-east of Gianyar, on the road to Bangli, stands the small but remarkable **Pura Dalem of Sidan**. As everywhere in Bali, this Dalem temple is intended to keep at bay the dangerous powers of the underworld and the spirits of the dead, which have not yet been "purified" by ritual burning. It is dedicated to the Merajapati, the watchman of the kingdom of the dead. The fine reliefs on the base of the outer *Kulkul* tower show scenes from *Bhima's*

*Journey into Hell (*see also under Klungkung). Terrifying figures of Rangda with pointed teeth and pendulous breasts flank the *candi bentar* gates inside the temple.

A little further north stands the ancestral temple of the rajas of Gianyar, the **Pura Merajan Agung** of Sidan. Some modern motifs have found their way into the reliefs: an aircraft and its pilot, a soldier with binoculars and a uniformed man on a bicycle. To the north, the classic triad of temples is completed by the **Pura Puseh Sidan**, facing towards the mountains; a "temple of origin" with a seven-tiered *meru*.

Kutri and Bedulu

Between Gianyar and Ubud lies a land of ancient culture, rich in architectural finds and monuments of artistic importance. It lies between the rivers Pakerisan and Petanu ("blood river"), which rise near Penelokan in the Batur region. Traveling from the town of Gianyar to Ubud, one can visit Bali's most important

sacred places, one after the other – the Bukit Dharma, the cave shrine of Goa Gajah and the "Moon of Pejeng."

Bukit Dharma is the name of a sacred hill near **Kutri,** about 2 1/2 miles (4 km) west of Gianyar, on which Queen Mahendradatta, the "wicked widow" of the Balinese king Udayana, is said to have been cremated in 1006 AD. According to legend, Mahendradatta attempted, with the aid of black magic, to destroy her son, King Airlangga, together with all his retinue, by means of a plague. Many claim that she is the archetype of the dreaded witch Rangda. Be that as it may, the summit of the hill is crowned with a a weathered stone relief from the 12th century, portraying the six-armed goddess, Durga. It can be found amongst a stand of banyan trees. Durga represents the female energy of Shiva, who can be both destructive (Kali) and creative (Parvati).

Above: Entrance to the elephant cave of Goa Gajah. Right: Praying before the Yehpulu relief.

A few miles to the north, near **Bedulu,** is the **Goa Gajah**, or "Cave of the Elephant" – the name given to this cliff grotto by Dutch archaeologists who rediscovered it in 1923. It was probably inspired by the oversized ears of the gigantic demon-face which has been carved out of the rock surrounding the entrance to the cave. If you have a flashlight with you, in the dark, T-shaped interior you will find a real elephant-god: in one of the 15 niches stands a four-armed Ganesha, barely 3 ft (1 m) high. He is the elephant-headed son of the god Shiva, in the Hindu pantheon.

This shivaitic shrine, which was probably a place of meditation, dates from the 11th century and contains several stone *linggas*, or phallic symbols, which symbolize Shiva's procreative power. Buddhist monks have also left behind evidence of their activity in Goa Gajah: two severely weathered stone Buddhas, in the lotus position, can be found on a narrow path on the far side of the little stream in the south-east corner of the site. The

Hindus of Bali still come and place sacrificial gifts before them. In 1954, a large bathing-pool, about 1000 years old, was excavated in front of the Elephant Cave. It is fed by six gargoyles in the shape of water-nymphs (*widadari*).

Another historic bathing-pool was discovered at **Yehpulu**, south of Bedulu; it can be reached on foot through the rice-fields, in about half-an-hour from Goa Gajah. There you will find a 30 ft (27 m) long **stone frieze** from the 14th century, which is unique in Indonesia. The life-size figures carved from its gray-brown lava stone include a yogi, an attacking bear, a hunter stabbing an animal; other hunters carrying their "bag" slung on a pole over their shoulders, and a rider on a horse, with a woman pulling the tail. These are probably figures from the Hindu epic, *Mahabharata*, and may specifically relate to Krishna's hunt for the magic jewel of the bear Jambavat (Krishna is the corporeal form of the god Vishnu). The relief is completed by a two-armed figure of Ganesha.

Pejeng

Until its conquest by the East Javanese general Gajah Mada, in the 14th century, the area around Bedulu and Pejeng, a little way to the north, was the center of of a prosperous kingdom whose cultural blossoming is evidenced by the numerous Buddhist and Hindu statues. Considerably older even than these is the famous **Moon of Pejeng**, a gigantic bronze gong measuring 3 ft 7 inches in diameter (1.1 m) and just over 6 feet (1.86 m) long, which is believed to date as far back as the 3rd century BC, that is to say the beginning of the Bronze Age in Indonesia. Its provenance is not clear. The Balinese insist that it fell from heaven, which would certainly explain the long dent in it. In style it is reminiscent of the Dongson Culture of Indo-China, but the ancient Indonesians were also well-versed in the art of gong-making. Unfortunately, this gong, endowed with magic power and woven around with legends, is kept on the top storey of

99

the tower-like shrine of the royal temple of **Pura Penataran Sasih**. This means that its magnificent, finely engraved ornamentation – spirals, circles and an eight-pointed star – can only be admired through a pair of binoculars.

On the south side of Pejeng is the **Archaeological Museum**, with displays of sarcophagi, neolithic axe-heads, bronze statues from the pre-Christian era and Chinese porcelain.

In the **Pura Kebo Edan,** the "Temple of the Wild Buffalo," stands the "Giant of Pejeng." This is a 13 ft (4 m) high statue, nearly 700 years old, representing the god of fertility, called Bhima by the Balinese, dancing on the head of a demon. The enormous penis of the deity and the two bulls kneeling at either side of him, are characteristic of the ancient Indian cult of Shiva-Bhairava, which in Bali was enriched with tantric elements. The four round-headed nails in the Bhima's sex-organ, designed to increase the pleasure of his female partner, clearly show the sexual refinement of the tantric Hindus of the 14th century, who sought enlightenment through orgasm. They also believed that by breaking tabus – such as drinking blood from a human skull, as demonstrated by the Raksasa standing in front of Bhima – they would be raised to new levels of ecstasy and heightened perception. Whether human sacrifice also took place is a matter for speculation.

Equally lurid forms of fertility symbolism are shown by the sculptures in the **Pura Pusering Jagat** ("Navel-of-the-World Temple"): four moustached demons in a cudgel-swinging dance around a central *lingga* of Shiva. This temple, which dates from 1329, also contains a remarkable stone vase, 2 1/2 feet (75 cm) high, with a relief depicting the "The stirring of the Ocean of Milk." The Hindu

Right: A traditional Balinese motif painted in a modern manner.

gods wind the serpent of the world around the mountain of Mandara, which is held to be the axis of the world, then set it spinning and thus obtain the elixir of life, *Amrita*, by a process of "churning."

The Ubud region

To walk along rich green rice-terraces from Ubud to Keliki, to watch a procession of ducks solemnly following their duckherd, or peasants cosseting their champion fighting-cocks, to enjoy a meal of grilled *Sate ayam* at "Murni's Warung" in Campuan, to visit one's favorite painter in Penestanan or Pengosekan, to sip tea in the Café Lotus at the Pura Saraswati, or to witness a *Legong* dance on a warm night in Peliatan: all this awaits you in Ubud, which, in spite of the tourist boom of the last few years, is still an absolute "must" for anyone visiting Bali. Art-lovers can book into a *losmen* with the promising name of *Painter and Homestay;* and in little hotels, set apart in the middle of the rice-fields, romantics can still sniff the spice-laden air of a tropical paradise, which had already disappeared from Kuta twenty years ago.

It was the Ubud region which gave Bali its image as an island of artists. Many of the most famous painters, dancing-girls, musicians and wood-carvers have their roots in the peasant villages around Ubud. Fertile soil and an abundance of water for irrigation have since time immemorial provided the rice-farmers of central Bali with good harvests. The agricultural surplus gave the farmers enough leisure to release their creativity, and also guaranteed the survival of the feudal court of the Rajas of Gianyar, who saw themselves as heirs to the lost Javanese empire of Majapahit, and generously promoted the arts. Around 1890, Cokorda Gede Sukawati of Ubud brought craftsmen from all over Bali to work on temple and palace decoration and persuaded them to settle in

his village – with great success. But until the early 20th century, craftsmanship, painting and dance had a purely religious inspiration; statues and paintings only portrayed Hindu gods, and dances were considered merely as part of temple festivals. That all changed in the 1920s, when the *Cokorda* (prince of the Ksatriya caste) Gede Raka Sukawati began inviting foreign artists to his residence in Ubud. This generated a creative climate, particularly in the inter-war years, when the Berlin-born painter and musician, Walter Spies, gave valuable encouragement to the naive, naturalistic painting style and also to native music and dance. Spies came to Ubud in 1927 after an assignment as court conductor to the Sultan of Yogyakarta. The house he lived in is near the bridge over the Campuan river, and above the Subak temple **Pura Gunung Lebah**. Today it is one of the more expensive hotels in the area. Ubud was visited at that time by the Mexican artists, Miguel and Rosa Covarrubias, who immortalised its village culture in their classic book, *Island of Bali*. The Dutch painter Rudolf Bonnet set up a studio in Ubud in 1931, and the village soon became known as the "in" place for art-loving travellers. The hospitable Walter Spies often acted as tour-guide and arranged the sale of Balinese paintings. Backed by Prince Sukawati, he and Bonnet founded the artists' association *Pita Maha* in 1936 (revived in 1947 as *Ratna Warta*), which was joined by some 150 local artists, including such talented and versatile figures as I Gusti Lempad, who not only produced highly-prized ink drawings and masterly *Barong* masks, but also created the stone lotus-throne in Ubud's **Saraswati temple**.

After the war the Dutch ex-colonial soldier, Han Snel, arrived in Ubud, began painting, married a village girl called Sita and stayed for ever. The couple run a restaurant near the lotus-pond; and Han-Snel's own gallery is worth a visit.

In 1956 another Dutch artist, Arie Smit, settled in the neighboring village of **Penestanan**, west of Ubud; his gifted

Balinese pupils, known as the *Young Art-ists*, who developed a colorful, naive style of painting all their own, are now admittedly getting on in years, but their grandchildren are scarcely less productive. Near the Campuan bridge lives an eccentric painter from the Philippines, Antonio Blanco, who married his favorite Balinese model and to this day continues to capture her on canvas.

Pengosekan, south of Ubud, is the home of gifted painters like Mokoh (a lover of mischievous detail), Batuan (most famous work: *Turis dan Bali*), Kobot, Barat, Putra, Sana and Gatra. However, most of the inhabitants of Pengosekan are in the "wooden fruit business": the American furniture designer Linda Garland, once encouraged the artists to paint wooden frames for her pictures; and soon they were carving and painting fruit, even whole banana-plants

Above: The Puri Saraswati behind the Lotus Café. Right: This descendant of Hanuman, specializes in stealing sacrificial gifts.

and four-poster beds – an activity which has now become the backbone of the village economy.

Before buying a painting or wood-carving, one should get an overview of the different artistic schools – best done by visiting a large gallery or museum. The **Agung Rai Gallery** in **Peliatan**, in the south-east of Ubud, offers a broad spectrum and has an excellent reputation. Also in this area there are still painters, who follow the traditional *Wayang* style, such as Made Kuanji, Ketut Madra and Nyoman Kuta. Two well-known and creative woodcarvers working here are Nyoman Togo and Wayan Pasti. And while you are in Peliatan, you should ask when the next dance performance will take place, since the district has a famous *Legong* group which has toured Europe and the USA. No less than 15 *gamelan* orchestras take turns to play every evening in Peliatan and the neighboring village of **Teges.**

The **Puri Lukisan,** or "Palace of Pictures," was built in 1956 in a small park

by Prince Sukawati, and contains what its name suggests: exhibits spanning the whole period of painting in this region from 1930 until 1978, the year in which Rudolf Bonnet died. He had been instrumental in setting up the museum. One can clearly trace the stylistic development from the classic *Wayang* painting, with its formalized profiles, right up to modern works which portray people with astonishing realism. The modest entrance fee seems sadly inadequate to cover professional conservation of the paintings and sculptures. In the next-door building a co-operative runs an exhibition of works for sale.

The **Museum Neka,** north-east of Ubud, beyond Campuan on the road to Kedewatan, was opened in 1982 and presents works in better conditions. Here you can see not only work by the "old Europeans" such as Spies, Bonnet, Hofker and Smit, but also that of the Indonnesian avant-garde, including Ubud's own Lempad (d. 1978), Sujono and the very modern Affandi. If you have a gold credit-card on you, you can choose from the best collection on the island. The **Neka Gallery,** close to the post-office, is also a treasure-trove for art-lovers.

Walks in and around Ubud

Ubud is included in the expedition programs of all the large beach hotels, and consequently the innumerable souvenir-shops along the "Shopping Highway" between Peliatan and Campuan, and on the road to the **Monkey Forest**, believe they can get away with charging ridiculous prices. You are foolish if you do not bargain: negotiation is the first duty of every tourist! In fifteen minutes you can reach the *Hutan Kerah* (Monkey Forest) from the center of Ubud. The children of Hanuman love romping in the great banyan tree in front of the **Pura Dalem Agung Padang Tegal.** This temple to Durga, goddess of death, features a remarkable *Candi Kurung* gate, which is only opened for sacrificial ceremonies.

The monumental temple gate stands on

the giant turtle Bedawang, which represents the underworld, guarded by seven terrifying, slack-breasted Rangdas – the two witches at either end appear to be in the act of devouring children.

From the Monkey Forest you can continue walking to the wood-carvers' village of **Nyuhkuning**, where you cross the river Wos in a westerly direction, then head north through the rice-fields, past **Klatikuning**, to the painters' village of **Penestanan**. A short, well signposted path leads from there, via Campuan, back to Ubud. Another path goes through Penestanan to the **Yeh Ayung gorge** where luxury hotels are under construction, and on to the Monkey Forest of Sangeh.

Walkers who take the path northward from the Campuan temple (near the Kecak Inn) will encounter village culture as it was before the advent of tarmac roads and tourists. The path first winds

Above: The Candi gate to the shrine of Gunung Kawi. Right: At the sacred spring of Tirtha Empul.

along the picturesque rice-terraces in the steep-sided valley of the river Wos, then widens and leads through the villages of **Bangkiangsidem** and **Sebal**i.

There one can either cross the Wos eastwards and walk back to Ubud along the field path via **Batuyung** and **Sakti,** or one can stroll on as far as Keliki, and pick up the tarmac road eastward to **Tegalalang**, from where a *bemo* will take you back.

En route it is worth stopping in **Petulu**, especially in the late afternoon. There is an interesting **bird-sanctuary** here, in which thousands of white herons come to roost, after a day's fishing.

North of Tegalalang are the two villages of **Pujung** and **Sebatu**, famous for their talented wood-carvers. If you are a good walker, and set out before sunrise, you can, in a day, complete the 19 mile (30 km) walk from Campuan, via Keliki, Taro (coffee plantations) and Pisang right up to **Penelokan** (see also p.138), at the foot of the Batur volcano. On the way you will get to know rural Bali at first

hand – but beware the dogs which roam around the villages in large numbers!

Gunung Kawi and
Tirtha Empul

Roughly half-way to Penelokan you come to the wood-carving village of **Tampaksiring**, and about a mile (1.5 km) south of it is the shrine of Gunung Kawi, set idyllically in the gorge of the *Sungai* (river) Pakerisan. There are a total of ten *candis* in the Javanese style, standing in 23 ft (7 m) high niches in the sheer rock walls on either side of the river.The giant Kebo Iwo must have been pretty busy: he is said to have hewn not only Goa Gajah, but also these *candis*, from the solid volcanic rock with his thumbnail. The shrine was probably built at the end of the 11th century, after the death and in honor of King Anak Wungsu. A group of four *candis* on the left hand side of the steep staircase leading down from the car-park, are said to be in memory of the monarch's four favorite concubines.

The *candis* on the opposite side of the river are dedicated to the king and his four chief wives, and the one on the left, slightly raised, is dedicated to the deified Anak Wungsu. To the right of the group of five *candis* is a narrow gap leading to a Buddhist refuge which may only be entered barefoot. Its rock walls conceal niches for meditation, probably built by Buddhist monks over 900 years ago. At the foot of the staircase is a gate leading to a path which takes you south-west through rice fields for just over half a mile (1 km) to the so-called "Tenth Grave." This is supposed to have been built for a Brahman who was one of Anak Wungsu's ministers, but the word "grave" is misleading, since the dead were burnt and their ashes subsequently scattered in a river – in other words consigned to the goddess Ganga in order to exert a favorable influence on the cycle of rebirth.

To the north of Tampaksiring the sacred river Pakerisan has its source. Not far from this beneficent spring, which the

Balinese believe confers eternal youth, a bathing-place was created by one of the Warmadewa rajas in 960 AD. Later, in the 11th century, King Airlangga had it adorned with statues and shrines. In all, 31 gargoyles feed the three basins of **Tirtha Empul**; the left hand one is reserved for women and the middle one for men. The water in the small right-hand basin is said to be of exceptional purity.

Tirtha is derived from the Sanskrit word *amrita*, which means something like "nectar of the gods" or "elixir of life." The myth of the holy bathing-place, which draws thousands of pilgrims every year, is bound up with the Hindu god Indra: once this Indian god-king was fighting in Bali against the demon king Maya Danuwa. The evil ruler treacherously poisoned the water of the river Petanu, from which Indra's warriors drank and then died. Indra saved them by driving his cudgel into the ground a little further to the east, thus creating the spring of Tirtha Empul and the river Pakerisan. The god-king sprinkled this holy water over his dead comrades and so brought them back to life. A gigantic block of black stone was later consecrated as a throne to Indra: it can be seen in the middle of the inner courtyard of the temple, in which there are also some 20 small shrines, each with a beautifully carved little door, painted gold.

Holy water plays an important part in Hindu religious rites: the Brahmans of Bali prefer to obtain the water from Tirtha Empul, which they use in numerous sacrificial and purification ceremonies. On the other hand, water from the neighboring river Petanu was, until a few years ago, considered to be cursed, since the blood of the demon king, Maya Danuwa, had flowed into it, when he was laid low by Indra. Only after elaborate sacrificial ceremonies was the water of the Petanu recently declared ritually pure (*suci*) – which was a blessing for the rice-growers, because until then it had been tabu to use the water for irrigation.

BANGLI

Gianyar's neighbour to the east is the predominantly agricultural regency of Bangli. With only 175,000 inhabitants, it is the second smallest administrative district of Bali. The capital, with the same name, lies only 8 miles (13 km) northeast of Gianyar town, at the foot of the Batur massif, and thanks to its altitude of 1650 ft (500 m) it has a pleasant climate. Bangli's recorded history goes back as far as an inscription from the 9th century, in the Pura Kehen. In the 15th century, Bangli became a dependency of the kingdom of Gelgel. It gained its independence after 1700 and reached the height of its power in the 19th century – paradoxically after signing a treaty subordinating it to Dutch colonial rule.

It is still possible to live like a raja in Bangli today, by staying at the historic **Puri Denpasar** (Jalan Merdeka), which has been converted into the palatial **Artha Sastra Inn**, and is run by descendants of the ruling family. Gilt carving, flowers, *bales* and sumptuous decor await the guest, who can even reserve the original bed (or so one is told) of the last Raja of Bangli, who died in 1960.

Every three days the sleepy provincial town awakes to hectic activity, when the peasant women from the surrounding area come streaming into the *pasar* (market square) to sell their peanuts, cloves, sweet potatoes, passion-fruit, maize, citrus fruits (*jeruk*), coffee and tobacco. Herbal remedies of all kinds (known as *jamu*) are also on sale; the nature-healers (*balian*) of the district are widely known for their practice of inducing trances, and there are many dark mutterings about black magic.

Right: A Balinese village just before an important temple festival.

On the north-east side of the town, in a superb position on the slopes of Bukit Bangli, stands a temple, which is possibly the most beautiful in Bali, and is certainly the second largest on the island. This is the **Pura Kehen.** Founded in the 11th century and dedicated to Hyang Kehen, the god of the hearth, this became the state temple of the rajas of Bangli in the 18th century. The caste of the blacksmiths, the Pande, also come here to venerate Hyang Api, the god of fire. A flight of 38 steps, flanked by nearly life-size *Wayang* figures, leads up to the sanctuary that is laid out on eight terraces. In the first forecourt stands an ancient, spreading banyan-tree, which conceals a *kulkul* tower in its branches. Beside it, above the *candi bentar* gateway, a *kala boma* mask keeps away evil spirits. Passing through the middle courtyard, one reaches the *jeroan*, the holy of holies, whose walls are partly decorated with ancient Chinese porcelain plates. The *jeroan* is dominated by a *meru* with eleven *tumpangs*, or tiered roofs, which

is dedicated to Hyang Kehen, as one of the manifestations of Shiva. A *padmasana* (throne of the gods) for the Shiva-Brahma-Vishnu trinity stands in the north-east corner of the inner courtyard, and is decorated with remarkable stone carvings. Its base is in the form of a turtle round which a snake is coiled: a symbol of the underworld. On the rear side of the stone throne are some magnificent sculptures; half the Hindu pantheon is assembled there, including Shiva and his son Ganesha, Durga the goddess of death, Vishnu and his "personal transport," Garuda, the directional deities as well as Prince Arjuna and other figures from the Sanskrit epic *Mahabharata.*

In the **Budaya Art Center** (not far from the Pura Kehen), you can see temple-dancing and listen to *gamelan* music. As well as performances of *Kecak* and *Wayang,* you may occasionally be able to see unique local forms of dance, such as the *Baris Johor, Baris Dadap* or *Baris Tamiang,* which are reminiscent of archaic war-dances.

107

CENTRAL BALI

Most places in Central Bali are within easy reach of Denpasar – and often of each other – using bemos as transport. If you only wish to visit Tanahlot, you should join an organised tour in Kuta, Sanur or Nusa Dua or catch a bemo from Denpasar heading for Tabanan and change in Kediri. If you are using bemos, you should start the return journey about 4 pm, because very few bemos operate after that time.

TANAHLOT

Accomodation / Restaurants

There is a moderately priced losmen behind the market stalls. At the viewpoints for looking at the temple there are rows and rows of warungs and other restaurants and bars. In the high season, the place can get very crowded around sunset, when whole busloads arrive and spread themselves .

UBUD
and SURROUNDING AREA

Accommodation

(Prices always refer to double rooms)
LUXURY CLASS: **Amandari**, Sayan, P.O.Box 33,Ubud, Tel: 95333, Fax: 95335, fantastic position above the Yeh Ayung river, from US$ 200;
Cahaya Dewata, Kedewatan, Tel: 95495, lovely view of the Yeh Ayung, from US$ 45;
Kupu Kupu Barong, Kedewatan, Tel: 95478, Fax: 95079, relatively far from Ubud, superb position above the gorge of the Yeh Ayung, excellent restaurant, no children under 12, from US$ 225;
Pringga Juwita, Jl. Bisma, Tel/Fax: 95734, borders on rice-fields, quiet, central location, rooms from US$ 45;
Tjampuan, Campuan, P.O.Box 15, Denpasar, Tel: 95368, Fax: 95137, idyllic situation on the Cerik, walking distance to center, from US$ 45;
MID-PRICE: **Ananda Cottages**, Campuan, near the Neka Museum, P.O. Box 205, Denpasar, from US$ 35;
Oka Wati's Sunset Bungalows, Tel: 95063, central and quiet, from US$ 25;
Sayan Terraces, Sayan, nice view of the Yeh Ayung, from US$ 20;
Siddharta, Penestanan Kaja, Tel: 95748, in the middle of rice-fields, from US$ 20.
Siti Bungalows, P.O. Box 227, Denpasar, Tel: 28690, central and yet cosy, behind the Lotus Café, from US$ 30;
Ubud Village, Monkey Forest Road, Tel: 95069, central, from US$ 35.
BUDGET: There are very many small **losmens** in and around Ubud, some of which charge less than

10,000 Rps. for a double room.The simplest thing is to hunt for lodgings on either side of the Monkey Forest Road. We can recommend, for example, **Monkey Forest Hideaway**, Tel: 95354, with a view of the forest, from Rps. 20,000. A further budget accommodation is beyond the big crossroads on Jl.Suwata: The **Suci Inn** lets rooms for as little as Rps. 8,000.
In Peliatan, the **Sari Bungalows** has rooms for only Rps. 6,000. In Penestanan, you should ask at the **Hotel Tjampuhan**. If you are seeking solitude, head for the **Pugig Home-stay**, with accommodation from Rps.10, 000 in a Balinese farmstead.

Restaurants

Just about every connoisseur will find something to his taste in Ubud. Top of the list for quality and high prices is the **Kupu Kupu Barong** hotel restaurant (Indonesian, Japanese und international). In Ubud itself, we can recommend the restaurant of the **Tjampuhan** Hotel, **Murni's Warung** (not a warung in the normal sense), the **Café Lotus** (Pasta), **Oka Wati** and the **Nomad** (especially their steaks); all are in the middle price-range. There are good but cheap places on the Monkey Forest Road, like **Lilies**, **Bendi's** or **Dennis**.
Many travelers prefer to eat cheaply at the stalls in the night-market. In Peliatan, **Ibu Arsa's Warung** (near the big banyan-tree) is recommended to lovers of Balinese food. Unfortunately, it is right by a busy street. Ibu Arsa also knows all about dance performances and can get you tickets. Lovers of rich cakes will enjoy themselves at the **Café Wayan** ("Death by Chocolate") on Monkey Forest Road .

Shopping

The main street and Monkey Forest Road are lined with shops selling goods of all kinds. There is a covered bazaar in the town center. If you are staying in Ubud you should seek out the artists themselves, since the whole area is dedicated to the production of a wide range of handcraft items. Painters prefer to have their studios in Peliatan, Ubud and Penestanan. Wood-carvers work in Mas and Kemenuh, but also on the road that runs northward to Sebatu, from the east side of Ubud.
A maker of gamelans is to be found in Blahbatuh. Silver jewelry is made in Celuk. The market in Sukawati offers everything that is woven from rattan, including dolls, sun-shades and baskets, all in one place. However, the stall-holders are used to tourists and are not happy to be beaten down on price.

Evening entertainment

Ubud is the best place to visit if you are looking for native culture. The shows that are put on here night after night have largely lost their sacred character, since dancing has become a source of money. However, it has been replaced by a certain professional creativity. In a sense, Ubud could be called the "Broadway" of Bali. The individual gamelan-players and dancers vie keenly for the visitor's favor; dance-schools even instruct westerners in the intricacies of their art. The groups from Peliatan have taken a lead in this. The way they perform the *Kecak* surpasses even the dancers from Bona in its intensity and the harmony of their ensemble. The members of the excellent women's gamelan orchestra compose and perform their own solos, and girls join at an early age. One is struck by the earnest dedication of the dancers in these shows.

If you enjoy comic strips, you must not miss the Wayang-Kulit performance in the **Oka Kartini**. You can find out where a performance takes place, from the stall at the main cross-roads in the town center or from the hordes of young ticket-sellers roaming the area. Prices are around Rps. 5,000. When going to an out-of-town performance, such as the fire-dance at Bona, you should take advantage of the courtesy-buses provided, rather than using your rental car, since returning late at night on the narrow roads can be quite dangerous.

Museums and Galleries

In addition to the commercial galleries and artists' studios, which are basically there to attract passing trade, there are several interesting collections of Balinese painting and western art inspired by Bali. In the town center, the **Museum Puri Lukisan** is open daily from 8 am to 4 pm (entrance: 500 Rps.). This gives the best overview of all styles and periods. Also very good is the **Museum Neka**, north of Campuan, which is open daily from 8.30 am until 5 pm (entrance: 500 Rps.).

The **Neka Gallery** near the Post Office principally shows paintings for sale. Likewise, the **Agung Rai Gallery** in Peliatan and the **Agung Raka Gallery** at the northern end of the village of Mas.

A more intimate atmosphere can be found at **Antonio Blanco's Studio**, open nearly every day 9 am – 5 pm (entrance: 500 Rps.). A private collection of the work of Han Snel can be seen at his own hotel, the **Siti Bungalows**, behind the Café Lotus.

Walks and hiking

Ubud is an ideal starting-point for walks and longer expeditions on foot. The following are two relatively easy walking tours:

Tour 1) Ubud – Sangeh (one way, 7 1/2 - 9 miles, 12 - 15 km): Starting opposite the Hotel Tjampuhan you climb the steep steps and just keep going straight on until you reach the tarmac'd north-south road at Sayan. (Before that, you may come upon the little used tarred side-road that goes through Penestanan. If you do, follow it as far as Sayan, then head north.) From the Sayan Terraces Hotel, follow a narrow path westwards, which leads into the gorge of the Yeh Ayung river. The river is crossed by a swaying bamboo bridge. On the far bank, you have a choice of continuing northwards along the bank or heading south for a little way, then going westwards. If you go north, continue only as far as the village of Bongkasa, then turn west. A wide path through the forest and past rice-fields will bring you to Sangeh. For the return journey, you can take a bemo to Sayan via Lambing and Kengetan.

Tour 2) Ubud – Pejeng – Kelusu (there and back, about 9 miles or 15 km): At the point where the main steet of Ubud meets the road running north-south from Peliatan to Petulu, carry straight on eastwards and cross the Petanu river.

In the middle of Pejeng, continue eastward to Kelusu. Alternatively, head in a slightly more northerly direction and you come to the temple Pura Pengukur Ukuran and the river Pakrisan.

Here, by the river, is a little-known but moderately spectacular archaeological treasure, **Goa Garbo**, an overgrown miniature version of Gunung Kawi. Don't forget to bring a picnic.

For futher tours and walks we recommend you buy a map on sale in Ubud, called **Bali Pathfinder.** It is admittedly not always very accurate but does help you get your bearings.

If you opt for a cycle-tour, don't forget that there are some pretty steep hills, and be sure to avoid the very congested main Ubud – Peliatan – Teges road.

Important addresses

For any information required, apply to the **Bina Wisata**, a small public office near the central cross-roads.

The **Post Office** is on the south side of the main street, going east, set back a little from the road. It can be used as an address for poste restante mail, which should be addressed to: *Kantor Pos, Ubud.*

The **Telephone Office** is outside the center, on the north-south Peliatan – Petulu road. You can send and receive faxes there (Fax Nr: 0062-361-95120).

Vehicle rental

In Ubud, it is possible to hire jeeps, motor-cycles and bicycles. However, in the high season there is often quite a long waiting-list. There is a firm that hires motor-bikes and push-bikes, right on the central crossroads.

Other rental firms have their offices near the main street, usually combined with a bureau de change and a public transport operation.

BALI SEA

JAVA

Singaraja •

Gilimanuk •

Banyu-
wangi •

Western   Penga-
Bali   stulan

Northern
Bali

• Negara

Central
Bali

Eastern
Bali •
        Karan-
Ubud • Klung- gasem
        kung

BALI

Denpasar • • Sanur
Kuta •
    Southern
    Bali
        NUSA
        PENIDA

INDIAN OCEAN

A RESERVATION FOR WILDLIFE IN THE FOREST

JEMBRANA
WEST BULELENG
WEST BALI NATIONAL PARK

JEMBRANA

Western Bali extends over two administrative districts: in the south, the regency of Jembrana and in the north the western half of the regency of Buleleng. You can literally circle the whole area, if you drive from Gilimanuk on the coast road to Denpasar, as far as Penggragoan, then head for the north coast and from Seririt return to Gilimanuk along that coast.

The name Jembrana is derived from the Balinese *jimbar wana*, which means something like "great forest," and indeed more than half the 324 square miles (840 sq.km) of this district is thickly forested and forms part of the Bali Barat National Park. Under the Dutch, resettlement projects in the early part of the century brought Balinese villagers to this remote mountainous wilderness for the first time. With only 220,000 inhabitants, Jembrana is today still the most sparsely populated region of Bali.

Gilimanuk

In Java there once lived a king, who had a very badly-behaved son. In order to

Previous pages: Separating the rice from the chaff. Left: On the south coast, east of Negara.

be rid of him, the king took his wayward offspring far away to the east, to a point where the land became very narrow. There the king ordered the prince to keep on walking, and drew a line in the sand behind him: then the waters of the Java Sea and the Indian Ocean flowed together and Bali was henceforth an island of exile.

For backpackers arriving from Java, the ferry-harbour of Gilmanuk is the gateway to Bali. This little sea-port on the Bali Straits welcomes its visitors with a big **candi bentar**, or split gate, which is supposed to deny demons their entry to the holy island of Bali.

At dawn and dusk, you cannot fail to hear the loudspeaker of the mosque calling the faithful to prayer – a sign that Islam long ago made the leap across the water to the Hindu island. In the **Rumah Makan Padang** restaurant, near the mosque, you will not see pork on the menu, but you will find that followers of the Prophet in their voluntary Balinese exile have lost none of their culinary skill: the beef (*rendang*) is just as hot and spicy here as in Western Sumatra, where the chef comes from. If you spend a night in Gilimanuk, the night-market (*pasar senen*) will give you a taste of the culinary skills of the Balinese *Ibus* (*ibu* = mother) at their hot-food stalls.

113

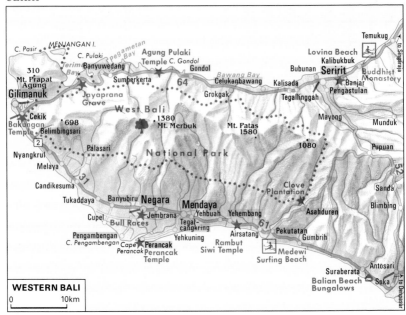

WESTERN BALI

0   10km

Little two-wheeled pony-carts, called *dokar*s, bring a Javanese atmosphere to the main street of Gilimanuk, lined with *warungs*, and whenever a ferry arrives the thoroughfare is crammed with over-loaded trucks, crowded long-distance buses, and hordes of foreign and Indonesian travellers.

Cekik

As suggested by the myth of Bali's origin, quoted earlier, there was indeed a land-bridge between Bali and Java during the great Ice Age; and this is demonstrated not only by the almost identical flora and fauna of the two islands. Objects excavated at Cekik, 2 miles (3 km) south of Gilimanuk, include stone axe-heads and pottery sherds which reveal the existence of a neolithic settlement, and point to Bali having been colonized at that time by people from Java.

Right: A representation of Christ in the Balinese manner.

The only monument in the area from a more recent period of Balinese history, is the little temple of **Pura Bakungan** on the north-eastern edge of the town of Cekik, which was built around 1450 AD – at the time when two princes from the Kingdom of Gelgel were sent to West Bali to reclaim the wilderness for cultivation: this was how the states of Gilimanuk and Negara came into being. However, rivalry between the king's two sons soon led to a civil war, which effectively wiped out all the early successes in developing the region. This at least is the traditional explanation for the fact that so few Hindus settled in western Bali, inspite of the pressure of overpopulation in the middle of the island – a more convincing reason, however, is the lack of water for irrigation, due to low rainfall, and the poor quality of the soil. However, this obviously did not deter seafarers and fishermen, and since the indigenous Balinese regard the sea with distinct suspicion, the west coast of Bali was settled in the 17th century by Bugis, who were

114

Moslem sailors from the Sunda Sea, especially from Java and Sulawesi (the Celebes Islands). In fact, exiles from the whole archipelago found a home here.

In Cekik is the headquarters of the West Bali National Park (see page 119), and its information center provides literature and a small exhibition about forest ecology.

Belimbingsari and Pelasari

Christian missionaries came from the USA and the Netherlands after 1930 and worked among the members of *Sudra* under-caste in the Hindu villages of southern Bali – with the result that the newly converted Christians were driven out of their villages, since they no longer fitted into the social hierarchy.

These religious refugees from the south made their home in forest clearings in the west Bali highlands, 6 miles (10 km) south-east of Cekik. In 1939 the village of **Belimbingsari** was established, in which today some 2,000 Protestants (*kristen protestan*) live. Their church (*gereja*) has incorporated some of the Balinese temple traditions.

Thus the bell-tower looks like a *kulkul-* tower and the church itself resembles a *bale*. Even the demon-repelling *candi bentar* has found its way into Christian church architecture. Here the very cross of Jesus is allowed to stand on a brahmanic lotus throne. The tradition of temple dancing is also maintained, though with the difference that in Belimbingsari, according to Christian principles, Good defeats Evil, whereas the Hindus of Bali seek the harmony which results from a balance between the forces of creation and of destruction.

Competition from Christianity of the Catholic persuasion has taken root further east: in **Palasari** (pop. 1,800) stands a Catholic church, built in 1960, which is the largest in all of Nusa Tenggara (Eastern Indonesia).

Negara

About 22 miles (35 km) south-east of Gilimanuk lies Negara, the capital of the Jembrana regency. The roads which approach it from the Java ferry in the west and Denpasar, 59 miles (95 km) away to the east, run through flat flood-plains with vivid green rice-fields, and little villages half-hidden under coconut-palms. The resettlement policy of the Indonesian government has transferred complete Javanese villages into this thinly populated region, which up to now has been spared from mass tourism.

At the most, tourist coaches heading for southern Bali will stop in Negara for a tea-break.The little market town has thus been able to retain its friendly backwoods atmosphere. The main sights to see include the new white **mosque** and the **Heroes' Cemetery**, which recalls those who fell in the struggle for independence from the Dutch. Negara's tourist infrastructure stretches along the two main axes, Jalan Diponegoro and Jalan Ngurah Rai: some

simple hotels, *warungs*, restaurants, fruit-stalls, the Post Office and a gas-station.

On the southern edge of Negara you can find the settlement of **Loloan Timur**, a *kampung* where Moslem descendants of Buginese seafarers live. Their rectangular dwellings, built on stilts, are quite untypical of Bali; whereas in Balinese peasant villages domestic life takes place at ground level, the living quarters of the maritime Bugis are on the first floor, to protect the occupants from exceptionally high tides.

A further 5 miles (8 km) south-west lies the fishing port of **Pengambengan.** Motorized outriggers land their sardine-catches there. The fish are immediately processed in a canning factory; and a crab-farming project has been successfully started up. So far, the beautiful beaches in this area have not been opened up to tourism.

Above: A water-buffalo race in Negara.
Right: Awaiting the start with relish.

The chief attraction of the Jembrana region are the **Water-buffalo races** (*mekepung*), which take place every year in September and October, after the rice-harvest. In these events, two teams of colorfully decorated water-buffaloes, each pulling a sort of sulky with a driver, race around a 1.25 mile (2 km) course. There are two main teams: the buffaloes (*kerbau*) of the rice-farmers living east of the Ijo Gading river, compete with those of the villagers on the west bank. Trial runs take place on Sundays from April to October: in Bayubiru (3 miles / 5 km west of Negara) and in Dlodbrawah (1 1/4 miles or 2 km south of Tegalcangkring).

The buffalo has an important place in the fertility- and ancestor-cults of the ancient Malay tribes all over the Indonesian archipelago: the Toraja in Sulawesi kill buffaloes for their burial ceremonies; the Karo-Batak of northern Sumatra decorate the gables of their houses with buffalo-horns, and in many aboriginal villages of Bali buffaloes are sacrificed to ensure the fertility of the rice-fields.

For lovers of *gamelan* music the Negara district offers something rather special: the *Gamelan Jegog*. The artistically carved and colorfully painted bamboo instruments of the *Jegog* orchestra are of a remarkable size and produce sounds which are so deep that one does not simply hear the vibrations but actually feels them physically. In the *Jegog Mebarung* several groups of musicians compete for the favor of the listeners – visitors from outside can easily get the impression that volume is the only decisive factor. Scarcely less noisy is the music of the *Kendang Mebarung*, in which two players with gigantic drums take part in a rythmical contest. The *kendang* drums can be as much as 8 feet (2.5 m) long with a diameter of 3 feet (1 m), and produce a deep sound that is so penetrating that at night it can be heard for miles. The musical domain of the women is the *Bumbung Gebyog*. The wives of the rice-farmers pound the ground with bamboo pipes of different lengths, which produce sounds of varying pitches. The name *Bumbung* is onomatopoeic, and reproduces the sound of this orchestra rather well – the treading of the rice seems to have been the inspiration behind this particular form of *gamelan.*

Temples and beaches of the south-west

In the 16th century the Sanskrit scholar and holy-man, Nirartha, emigrated from East Java to Bali, because Islam was gradually gaining the upper hand in his homeland. In Bali he revived Hindu learning and his work is still remembered. Two sea-temples in the Negara region recall his ministry: Pura Gede Perancak and Pura Rambut Siwi.

The little white **Temple of Perancak** is seldom visited, as it is located 6 miles (10 km) south-west of **Mendoyo** beside a remote lagoon that is bordered by off-shore coral reefs. The walls of the *Pura* are built of light-colored coral stone; the *meru* in the central court has only three palm-thatched tiers and is dedicated to

117

the Javanese divine, Nirartha, whom the Balinese call Pedanda Bau Rauh.

The most important temple on the south-west coast is without doubt **Rambut Siwi** (near **Yehembang**, 5 miles / 8 km east of Mendaya). Its name means, roughly, "Sacred Hair": Nirartha is said to have cut off his own hair and left it as an object of worship in a shrine of the Pura Rambut Siwi in 1546. The notion that hair possesses magic powers is an element of the Indian cult of Shiva; a turban around the hair is the distinguishing characteristic of Shiva as the supreme yogi. You approach the temple by steps leading down to a beach of black sand at the foot of a sheer cliff. Seen from the sea, the temple buildings of mellow brick and stone seem even more impressive, especially the Pura Luhur complex, shaded by frangipani trees.

Surfers from Australia have discovered the black sand beach of Medewi,

Above: The last expanse of wilderness in western Bali.

about 2 miles (3 km) west of Pekutatan, beside the mouth of a river. A few little *losmens* have already been set up to meet the needs of the surf-riders.

Just 12 miles (20 km) further westward Lalang Linggah attracts bathers with its palm-fringed beach.

If you have always wondered where the Indonesian national cigarette, *Kretek*, gets its inimitable flavor, you should make the trip north to the village of **Asahduren**, 9 1/2 miles (15 km) away, where clove-plants cover the hillsides as far as the eye can see. The cloves that are gathered there are taken to a factory in Java and mixed with sugar and tobacco to make the cigarettes whose aroma is as typical of Indonesia as incense is of the Vatican. You branch off from the coast road at **Pekutatan** and take the mountain road though attractive scenery to Asahduren and its clove and vanilla plantations, then past picturesque rice-terraces to **Pupuan** (coffee plantations), through Pengastulan and finally to Seririt on the north coast of the island.

WEST BULELENG

A well-built coastal road runs from Singaraja through the busy market town of **Seririt,** and westward on towards Gilimanuk. Bali's relatively dry north coast is thinly populated; the roads are bordered with kapok trees, stands of coconut palms, fields of maize, and – something you would never expect to see in the tropics – vineyards! The grapes are pressed to make *anggur*, a heavy, liqueur-like red wine, which is given to invalids to restore their strength.

At sea, one can see little fishing-boats with bamboo outriggers and colorful sails, making for the small harbor of **Celukanbawang.** Further west, on the Bay of **Gondol**, a gorgeous white shell-sand beach tempts one to stop for a swim. At Cape Gondol there is a an establishment for breeding sea-turtles.

A cluster of stalls selling lemonade and take-away food marks the point where the road forks for the **Pura Agung Pulaki.** This ritually significant temple, devoted to the religious reformer Nirartha, has recently been renovated and given a new gateway and shrines. Its beautiful position on the cliff-top, with a view over the sea, the beach and the volcanoes of Java, is something to savor, but you must be prepared to share it with a horde of wild monkeys. These are not as uncouth as their cousins in Sangeh, but should nevertheless be treated with a healthy mistrust.

People suffering from skin complaints are sent by local doctors to the **Air Panas of Banyuwedang,** a very hot sulphur spring not far from Sumberkerta, which has powerful healing properties.

West Bali National Park

Just too late to save the Balinese tiger, which had already been hunted to extinction in the 1930s, a wildlife reserve was designated in western Bali in 1941. The original intention was to preserve the rare Balinese white starling (Indonesian name: *jalak putih*; zoological name: *Leucopsar rothschildi*) and the Balinese wild cattle (*banteng*) from extinction. Then, in the 1980s, the area was enlarged to create the **Taman Nasional Bali Barat**. The Javanese wild buffalo (*Bos javanicus*), Muntjak deer, leopard, civet, wild boar, monkeys, snakes – including some highly poisonous varieties – and many species of birds now inhabit the reserve.

The national park covers about 300 square miles (765 sq. km), of which 200 sq miles (500 sq. km) is forest: on the well-watered southern slopes of the central highlands up to an altitude of 5000 feet (1500 m) there is evergreen primeval rain-forest; on the dryer northern slopes are less dense, deciduous monsoon forests and palm savannah. In the northwest of the park is a marine reserve, which includes mangrove-swamps, and coral reefs full of fish off the coast of the **Prapat Agung peninsula** and **Menjangan Island**, as well as bird sanctuaries on the small islands in Gilimanuk bay. The park authorities aim to achieve a controlled exploitation of the forest. An especially watchful eye is kept on wood-clearing by farmers from the villages bordering the park. The boundaries of the park were redefined in 1984 and plantations of coconut and eucalyptus, lying within those boundaries, are being returned to a wilderness state – a sensible but distinctly unpopular measure. In the coastal park, fishing and coral collecting are banned.

A "soft" form of nature tourism is to be established in the long term, designed for quiet walking rather than scheduled presentations of wildlife, viewed from a jeep. In the tropical jungle, it is a matter luck, whether or not you see wild animals, because, unlike those in the East African bush, they are not encouraged to seek out well-known water-holes at certain hours of the day.

The information center is at the **Park Headquarters** in Cekik. Here, and also in **Labuhan Lahang** on Terima Bay and in Denpasar, you can obtain the visitor's permit which costs nothing but is compulsory and entitles you to an obligatory official guide. Anyone planning to trek and spend the night in the national park must take a sleeping-bag, mosquito-net, water and provisions. Boots with a good, gripping sole are needed for walking on the slippery earth. Food is cooked on camp-fires and one sleeps in very basic huts. If you want to be more comfortable, you can rent a *losmen* in Labuhan Lahang, Gilimanuk or Negara and make expeditions into the mountains.

Trekking in the Taman Nasional is still something of a novelty. However, word is getting around that Pulau Menjangan is the most fascinating place in Bali for diving and snorkelling. In Labuhan Lalang there is an office of the park authority,

which rents out little outboard motor-boats for trips to "Deer Island." For Menjangan is indeed a refuge of the Java deer, and also of the protected Bali starling. However, the rangers advise against walking in this area because of the poisonous snakes. Fortunately the undisturbed beaches of this paradise island are reptile-free. You only need a pair of goggles to enter a completely new cosmos: Just 5 feet (1.5 m) below the surface the tropical underwater world is populated with an unbelievable variety of brightly colored fish romping among the petrified branches of white coral. Strange as it may sound, you should always wear a shirt in the water, because the UV-rays of the tropical sun can do terrible things to a naked back – and one loses all sense of time, so bewitched is one by the undersea magic. Snorkelling equipment can be hired in Labuhan Lalang, but for scuba-diving you must bring your kit with you from Sanur, Kuta or Nusa Dua.

If you have plenty of time, you can walk right round the peninsula of Prapat Agung in a longish day (15 1/2 miles or 25 km), and here you can snorkel among undisturbed coral reefs.

A little way inland from Terima Bay lies a tomb which is highly revered, both by the Balinese Hindus and by the syncretic Javanese Moslems: the **Makam Jayaprana.** A steep climb over several terraces brings you to the temple which rewards your exertion with a superb view – across the Bali Strait to the Merapi volcano in Java.

A tragic love story is connected with the temple: the orphan Jayaprana, who rose to become the favorite of his raja, took the extraordinarily beautiful fruit-seller, Leyonsari, as his wife. Unfortunately she also caught the eye of the old raja, who sent Jayaprana into the mountains and had him murdered. When Leyonsari saw the murder in a dream, she killed herself, rather than submit to the unwelcome embraces of the king.

Above: The fascinating underwater world off the coast of Menjangan Island.

WESTERN BALI

Large parts of Western Bali are sparsely populated and unknown to tourists. Buses and bemos run regularly on the main roads: Gilimanuk – Denpasar, Gilimanuk – Singaraja, and Singaraja – Denpasar. The best way to get to know Western Bali really well is by rental car or motor-cycle.

GILIMANUK
Accommodation

Gili Sari, **Kartika Candra** (both from Rps. 6.000), **Surya** and **Lestari** on Jl. Raya, which runs down to the harbour, offer very simple accommodation. The same applies to the **Putra Sesana**, right by the bus terminus.

Ferry to Java

Up to 16 ferries a day run between Gilimanuk and Ketapang in Java. The crossing takes about half an hour. Prices: adults Rps. 2,000, motor-cycles Rps. 3,000, cars around Rps. 25,000, according to size.

CEKIK
Accommodation

The **headquarters of the West Bali National Park** is located in Cekik. Anyone wishing to trek in the National Park, can pick up their permit and information pack here. These are also available at an office in Denpasar: PPHA, Jl. Suwung 40, P.O. Box 320.

NEGARA
Accommodation / Restaurants

BUDGET HOTELS: **Cahaya Matahari**, 1/2 mile/1 km east of the town, breakfast only, no main meals;
Hotel Ana, Jl. Ngurah Rai 75, very basic, rooms from Rps. 3.000;
Hotel Ijo Gading, Jl. Nakula 5, from Rps. 10.000;
Losmen Taman Sari, Jl. Nakula 18, in-house restaurant, rooms from Rps. 6.000;
Hotel Wirapada, Jl. Ngurah Rai 107, in-house restaurant, rooms from Rps. 12.500.
You can also eat simply and well in the **Rumah Makan Puas** on Jl. Ngurah Rai.

YEHEMBANG
Accommodation / Restaurants

On the main Negara – Tabanan road, about 3.75 miles / 6 km beyond Yehembang, a road branches off to the south, leading to a long, remote beach of black lava sand. In the village, a *losmen* offers simple overnight accommodation; and there is a small restaurant close by. Also in Yehembang, the well-known painter Putu Windya Anaya runs the *Sangar-Nirartha* painting school.

MEDEWI
Accommodation

Hotel Nirwana, on the beach, rooms from Rps. 15.000; **Medewi Beach Cottages**, on the beach, new and luxurious bungalows, rooms from Rps. 65.000; there is also a simple **losmen** in the main street, rooms from Rps. 8.000.
The beach is a favorite place for surfers.

LALANG LINGGAH
Accommodation

Balian Beach Club, surrounded by coconut-palms, with a lovely view over the Yeh Balian river, rooms from Rps. 10.000.

SERIRIT
Accommodation

Hotel Singarasari, by the bemo terminus, rooms from Rps. 7.000.

CELUKANBAWANG
Accommodation

The **Hotel Drupadi Indah**, with restaurant, is the only place you can stay in Celukbawang.

TERIMA-BUCHT
Accommodation

Margarana Accomodations, with restaurant, rooms from Rps. 15.000.

LABUHAN LALANG
Accommodation

Labuhan Lalang only has a few simple tourist bungalows near the beach, rooms from Rps. 7.500.

Excursions

At the tourist bungalows in Labuhan Lalang you can hire a boat for the trip out to Menjangan Island. Prices per person per hour: 5.000 Rps. For a guide, one pays a further Rps. 5.000. The journey takes half an hour. The island of Menjangan is the gateway to a fascinating underwater world, and this provides wonderful opportunities for divers. Since Labuhan Lalang lies within the borders of the West Bali National Park, there is a charge of Rps. 500 to go on to the beach.

Scuba-diving tours can be organised from the resorts of Kuta, Sanur, Nusa Dua or Lovina Beach. However, you have to bring your own diving equipment with you. Snorkels and goggles can be hired in Labuhan Lalang for a small charge.

A **walk** lasting about 10 hours will take you right round the Prapat Agung penisula. You will see macaque monkeys cavorting in the mangroves. There are refuge-huts along the route. Remember that you have to bring along your own food and water!

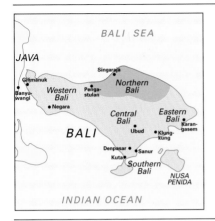

BALI SEA

JAVA

Singaraja

Gilimanuk

Banyu-wangi

Western Bali

Penga-stulan

Northern Bali

Negara

Central Bali

Eastern Bali

Karan-gasem

BALI

Ubud

Klung-kung

Denpasar

Sanur

Kuta

Southern Bali

NUSA PENIDA

INDIAN OCEAN

VOLCANOES, TEMPLES
AND BEACHES OF
BLACK SAND

SINGARAJA
LOVINA BEACH
EAST BULELENG
LAKE BRATAN
BATUR VOLCANO

SINGARAJA

Singaraja, on the north coast of Bali, is the administrative capital of the regency of Buleleng, which stretches from the Prapat Agung peninisula in the West Bali National Park as far as Cape Ngis in the east. The coastal region lies in the rain-shadow of the great volcanoes of the interior and therefore – in comparison with the south – has a considerably drier and hotter climate. On the plains the farmers of northern Bali grow not only rice, by the irrigated and non-irrigated methods, but also maize and grapes. At higher altitudes they cultivate fruit, coffee and cloves. They also raise pigs, buffalo and cattle for the market.

In the 17th century, the domain of the Raja of Buleleng, Ki Gusti Panji Sakti, extended as far as eastern Java. The name Singaraja means "Lion King"and recalls that terrible ruler of the feudal age, under whose aegis Balinese slaves were shipped over to Java in exchange for gold and opium. The trade was extremely profitable and made Singaraja a rich city as well as royal capital.

Previous pages: The Meru of the Pura Ulun Danu in Batur, with the sacred Mt. Gunung Agung behind. Left: A Balinese, with the ob-ligatory festival headgear, the "destar."

This was the part of Bali where the Dutch first set foot, in 1849, and from then on, until Indonesian independence a century later, European influence was much deeper and more lasting here than in the south. Consequently, the rigid caste-system and the rajas, scarcely less exalted than the Hindu gods, lost much of their influence. The local feudal rulers were turned into Dutch colonial adminis-trators, fettered by regulations. In 1882, Singaraja was granted the status of capi-tal of the colony of Bali, and gained fur-ther importance through its flourishing port. But after the Second World War, measures introduced by the new nationa-list government deprived the Dutch-in-fluenced capital of its importance: the port was transferred westward to Celu-kanbawang, the government offices were moved down to Denpasar, and an inter-national airport was opened in the south of the island. The development of beach resorts in Sanur, Kuta and Nusa Dua led to the further downgrading of the former colonial capital.

At the **Old Port,** dilapidated ware-houses remind one that in colonial times this was the main commercial crossroads, not only of the island, but for the whole of eastern Indonesia. And until 1940, tourists visiting Bali arrived here on ocean liners. However, the anchorage in

125

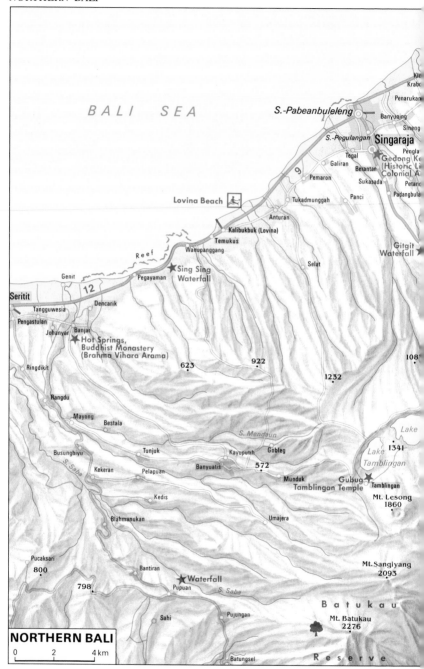

BALI SEA

S.-Pabeanbuleleng

Klc
Krabc
Penarukan
Banyuning
Simeng
S.-Pegulangan **Singaraja**
Pengla
Gedong Ke
(Historic Li
Colonial A
Tegal
Galiran
Berantan
Pemaron
Sukasada
Petanc
Padangbula
Panci

Lovina Beach

Tukadmunggah

Anturan

Kalibukbuk (Lovina)
Temukus
Reef
Wanupanggang
Selat
Gitgit
Waterfall
Genit
Pegayaman
Sing Sing
Waterfall
12
Seritit
Tangguwesia
Dencarik
Pengastulan
Johanyar Banjar
Hot Springs,
Buddhist Monastery
(Brahma Vihara Arama)
Ringdikit
623
922
108
1232
Rangdu
Mayong
Bestala
S. Mendaun
Lake
Busunghiyu
Tunjuk
Kayuputih
Gobleg
1341
Lake
Kekeran
Pelapuan
Banyuatis
572
Tamblingan
S. Saba
Munduk
Gubug
Tamblingan Temple
Tamblingan
Kedis
Mt. Lesong
1860
Blahmanukan
Umajera
Pucaksari
800
Bantiran
Mt. Sangiyang
2093
798
Waterfall
Pupuan
S. Saba
B a t u k a u
Sahi
Pujungan
Mt. Batukau
2276

NORTHERN BALI

0   2   4 km

R e s e r v e

Batungsel

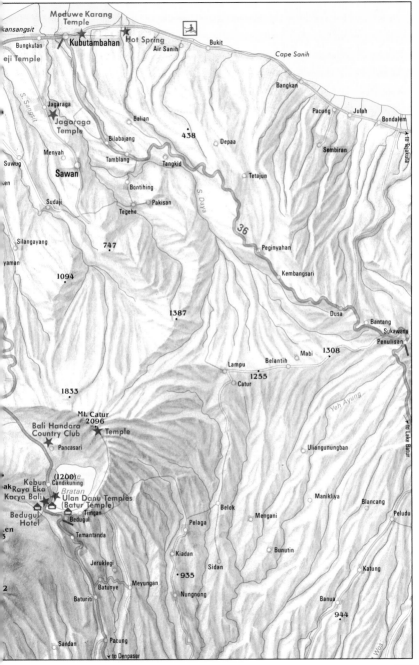

the estuary of the River Buleleng became silted up, and the export trade in livestock, coffee, spices and maize moved to Celukanbawang. Now only the local fishermen bring their little outriggers in here. In the Sukarno era, a statue to a famous freedom fighter, called the **Yuddha Mandalatama**, was erected on the harbor. In style and form it is reminiscent of the social-realist heroic mode which can be seen in so many monuments in the emerging nations of the Third World.

In the wake of the Dutch colonists Chinese traders and artisans came to Singaraja, and by their industry and business acumen they rose to become the economic elite of the city. In the **Chinese temple** by the Buleleng Bridge, Confucian merchants and their families come to pay homage to their ancestors. A colorful relief above the entrance to the temple illustrates the "Legend of the Eight Immortals." The **Chinese cemetery**, which has some tombs of very unusual design, can be found near Lingga Beach on the western edge of the city.

Long before the voyages of Vasco da Gama, Arab seafarers already had a firm grip on the spice-routes across the Indian Ocean. When the Moroccan traveler Ibn Battuta visited Sumatra in 1340, he encountered an already well-established Islamic sultanate there. The long-standing Moslem community in Singaraja can also be traced back to Arab, Javanese and Buginese antecedents. Their Friday mosque is located to the south of the harbor in Jalan Imam Bonjol, and can be recognized from a long way off by its zinc-covered dome. The **Masjid Agung,** or Great Mosque, dates from the 19th century. To the east of it lies the market quarter, or **Pasar Anyar**. At night, many people also visit the **Pasar Banyusari**, by the bus-station of the same name, at the western end of Jalan Ahmed Yani.

In Jalan Veteran, on the south side of the town, is a building which, until the Japanese invasion of February 1942, was the residence of the Dutch governors – who no doubt enjoyed the change from the cold, damp climate of their North Sea homeland. Until the 1930s, they were successful in protecting the Hindu Balinese, for tactical reasons, from the missionary zeal of their Christian countrymen. At sunset, the **Colonial Residence** offers a fine view of the Old Port and the sea. Not far from this building, which today houses the administrative seat of the Regent (*bupati*) of Buleleng, stands the emblem of the city, the statue of the winged lion **Singambaraja**, which dominates the junction of Jalan Ngurah Rai and Jalan Veteran.

A "must" for bibliophiles is the **Gedong Kertya Historical Library** (only open in the mornings), situated a little further east along Jalan Veteran. Here you can see over 3000 ancient manuscripts, written on the leaves of *lontar* palms. There is also a collection of *prasastis*, which are copper plates inscribed with the edicts of the rajas, dating from the 14th century. In part of the former Rajas' Palace, the **Puri Kawan**, immediately behind the libraray, you can now see sarongs being woven.

On high ground by the Jalan Gajah Mada stands the **Temple of Shiva**, the Pura Dalem of Singaraja. The steps leading up to the inner courtyard are flanked by terrifying reliefs of the witch Rangda. And Durga, the female embodiment of Shiva's destructive energy, watches over the nearby place of cremation. Maintaining the balance between creation and destruction, death and birth, is the underlying theme of Balinese Hinduism.

In the village of **Bratan**, about 1 1/4 miles (2 km) futher south, silversmiths can be seen at work. Some 6 miles (10 km) southward at **Gitgit**, a path leads off the main road to a 30 ft (10 m) high waterfall (*air terjun*) on the upper reaches of the river Buleleng – these cascades are of course at their most impressive during the monsoon season.

Lovina Beach

In 1970 the last Raja of Buleleng, Anak Agung Panji, built the first hotel on the 4 1/2 mile (7 km) long, gray-black beach of Lovina, which runs from Pemaron, through Kalibukbuk, to Temukus. Word of Bali's new rendez-vous soon spread among the backpacking fraternity: it was a quiet, palm-fringed, low-budget beach resort with beautiful underwater coral reefs offshore. True, the sunsets are just as impressive as ever, but apart from that quite a lot has changed. In the 1980s, simple *losmens*, cheap compared to those in Kuta, sprang up like mushrooms – followed by more than 40 modest bungalow hotels. At night, heavily loaded trucks rumble along the Singaraja – Gilimanuk – Java highway, which runs parallel to the beach, but in spite of this Lovina Beach is still a quieter and more restful place than Kuta or Legian. You will not find any culinary sensations in the numerous little restaurants, but at least the fish is good and fresh. For variety, you can get authentic Chinese cooking at the **Aditya Restaurant**. There is still a lack of accommodation in the higher price-range, but plans are in hand to remedy this.

In the early morning the sea-water is clear, even close to the beach; otherwise you can get a fishing-boat to take you out to the snorkelling areas on the coral reefs. There, around dawn, you will see dozens of dolphins playing among the outriggers with which they have become familiar.

From midday onward, the heat tends to reduce beach activity to a somnolent minumum, so it makes a nice change to take an excursion to the village of **Banjar.** On a hill above this Hindu village stands the Buddhist monastery of **Brahma Vihara Arama**, which was founded in 1958. It is 8 miles (13 km) from Lovina, and is worth a visit, not just for its beautiful outlook over rice terraces and down to the sea.

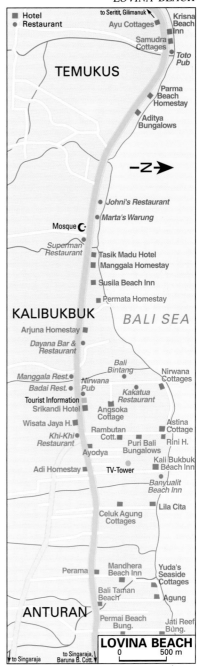

129

Taxi-mopeds wait in Dencarik to take you the last 2 miles (3 km) up the hill to the monastery. The staircase leading up to it is flanked by watchmen of stone. A lotus pond adorns the outer courtyard. The main hall of the white-walled Vihara is decorated with reliefs showing scenes from the life of the Buddha, from his birth until his ascent into the Parinirvana. A *stupa* symbolizes the stages of enlightenment according to the teaching of the Buddha. In the next hall stands a gilded Buddha figure, flanked by two statues of Avalokiteshvara, the savior in Mahayana Buddhism, who lives on today in Japanese Zen and certain other religions. However, the yellow-garbed monks who live in the monastery follow the rather puritanical meditation regime of Theravada Buddhism, which is widespread in Sri Lanka, Burma and Thailand. Visitors

who are interested can take part in a two-week course in meditation.

The **hot springs** (*air panas*) near Banjar have been recently revovated and are a popular bathing-place for the Balinese. A hot sulphur spring gushes out at a temperature of 38° C from the stone heads of eight sacred snakes and into three tiered basins. Recently installed changing-rooms, showers, a restaurant and a *losmen*, add considerably to the comfort and enjoyment of bathers.

The temples of eastern Buleleng

A particularly fine example of the almost Baroque temple architecture of northern Bali can be found at **Sangsit,** 4 1/2 miles (7 km) east of Singaraja. The **Pura Beji** of Sangsit is a *subak* temple for the local farmers, who for generations have been organized into irrigation associations. A closed *gedong* or shrine is dedicated to the rice-goddess, Dewi Sri, who is responsible for the fertility of the fields. Phallic *linggas* symbolize the pro-

Above: The catch is landed on the beach near Lovina. Right: A serpent's head spews out water at the thermal spring in Banjar.

130

creative power of the god Shiva. The temple has become famous for its extravagant reliefs and highly detailed sculptures, which, unlike the dark volcanic stone of southern temples, are carved from pink sandstone. The wide temple gate of the Pura Beji is covered with arabesques, and heads of demons and Garudas, and crowned by so-called *kayonans*, symbols of the Tree of the World and the Mountain of the World, which have become familiar through the shadow-plays.

About 3 miles (5 km) south-east of Sangsit lies the village of **Jagaraga**, whose **Pura Dalem** is worth a visit to see its unusual reliefs: two rather corpulent Dutchmen are sitting in a Model T Ford that has been reproduced in loving detail. They are being stopped by a Balinese who is threatening them with a peculiar-looking revolver. The richly ornamented statues of the bloodthirsty witch Rangda indicate that the temple is dedicated to the goddess Durga.

About 2 miles (3 km) further south is the village of **Sawan**, lying picturesquely among *sawah* fields. Here, smiths still practise the traditional art of making bronze gongs.

Back on the coast road, the next stop is **Kubutambahan**. In the **Pura Meduwe Karang** (3/4 mile / 1 km east of the fork to the Batur volcano) farmers bring offerings to the sun-god Surya, the "Lord of the Fields," and to Mother Earth (*ibu pertiwi*), to ask that fertility may come to the fields which they are unable to irrigate. There is a famous relief, which can be found in the third courtyard, the Holy of Holies, to the left of the stone plinth which supports the shrines: at first glance the figure it shows seems to be a Balinese, since the straight-backed cyclist is wearing a sarong printed with a floral pattern, and some Indonesian-looking headgear. But in fact it is a Dutch ethnologist named Nieuwenkamp, whose long nose – the typical mark of a wester-

ner to Southeast Asian eyes – remains clearly visible, having survived restoration following an earthquake. Nieuwenkamp explored the island by bicycle in 1904, and one can imagine the excitement which his appearance must have caused in the villages. In the Balinese interpretation, the back wheel of the bicycle becomes a lotus-flower, the chain is left out as being superfluous, but instead a rat and a dog have been placed under the chain-guard, which itself bears a marked resemblance to a circular saw.

Continuing along the coast road, shaded by avenues of trees, one arrives, 11 miles (18 km) east of Singaraja, at the pools of cool spring water of **Air Sanih,** by a quiet beach of black sand. This is a wonderful place to relax, mainly visited by Indonesian tourists. It has beautifully laid-out gardens and a hotel and restaurant waiting to greet you.

The Bali-Aga village of **Sembiran**, high up in the hills (19 miles / 30 km from Singaraja) is not necessarily worth a visit, because – unlike Tenganan in east-

ern Bali – the indigenous villagers no longer keep up their pre-Hindu traditions. On the contrary, they are obviously anxious to be regarded as perfectly normal Balinese. The very name "Bali-Aga" they feel to be a form of discrimination. Nowadays they cremate their dead and no longer, as they once did, leave them in nearby megalithic hill- temples to be eaten by birds. Nevertheless, the tortuous mountain road to Sembiran certainly offers a superb panorama over orange-groves and fields of maize to the sea.

Tejakula, 22 miles (36 km) from Singaraja, is a sleepy village with a Chinese character. In the Banjar Pande silver-smiths make personal ornaments and ritual objects. A **horse-bath** recalls the feudal era, when the raja's mounts used to be washed there. Nowadays, even the common people are allowed to bathe in it.

Above: The Meru of the Pura Ulun Danu stands in the middle of Lake Bratan.

LAKE BRATAN

If you are tired of burning your feet on the scorching black sands of the north coast, you can go and cool off in **Lake Bratan**, in the nearby volcanic mountains. There are two roads leading to it. The fastest route into the mountains is the well maintained Singaraja – Bedugul road (19 miles / 30 km). But since, as the Buddhists say, the road is itself the destination, we would recommend a longer route which, although more challenging for drivers, goes through much more attractive landscape: via **Pengastulan**, **Rangdu** and **Banyuatis** to **Munduk** in the highlands, and then steeply up to the twin lakes of Tamblingan and Buyan. The two lakes were one until separated by an earthquake in the 19th century; they lie on the thickly jungle-covered north slopes of Gunung Lesong (6100 ft / 1860 m) and Gunung Tapak (6250 ft / 1905 m). From the village of **Tamblingan** a road leads up to **Lake Tamblingan** (4260 ft / 1300 m) – a forgotten oasis of silence. A few farmers have planted fields of maize and built huts on the shore of the lake; they are genuinely pleased to see visitors, provided they have mastered a few words of Bahasa Indonesia. Here and there, you can see fishermen crossing the lake in dug-out canoes. On the southern shore the **Pura Gubug Tamblingan** stands among the reeds, recognizable by its new *merus*. This temple is dedicated to the ancestors of the rajas of Buleleng and Tabanan.

A road which was not asphalted until the 1980s, runs high above the north shore of **Lake Buyan** and continues westward until it joins the main Singaraja – Denpasar road, about 37 miles (60 km) away. Soon, **Lake Bratan** appears to the south, lying picturesquely in an extinct volcanic crater. On the western shore, the **Pura Ulun Danu** indicates the religious significance the lake has for the Balinese. The lake-temple complex, which includes two islets, is where sacrifices are made to the water-goddess Dewi Danu (the three-tiered *meru*), as well as to Shiva (the seven-tired *meru)* and Vishnu (the eleven-tiered *meru*). Even the Buddha is honoured with a pagoda temple containing five meditating Dhyani Buddhas, to the left of the split *candi bentar* gate; Balinese Hindus consider Gautama Buddha to be one of the many manifestations of Vishnu, the preserver of cosmic continuity.

The cool mountain climate, with minimum temperatures of 11°C at this 4000 ft (1200 m) altitude, is particularly attractive to the foreigners who live and work in Bali. They come to relax in the elegant **Handara Country Club**, which has a good restaurant and an 18-hole golf-course, and is open to ordinary mortals! In the middle of the sacred Lake Bratan there is a water-ski jumping-ramp belonging to the **Hotel Bedugul**. This hotel, popular with Indonesian tourists, also offers para-sailing. Moderately-priced bungalows (e.g. "Lila Graha") can be found

in the village of Candikuning. There is also a colorful flower-market there, where peasant women offer ornamental tropical plants including many rare species of orchid. The broad bowl of the crater with its fertile soil and ample rainfall, provides ideal conditions for growing fruit and vegetables; strawberries, passion-fruit, pineapples and apples all thrive amazingly here. Garden enthusiasts take delight in a 320-acre (130 ha.) botanical garden, the **Kebun Raya Eka Karya Bali**. Over 600 types of tree and some 400 different species of orchid can be seen there.

If you have brought stout walking boots, with good gripping soles, and are prepared to set out at sunrise, you can brave the ascent of **Gunung Catur** (6875 ft/ 2096 m), whose summit is crowned by a temple, the Pura Pucak, dedicated to Shiva. It is advisable to take a guide on this trek, which starts at the Hotel Bedugul and initially follows a path through the fields to village of **Tihingan**. From here, a path leads uphill through constantly changing rain-forest, where you have to climb over fallen trees. Soon the going becomes so steep that you, as an *orang putih* ("white man"), wonder how the locals, wearing only slippers, can make any headway in the loamy red soil, made sticky and slippery by the rain. One hauls oneself up the slope, from one palm-vine to the next, until after a good six hours, one reaches the tree-clad summit and the Pura Pucak. Having negotiated the descent in series of skids and slides, there is an alternative route, branching westward, high above the north shore of Lake Bratan, to Candikuning and from there along the lake shore back to Bedugul.

ROUND THE BATUR VOLCANO

The name **Penelokan** (35 miles/57 km from Singaraja and 19 miles/30 km from Ubud) means "beautiful view," and it

keeps its promise – although the famous view is often distorted by souvenir-sellers, touts, volcano-guides and boatmen. If you can ignore these, Penelokan, at a height of 4750 ft (1450 m), does indeed offer the best view over the Batur region: far below, in a gigantic volcanic crater, lies the long, narrow Lake Batur, flanked by the still active Batur volcano (5630 ft /1717 m) to the west and Gunung Abang (7060 ft / 2153m) to the east.

Following the volcanic eruptions of 1917 and 1926, which cost thousands of lives, the inhabitants of the threatened village of Batur chose to move their settlement and its lake temple from the lake shore to the edge of the crater. Thus was born the **Pura Ulun Danu Batur**, an extensive complex comprising nine major temples on the ridge beside the road to Kintamani. The lake goddess Dewi Danu (a Sanskrit word which is related etymo-

Above: A winged monster in the Pura Ulun Danu Batur. Right: Morning mist over the new town of Batur on the edge of the crater.

logically to the European river names Danube and Don) is worshipped with sacrifices, even by rice-farmers from the south of Bali, since Lake Batur feeds many of the springs which emerge some distance away in the regencies of Bangli and Gianyar.

Every three days, in **Kintamani** (altitude 4900 ft / 1500 m), there is a bustling fruit and vegetable market; the cool climate may make the sun-sated beach tourists shiver, but it is ideal for horticulture. Kintamani also "produces" dogs in very large numbers, who make their presence impossible to ignore at night. The view is not as magnificent as from Penelokan, but to compensate for this the people of Kintamani generally seem rather more friendly.

Less than 4 miles (6 km) further north, in Sukawana, not far from **Penulisan**, there is a fork in the road leading to the mountain temple of **Pura Tegeh Koripan**, which is not only the highest temple in Bali, but also one of the most important. It may well also be the oldest, since you will not find any *merus* here. A seemingly interminable flight of steps leads up to a height of 5725 ft (1745 m), but it is well worth the climb: in the morning you can see as far as Java and, the other way, to Lombok, but unfortunately, after midday a cold damp fog often blows in.

In the highest group of temples, the **Pura Panarajon**, you will find numerous stone phallic symbols (*lingga*), over 1,000 years old, and mounted on plinths which are said to represent the female sex-organ (*yoni*): they symbolize the Hindu god Shiva and his female energy-principle, Shakti. In Tantric imagery, this expresses both the worship of sexual energy and creative force, as well as the uniting of opposites in an abstract sense. There is a row of vine-covered and much-weathered sculptures of the god Vishnu and his consort Lakshmi, and of Shiva and Parvati – not forgetting their

elephant-headed son Ganesha. You can also see a stone portrayal of a couple who may be presumed to be King Udayana and his wife Mahendradatta (11th century AD). The statue of Brahma, Creator of the World, shows an East Javanese influence, and can be recognized by its four faces, looking to the four points of the compass – statues like these are found at many crossroads on the island. It · is possible that before the Pura Tegeh Koripan assumed its function as royal temple of Pejeng, it was a megalithic sacrificial site, since to this day unidentifiable stone fragments are still to be found near the temple.

The climb to Gunung Batur

Seeing the sunrise over the Batur volcano must be one of the most vivid impressions you can come away with from a visit to Bali. The best base-camp for this mountain tour is the little village of **Toya Bungkah** (also called Tirtha) on the shore of Lake Batur, which has res-

taurants and simple *losmens*. You reach it by a winding road which runs from Penelokan down into the wide crater. Beside the lake the nights are milder than on the edge of the crater. And in Toya Bungkah you can also revive tired joints in the hot sulphur-water of an **air panas** at the waterside.

For the climb up Gunung Batur you need a flashlight, sweater, water and strong footwear with a gripping sole, since the upper slopes are covered with slippery lava sand. It is best to start out before 4 am; you can climb the first 2000 ft (600 m) in two to three hours. The shortest path begins in Purajati; the ascent from Toya Bungkah takes rather longer. To be on the safe side, you should hire a guide at the hotel. When you reach the rim of the crater you have a wonderful view over the whole surrounding area; for Gunung Batur is in fact a volcano within a volcano: it rises out of a larger crater bowl, which was created millions of years ago by an explosion of gases which blew the top off the huge

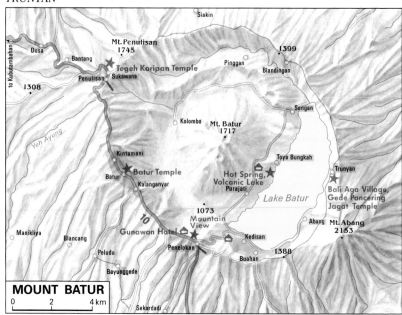

MOUNT BATUR

0 2 4 km

original volcano. In the bowl or *caldera* thus created, the "little" Mount Batur was formed, and is still growing: plumes of yellow sulphurous steam rise into the air and to the south-west stretches a broad black lava-field which was created relatively recently, between 1965 and 1974. At sunrise, if visibility is good, you can see another volcano, Gunung Rinjani, on the island of Lombok to the east, and westward one can make out the volcanoes of Java.

Trunyan

Lake Batur is about 1 1/2 miles (2.5 km) wide, 4 1/2 miles (7 km) long and 230 ft (70 m) deep. Because the lake provides water and therefore fertility for the rice-fields of the south, every year the *subaks* (irrigation associations) from the Ubud region come and sacrifice a water-

Right: Beyond Lake Batur lies the Bali-Aga village of Trunyan.

buffalo here. "Stars of the Lake" is the name given to the ancient Balinese villages which lie right beside the lake: Kedisan, Buahan, Abang, Trunyan and Songan. The only one of these which still has no road to it is the Bali-Aga village of Trunyan. So, visiting it means either a trek or a boat-trip. One can hire a motorboat in Toya Bungkah for the crossing which takes less than an hour. If you have already hired a skipper in Penelokan, he will probably put you ashore in the fishing and farming village of **Kedisan**, which boasts not only *losmens* and hot food stalls but also a jetty with a ticket office. If you have had enough of boats when you get to Trunyan, you can walk back to Kedisan via Abang in a little less than two hours.

There is no doubt that the most important things to see in Trunyan are connected with its ethnic history: the ancient Balinese villagers do not cremate the bodies of their relatives, but lay them out under a spreading sacred banyan-tree, to be eaten by the birds and animals of the

jungle. This explains the many skulls and bleached bones that can be seen lying around. Although foreigners may find it rather disconcerting, this ancient Mongolian and ancient Malay manner of dispatching the dead is still customary today among the Parsees of India and the tantric-influenced Buddhists of Tibet. The notion behind it is that the birds carry the dead souls up to heaven and thus favorably influence the cycle of rebirth.

Beside the cemetery stands the **Pura Gede Pancering Jagat** (literally: temple at the navel of the world). Its principal shrine houses the 13 ft (4 m) high statue of the god Da Tonte, who embodies the creative and destructive forces of nature – and indeed the people of Trunyan, living in the middle of a volcanic *caldera*, have good reason to know all about natural forces. Only once a year, at the full moon in October, is the Jagarat statue, which resembles a megalithic *menhir,* displayed to the faithful.

The fertility cult of Da Tonte/Jagarat is reminiscent of the ancient Indian cult of Shiva, and it is true that the Bali-Agas of Trunyan came into contact with Hinduism as early as the 10th century AD. However, due to the remoteness and inaccessibility of their village, they remained unaffected by the further conversion of the island to Hinduism under the empire of the rajas. Even today the villagers are anxious to preserve their Bali-Aga traditions and cling to their isolation: any villager who wishes to marry a partner from outside has to leave Trunyan. Thus, anything foreign and unfamiliar is held to be of little value in the eyes of the villagers. Sometimes the tourist visitor is made very aware of this. It is therefore a good idea to bring a guide from the hotel with you on this boat-trip. Trunyan has always been a poor community, since the steepness of the volcanic slopes makes cultivation very difficult. The village is unattractive by Balinese standards, with many modern tin-roofed shanties among the older thatched huts. There is an oppressive amount of begging, unlike in the rest of Bali, and prices are exorbitant.

137

SINGARAJA

Accommodation

As all accommodation in Singaraja is rather modest, most people drive 6 miles (10 km) further on to Lovina Beach. Nevertheless, the following can be recommended: **Duta Karya**, Jl. Jen Achmad Yani 59, from Rps. 10,000; **Garuda**, Jl. Jen Achmad Yani 76, Tel: 41191, from Rps. 7,500; **Saka Bindu**, Jl. Jen Achmad Yani 104, and **Gelar Sari**, Jl. Jen Achmad Yani 87, near the bus-station, both from Rps. 5,000; **Sentral**, Jl. Jen Achmad Yani 48, from Rps. 9,000; **Singaraja**, Jl. Veteran 1, former residence of the Dutch colonial governor; **Tresna Homestay**, Jl. Gajah Mada, Tel: 21816, from Rps. 3,000.

Restaurants

Gandhi, set back a little from Jl. Jen Achmad Yani in a little market-place, not particularly cheap, but reckoned to be the best Chinese restaurant in town; **Segar II**, opposite, is challenging Gandhi for the top spot; **Kartika**, nearby, also serves Indonesian food.

Important addresses

The **Post Office** is located at the T-junction of Jl. Jen Achmad Yani and Jl. Imam Bonjol.

The **Telephone- and Telegraph Office** is a little further south in a side-street off Jl. Diponegoro.

There are two **Bus-stations**: one in the west on the road leading out to Lovina Beach, Jl. Jen Achmad Yani (for buses to Denpasar und Gilimanuk) and one in the east on the road going out to Sangsit (for buses to Kintamani and Amlapura). Bus fares: to Lovina Beach, 400 Rps.; to Gilimanuk, 2,500 Rps.; Denpasar, 2,500 Rps.; Kintamani, 1,800 Rps.; Amlapura, 2,500 Rps. Near each of the bus-stations there is a **gasoline (petrol) -station**.

There is a **hospital** on Jl. Diponegoro.

Evening entertainment

In Singaraja, in the evening one either strolls around the bombastic Independence Monument and enjoys the sunset, or one goes to the cinema to see schmaltzy romances Indonesian-style or Kung-Fu thrillers. The **cinema** is on the far side of the river, east of the monument.

LOVINA BEACH

Accommodation

Lovina Beach is the name of the stretch of black sand, nearly 6 miles (10 km) long with plenty of accommodation. The tourism center is **Kalibukbuk**. Out of season it is easy to find good, cheap accommodation. At Christmas-time and in August, especially at weekends, there is a serious shortage of rooms. There are still no luxury hotels. But here is a small selection of hotels and bungalows (from east to west, as far as the big radio mast): **Baruna Beach Cottages**, one of the most expensive establishments, right beside the sea, with swimming-pool and sail-boards for hire at Rps. 12,000 per hour, from US$ 40; **Permai Beach Bungalows**, among rice-fields, not directly on the beach, from Rps. 10,000; **Jati Reef Bungalows**, the reef, in the sea right in front of it, is said to be the most beautiful on this stretch of coast, from Rps. 15,000; **Bali Taman Beach**, Tel: 41125, from Rps. 20,000; **Homestay Agung**, with bathrooms downstairs and bedrooms upstairs, restaurant on the premises, from Rps. 10,000; **Perama**, in the main street, with restaurant and office of the Perama Bus Compnay, from Rps. 10,000; **Celuk Agung Cottages**, with swimming-pool and tennis-courts, not directly on the sea, from Rps. 27,000; **Lila Cita**, simple, right on the sea, from Rps. 10,000; **Adi Homestay**, other side of the main road, some distance from the sea, from Rps. 6,000; **Kali Bukbuk Beach Inn**, with restaurant, right by the sea, from Rps. 15,000.

Hotels and bungalows beyond the big radio-mast: **Ayodya Accommodation**, traditional setting, on the main road, from Rps. 5,000; **Rambutan**, on the road to the beach, attractive rooms, from Rps. 15,000; **Puri Bali Bungalows**, nearer the beach, from Rps. 10,000; **Rini**, on the beach, very clean, from Rps. 15,000; along the main road there is a series of very cheap lodgings such as **Wisata Jaya Homestay**, from Rps. 5,000; **Nirwana Cottages**, Tel. 41288, spread over a large area by the beach, restaurant with view of the sea, from Rps. 12,000, two-storey bungalows from Rps. 35,000; **Angsoka Cottages**, good value considering closeness to beach, from Rps. 6,000, but more expensive rooms available; **Aditya Bungalows**, one of the most luxurious places, right by the sea, with swimming-pool and shops, from US$ 13; **Parma Beach Homestay**, nice location by the sea, from Rps. 5,000; **Toto Pub**, good position, simple rooms, from Rps. 7,000; **Samudra Cottages**, some distance from the sea, from Rps. 30,000. Further west there are a few more smaller, cheap establishments.

Restaurants

The two-storey **Nirwana Pub** has long been the gastronomic and social hub of Kalibukbuk. It is now reckoned to be overpriced but is still a good place to go for a drink at sundown. The **Badai** nearly opposite is good and relatively cheap. The decor is very basic but that does not seem to worry its many patrons. Going towards the beach you will find two restaurants with reasonable prices: the **Bali Bintang** and the **Kakatua**.

The **Khi Khi** in the main street is praised for its fish dishes. But the restaurants further out of town are also worth visiting. For lovers of seafood, the **Banyualit** on the beach going towards Singaraja is recommended. In the other direction, **Marta's Warung** and **Johni's** are very popular. Many restaurants advertise special evening buffets, but these do not always live up to their promise.

Important addresses

In Kalibukbuk there is a **Tourist Bureau**, open daily except Sun, 7 am – 2 pm (Fri until 11 am and Sat until 12.30 pm).
There is no **Post Office**. However, you can make **telephone calls** from the Aditya Bungalows.

Activities

No sooner have you arrived than you are lured into making the **boat-trip to see the dolphins**. This begins at daybreak and costs Rps. 8,000 per person, unless you negotiate a group rate. The price usually includes one or two stops for snorkelling on the reef. A boat-trip to the reef alone, for snorkelling, costs Rps. 4,000 per hour. Lovina Beach is also a good base for **scuba-diving**. West of the center of Kalibukbuk on the main road to the mosque is the diving sports agency **Spice Dive**. It offers the best opportunity for diving on the reef off Lovina Beach. But they also organise diving expeditions to Pulau Menjangan. These cost around US$ 60 per person.

On 16th August and on the day after Galungan, **buffalo-races** are held in Kaliasem.

BEDUGUL

Accommodation / Restaurants

LUXURY CLASS: **Bali Handara Country Club**, beautiful view of the lake, tennis-courts and an 18-hole golf-course, from US$ 45. Prices in the good restaurant begin at US$ 12.
MID-PRICE: **Bedugul Hotel**, Tel: 26593, within the Taman Rekreasi Bedugul Zone at the southern end of the lake, from Rps. 25,000; the restaurant attached is a bit overpriced and has a rather dull menu.
Bukit Mungsu Indah Hotel, from US$ 20; **Lila Graha**, old colonial building forms part of the hotel, from Rps. 30,000.
BUDGET: **Hadi Raharjo**, very simple, in the main street, from Rps. 10,000; **Losmen Mawa Indah**, on the road to the Botanical Garden, from Rps. 10,000; **Hotel Ashram**, on the lake, from Rps. 15,000.

Activities

In **Bedugul** motor-boat trips (at Rps. 35,000 per boat per hour), water-skiing and paragliding are on offer. In order to enjoy the delights of the scenery to the full, trips in rented paddle-boats (Rps. 6,000 for 4 hours) are absolutely ideal.

LAKE BATUR

Accommodation / Restaurants

KINTAMANI: There are some losmens right on the main street, such as the modest **Superman's,** from Rps. 4,000 and the comfortable **Hotel Miranda** from Rps. 6,000.
Approximately 550 yards (500 m) into the crater itself is the **Puri Astin Inn**, from Rps. 12,000. From the new rooms you can get a magnificent view of the sunrise. The hotel has its own restaurant.
PENELOKAN: Losmen Gunawan, superb view over the lake, with restaurant, from Rps. 10,000; **Lakeview Homestay**, Tel: 32023, the cheap rooms are extremely cramped, but there is a magnificent view, own restaurant, from Rps. 12,000.
KEDISAN: Segara Bungalows, out towards Toya Bungkah, simple, from Rps. 8,000; **Segara Homestay**, near the center of town, from Rps. 8,000; **Surya Homestay**, in the direction of Toya Bungkah, with restaurant, from Rps. 8,000.
BUAHAN: Baruna Cottages, new, with restaurant, very quiet, from Rps. 8,000.
TOYA BUNGKAH: Alina, bathing-grottoes are a feature, from Rps. 8,000; **Amerta Homestay**, near the hot springs, from Rps. 8,000; **Awangga Bungalows**, the cheapest accommodation available, from Rps. 5,000; **Balai Seni Toya Bungkah**, located higher up, reckoned to be the best accommodation in the town, has a small but interesting library, from Rps. 15,000; **Under the Volcano Homestay**, popular, has its own restaurant, from Rps. 8,000. In addition, there is further reasonably-priced accommodation and several new bungalow-resorts.

Excursions

Mountain tour of Gunung Batur: You can ask for a guide at your accommodation. Anyone needing advice about tours should go and talk to the knowledgeable Jero Wijaya in the Awangga Bungalows. The usual ascent starts in Toya Bungkah and takes two to three hours.
Provided the visibility is good, you do not need a guide for this tour. Ideally, you should aim to reach the summit by sunrise, or at the latest by 10 am, because after that the summit often disappears in cloud. Towards the end, the climb gets very steep, and slippery underfoot.
Boat trip to Trunyan: A ticket for the boat-trip includes the visit to Trunyan, to the cemetery outside the village and to the hot springs in Toya Bungkah. Tickets, at about Rps. 35,000, are sold at the office on the jetty at Kedisan.

UNDER THE VOLCANO

KLUNGKUNG
SOUTH-EAST COAST
TEMPLE OF BESAKIH
AMLAPURA

Looming over eastern Bali is the volcano of Gunung Agung, which in a devastating eruption in 1963 buried three-quarters of the region under streams of red-hot magma and a rain of ash. More than 80,000 Balinese were made homeless. Because so much farmland had been turned into a permanent desert, the Indonesian government re-settled many of the victims in Sulawesi. Since then, there has been a successful program of reforestation in Bali, and the natural ecology is slowly establishing itself again.

Eastern Bali comprises the regencies of Klungkung and Karangasem and its culture and landscape offers many attractions: Klungkung town, the former capital of the rajas, with its lively traditions of craftsmanship; the black sand beach of Kusamba and the bat-haunted caves of Goa Lawah; the beach resort of Candi Dasa and the Bali-Aga village of Tenganan; the mother-temple of Besakih in the shadow of the island's highest volcano (10,305 ft / 3,142 m); the royal baths of Tirthagangga in the middle of a superb landscape of rice-terraces, and not least, the lonely mountain temple on the Seraya massif, at the eastern tip of Bali.

Previous pages: The coast near Candi Dasa. Left: Rice-fields near Tirthagangga.

KLUNGKUNG

The administrative district of Klungkung, which includes the islands of Nusa Penida and Lembongan, is today admittedly the smallest of the island's eight *kabupaten* or regencies; but its former influence has left a lasting mark on the whole of Bali. For with the collapse of the Majapahit empire in Java, Klungkung became the religious, cultural, political and intellectual center of the Hindu elite in the island. At that time the raja, who was known as *Dewa Agung* ("Great Divine One"), ruled from Gelgel, a few miles south of Klungkung. In the mid-16th century his domain extended from eastern Java, over Bali, Lombok and Sumbawa as far as southern Sulawesi (Celebes Islands). In 1685, the capital was transferred to Klungkung, which, following the fragmentation of the Gelgel dynasty, was no longer the mightiest city in Bali, but nevertheless remained the seat of the supreme court of justice and guardian of the Hindu tradition.

The main street of Klungkung, **Jalan Diponegoro,** is a hot, noisy shopping-street, lined with antique-, souvenir- and video-shops. A remarkable number of shops are owned by Chinese, since Klungkung is the main center for trade between Lombok and eastern Java.

143

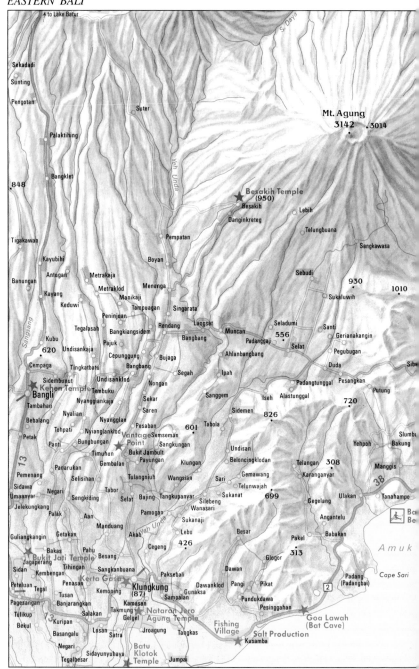

↑ to Lake Batur

Sekadadi

Sunting

Pengotan

Suter

Mt. Agung
3142 .3014

Palaktihing

Bangklet

.848

Besakih Temple
(950)
Besakih

Lebih

Danginkreteg

Telungbuana

Tigakawan

Pempatan

Sangkawasa

Kayubihi

Boyan

Sebudi

930

1010

Antugan

Metrakaja

Banungan

Metraklod

Menanga

Sukaluwih

Kayang

Manikaji

Keduwi

Tampuagan

Singarata

Peninjoan

Langsat

Seladumi

Santi

Tegalesah

Rendang

Muncan

556

Gerianakangin

Kubu

Bangkiangsidem

Bangbang

Padanggaji

Selat

Pegubuan

620

Undisankaja

Pajuk

Ahlanbangbang

Cepunggung

Bujaga

Duda

Sibe

Cempaga

Tingkatbatu

Bangbang

Segah

Ipah

Padangtunggal

Pesangkan

Putung

Sidembunut

Undisanklod

Nongan

Kehen Temple

Tembuku

Sekar

Sanggem

Iseh

Alastunggal

720

Bangli

Nyanggiankaja

Saren

Sidemen

826

Tambahan

Nyalian

Nyangglan

Bebalang

Tohpati

Nyianglanklod

Pesaban

601

Tabola

Slumbi

Petak

Panti

Bungbungan

Semseman

Vantage
Point

Sangkungan

Undisan

Yehpoh

Bakung

Timuhun

Bukit Jambult

Beloncingklodan

Telangan

308

Manggis

Pemenang

Panarukan

Gembalan

Payungan

Klungan

Karanganyar

Sidawa

Selisihan

Tulangniuh

Wangsian

Sari

Gemawang

Umaanyer

Negari

Tabor

Bajing

Tangkupanyar

Telunwajah

Sukanat

699

Gegelang

Ulakan

Tanahampo

Jelukungkang

Palak

Selat

Silebeng

Wanasari

Ba
Be

Guliangkangin

Getakan

Aan

Manduang

Pamogan

Sukanaji

Besar

Angantelu

Babakan

Amuk

Bakas

Pahu

Lebu

Pakel

Bukit Jati Temple

Besang

Cegeng

426

Glogor

313

Jagaperang

Tihingan

Sangkanbuana

Pakfor Cape Sari

Sidan

Kembengan

Penasan

Kerta Gasa

Padang
(Padangbai)

Peteluan

Tegal

Kemoning

Klungkung
(87)

Dawanklod

Pangi

Pikat

2

Pagesangan

Banjarangkan

Gunaksa

Pundukdawa

Tulikup

Kuripan

Salakan

Takmung

Sampalan

Pesinggahan

Bekul

Basangalu

Gelgel

Nataran Jero
Agung Temple

Goa Lawah
(Bat Cave)

Negari

Losan

Satra

Jroagung

Tangkas

Fishing
Village

Salt Production

Tegalbesar

Sidayunyuhaya

Batu
Klotok
Temple

Jumpai

Kusamba

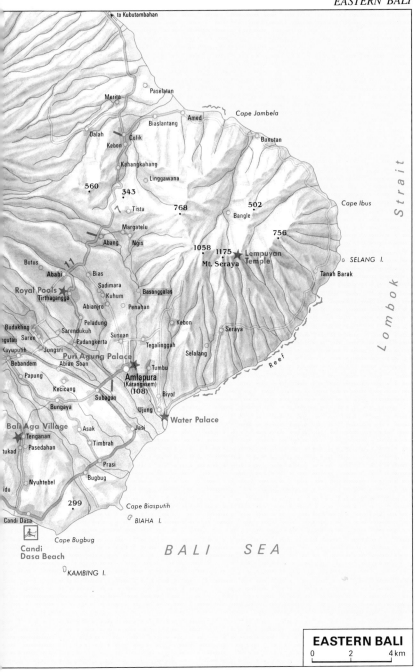

to Kubutambahan

Paselatan

Merita

Biaslantang

Amed

Cape Jambela

Dalah

Culik

Bunutan

Kebon

Kahangkahang

Linggawana

560

343

Tista

768

502

Bangle

Cape Ibus

Strait

Margatelu

756

Abang

Ngis

1058

1175

Mt. Seraya

Lempuyan
Temple

SELANG I.

Butus

Bias

Ababi

Sadimara

Kuhum

Basanggalas

Tanah Barak

Lombok

Royal Pools

Tirthagangga

Abianjro

Penahan

Budakling

Peladung

Kebon

Seraya

ngutan

Saren

Sarendukuh

Susuan

Kayuputih

Padangkerta

Tegalinggah

Selalang

Jungsri

Puri Agung Palace

Bebandem

Abian Soan

Tumbu

Reef

Papung

Amlapura
(Karangasem)
(108)

Biyol

Kecicang

Subagan

Bungaya

Ujung

Bali Aga Village

Asak

Jasi

Water Palace

Tenganan

Timbrah

tukad

Pasedahan

Prasi

Nyuhtebel

Bugbug

idu

299

Candi Dasa

Cape Biasputih

BIAHA I.

Candi
Dasa Beach

Cape Bugbug

BALI   SEA

KAMBING I.

It is well worth paying a visit to the busy **market** on the south-east side of Jalan Diponegoro.

Its is difficult to believe that as recently as 1950 the venerable Supreme Court of Bali still sat in the **Kerta Gosa** law-courts. The rectangular *bale* stands slightly raised immediately behind the entrance of the **Taman Gili**. This "island garden" belonged to the rajas' palace, which was destroyed by the Dutch in 1908. It is impossible to miss, since it is right by the main crossroads in Klungung. The *bale,* where the law-courts were held, is famous for its paintings in the *wayang* style, which portray not only the joys of heaven, but also the agonies of hell, with some very vivid scenes of torture. With help from the Dutch, the paintings were restored in 1930; in 1960 the roof of the hall was renewed and the paintings reproduced on asbestos sheets.

Above: The Bale Kambang in the island garden of Klungkung. Right: A Wayang painting in the Kerta Gosa.

The latest general overhaul was carried out in 1984 – unfortunately using chemical paints in places, which do not allow for the same subtleties of color as the natural paints that were used formerly.

The ceiling-paintings, which are divided into nine rows of pictures, tell the story of *Bhima Suarga*, or Bhima's Descent into Hell – one of the *Mahabharata* legends about the five Pandava brothers, which teaches respect for one's father: while out hunting, Bhima's father brought down a deer, which, as ill-luck would have it, was one of the manifestations (*avatar*) of a Brahman. So Pandu and his second wife, Madri, had to boil it in the cooking-pot of the death-god Yama. To redeem his father, Bhima forces his way into the hell of sinners. (He is recognizable by his dark skin, moustache, jewel-encrusted club and black-and-white checkered sarong). In the third row of pictures, he sees dreadful tortures: sex-organs being burned off, women who have had abortions being thrown to the crocodiles; mothers who do not want to breast-feed being forced to suckle caterpillars; criminals being hacked to pieces with knives or trampled by elephants; the demons of Yama sawing into the living skulls of sinners who do not honor their parents or ancestors; homosexuals and sodomites being devoured by pigs. In contrast to all this, the top row of pictures show the joys of heaven, beckoning to the upright and the godly: after many setbacks – including being killed twice by his own father – Bhima succeeds in laying the bones of his parents properly to rest. With the help of Shiva, he finally comes to the holy water (*tirtha*) with which he can perform the cremation according to the prescribed Hindu rites, and thus release the soul of his father.

The **Bale Kambang** ("Floating Pavilion"), is a rectangular, open-sided hall, which stands like an island in the lotus-pond, right beside the Hall of Justice. Its colorful, highly-detailed ceiling-paintings by Balinese artists, show scenes from the *Sutasoma* legends and were last restored in 1983. The bottom row of pictures depicts Balinese astrology, and the one above tells a childen's fairy-story called *Pan Brayut*. In the third row there is the beginning of the story of Sang Sutasoma, a Tantric Buddhist holy-man, who symbolizes care and the renunciation of violence. In the course of his wanderings he converts the murderous elephant Gajah and the serpent-king Naga to Buddhism. When Sutasoma encounters a tigress about to devour her young for lack of food, he offers himself in their place – for Sutasoma personifies altruism and the victory over the strongest of all human instincts, the desire for self-preservation.

On the west side of the Taman Gili stands the **Pemadal Agung.** This gate, decorated with reliefs in which one can recognize Dutch figures, is the only building which has survived from the destruction by fire of the rajas' palace, Pura Semara, during the colonial war of 1908.

Artists' villages around Gelgel

In the village of **Tihingan,** 2 miles (3 km) west of Klungkung, you can watch smiths at work, using old techniques to cast bronze gongs and metal instruments for the *gamelan* orchestras. In the artists' village of **Kamasan,** the ancient Balinese tradition of painting in the *wayang* style is still practised. The village is 2 1/2 miles (4 km) south-east of Klungkung, near the former rajas' capital of Gelgel. The artists of Kamasan, who still mainly use natural colors, were responsible for the original 18th century paintings in the Kerta Gosa, as well as their recent restoration. The village children learn the artistic skills of their forefathers in the painting-school of the renowned artist, Nyoman Mandra. In the 14th century, the ancestors of the gold- and silversmiths of the Banjar Pande Mas district crafted the crown jewels of the rajas of Gelgel.

East of Kamasan, in the village of **Tangkas**, the time-honored musical tradition of the *Gong Luang* is kept alive.

A place that has always held a particular magic for the Balinese is the village of **Jumpai**, further towards the sea, and famous for its *Barong* dance troupe. In the temple of **Pura Batu**, on the quiet beach of **Klotok**, processions of the faithful make sacrificial offerings to the gods of the sea, while on their way to the mother-temple of Besakih.

There is little in **Gelgel** (2 1/2 miles or 4 km south of Klungkung) to remind one of the former splendor of the greatest of the Balinese royal dynasties, which ruled there from the 14th to the 17th century, and from which all the noble families or the island are descended. The dilapidated **Pura Nataran Jero Agung,** the ancestral temple of the rajas of Gelgel, marks the site of the palace which was abandoned in 1700. On religious holidays members of the ruling castes of Bali gather in the **Pura Dasar**, to worship some very weathered stone statues sitting on a throne of

Above: School's out – fun on the beach at Padangbai.

honor – but no amount of imagination can turn these into anything but pieces of worn stone. With its nine- and eleven-tiered *merus*, the Pura Dasar has a ritual significance, since it forms the counterpart to the great mountain temple of Besakih. The split *candi bentar* gate at the entrance is interesting, since its inner surfaces, which would normally be smooth, are decorated with carved snakes.

The nearby **mosque** is one of the oldest in the island; it is said to date from the 14th century, having been built by a raja of Gelgel as a refuge for unsuccessful Moslem missionaries from Java.

THE SOUTH-EAST COAST

With the exception of Candi Dasa, Bali's south-east coast has seen little tourist development. The route from Klungkung eastward into the old rajadom of Karangasem, brings one first to **Sampalan**, where valuable silk *ikats* and gold-embroidered *songkets* are woven. The next stop is the fishing-village of

Kusamba. On its black sand beach workers in simple straw hats build rectangular pans in the sand, where they leave sea-water to evaporate – a primitive method of extracting salt, which brings them only a small income. The brightly painted outrigger boats (*jukungs*) of the local fishermen are also very primitive, but in skilled hands quite seaworthy. The *prahus* are a bit bigger, with outboard motors as well as sails, but in the treacherous currents neither of these craft are exactly safe. They serve as ferries to the island of Nusa Penida, which can be seen in the distance. Boats also go there from Padangbai and Sanur.

The most easterly tourist attraction in the Klungkung regency is the bat-cave of **Goa Lawah**. Thousands of bats have made their home in the cavern which leads deep into the cliff, and right back – so the Balinese believe – as far as Besakih, 12 miles (20 km) inland. The air is filled with the shrill squeaking of these eerie creatures and with the acrid smell of their droppings. By the cave entrance stands the **Pura Goa,** one of the royal temples of the rajas of Klungkung. The group of buildings contains, among other things, a throne for the mythical serpent-king of the underworld, Basukih, who is said to inhabit the cave. Apparently there are indeed pythons living there, which feed off the little vampire-bats.

In a picturesque bay, whose blue waters are ringed by palm-covered hills, lies the little port of **Padangbai**, which comes alive for a short time each day when the car-ferry from Lombok arrives. Sometimes, even an international cruise-liner will drop anchor in the bay. The fishermen of Padangbai are mainly Moslem; their big outriggers, or *prahus*, are painted in vivid colors, and have bows of a very unusual design, resembling the gaping jaws of a crocodile. Although there is an inviting stretch of white sandy beach, only a few *losmens* have so far been built for the use of tourists.

Scuba-divers will find a fascinating submarine world on the coral reef off nearby **Pulau Kambing** ("Goat Island") – but may have to share it with a few cruising sharks.

On the wide, crescent-shaped Amuk Bay, lies the beautiful, very peaceful and sandy **Balina Beach**. Almost the only accommodation available here are the **Balina Beach Bungalows,** which are in the medium price range and cater principally for scuba-divers. Equipment, boat-excursions and even diving-instruction, are all provided. In the morning it is pleasant to take a walk into the traditional villages of the hinterland, for example through Manggis and Ngis to Tenganan (four hours) or up into the mountains to Putung (three and a half hours).

Foreign investors in Bali's newest beach-resort, **Candi Dasa**, unfortunately want to turn it from being a haven of tranquillity, known only to a few, into a tourist fun-fair comparable to Kuta. The name Candi Dasa means "Ten Temples," but perhaps not enough praying was done during the construction boom of the 1980s. For since the removal of the offshore coral reef, the vengeful gods of the sea have brought heavy surf to deprive the owners of *losmens,* restaurants, discos and gift-shops, of their one important asset: the beach. This strip of sand is now so narrow that only at low-tide can it be called a beach at all.

The bungalow-hotels were built much too close to the sea, and attempts are now being made to protect them from the breakers with thick, reinforced concrete walls - but it is doubtful whether this will succeed. Erosion by the surf continues unabated, and meanwhile the once famous little lagoon at the eastern end of Candi Dasa is turning an increasingly unattractive brownish-green color. In spite of this, *losmens* and shops continue to spring up like mushrooms all along the 2-mile (3 km) long "development axis" of tarmac'd highway.

Tenganan, 2 miles (3 km) north of Candi Dasa, is one of the most exhaustively researched villages in South-east Asia. Scientists in every field, starting with ethnologists, have examined all aspects of the Bali-Aga (aboriginal Balinese) of Tenganan, even down to the genetic details of their blood-groups. Imagine how it would be if a group of Tenganese were to visit a European city, such as Basel, and take blood samples from the original inhabitants, or observe their Mardi Gras celebrations and draw far-fetched conclusions about cannibalism among the ancestors of the Swiss from the Hindu Kush...

The village of Tenganan is surrounded by a wall and can only be entered through a narrow gateway. It is laid out on the ancient Malay pattern: the houses stand at an angle to the unusually wide "high street," in the middle of which are the individual rice-stores, shrines and *bales*. Outsiders are not allowed to enter the meeting-halls built on stone platforms and used by youth groups and clan associations, and also strictly off limits is the 50-yard long Bale Agung where the village council (*krama desa*) holds its meetings. The 300 or so inhabitants of Tenganan believe themselves to be the chosen people of the god Indra, and set themselves rigorously apart from the outside world. With property of over 2, 500 acres (1000 ha.), they are so prosperous that they can give their time entirely to leisure and the pursuit of their traditional customs. Their fields are cultivated by tenant farmers, including those banished from the village for having transgressed the complicated rules of cohabitation and ritual purity. Sacred stones play a major role in the belief-system of the Tenganese, inspired by ancient India and predating the Hindu Javanisation of the Majapahit era. At the upper end of the village square stands a megalithic throne of the gods. Unlike the rest of Hindu Bali,

Above: Sceptical observers of the temple festivities in Timbrah. Right: The simple merus of the "mother-temple" of Besakih.

the dead of Tenganan are not cremated, but buried.

The *ikat* fabrics of the village are both famous and expensive. The traditional *Kamben Geringsing* is woven by women in the double-*ikat* technique, which takes months. The pattern is one which the god Indra is said to have personally designed. It is a religious obligation to wear a temple-sash of *Geringsing* at all important ceremonies, such as name-giving, or marriage, *rejang* dancing and the playing of *Gong-Selonding* music.

BESAKIH: THE MOTHER OF ALL TEMPLES

An indispensable feature of the tour-schedule of every visit to Bali is a respectful visit to the temple of Besakih on the south-west slope of Gunung Agung, the fateful mountain of eastern Bali. Modest clothing should be worn, for the god Agung is quick to anger, and punishes the frivolous with red-hot streams of lava...

If you are driving to Besakih through Klungkung, you can stop in **Bukit Jambul** in the neighboring regency of Karangasem, from where there is a magnificent view over emerald-green rice-terraces – best of all from the **Panorama Restaurant**. However, since both Gunung Agung and Besakih are hidden in cloud by about midday, you should save the gastronomic treat until after you have visited the temple.

About 5 miles (8 km) further up the mountain, in **Rendang**, a lively fruit market is held every three days. Durians and salaks are the specialities. In the village a research-station has been established, where vulcanologists monitor the seismic activity of Agung.

The mother of all *puras*, the holy Besakih, stands in an imposing position some 3000 ft (950 m) up on the south-west slope of Agung – halfway to heaven, so to speak. But the gods certainly make you sweat for it: you climb steeply past a row of soft-drink shops in the warm sun, and wish you had started out earlier. Visitors, male or female, who are showing too much leg must borrow a sarong and put it on to avoid profaning the holiest place in Bali.

The Pura Besakih was probably founded in the 8th century as a shivaitic shrine, and in the 11th century it served as a Buddhist place of worship. After an earthquake in 1917 the buildings were fully restored; and in 1963 the lava-streams from the eruption of Agung spared the sacred shrines of Besakih – which, to the Hindus of Bali, seemed nothing short of a miracle. The central line of the extensive temple grounds, which contain more than 50 *merus*, is oriented towards the summit of Gunung Agung. The Balinese believe that the volcano of Agung is the *Mahameru*, the mountain of the gods and throne of the Sanghyang Widhi Wasa, who, in a contest for mastery of heaven, turned himself into a column of eternal fire – a kind of super-*lingga* – and thus trumped his rivals, Brahma and Vishnu. When he descends to earth as Shiva, he resides in Besakih, in the central complex of the **Pura Pentaran Agung**. A broad staircase, flanked by figures from the *Mahabharata*, including the five Pandava brothers, leads up to the Paduraksa Gate, through which only Hindus may enter. Non-Hindus can walk around the outer walls of the Pura Penataran Agung, and get a glimpse into the interior. The ritual center of the temple is the lotus throne in the first courtyard, only accessible to Hindus. The three chief gods, Shiva (center), Brahma (right) and Vishnu (left), seat themselves here when they visit the world of mortals on the holy day of *Turun Kabeh*.

It used to be one of the privileges of the royal families of Bali, to worship their deified ancestors in the individual Pura Padharman shrines. Nowadays, peasant

Right: The sacred mountain of Bali, Gunung Agung, seen from Lombok.

pilgrims come here, to sacrifice to the rice-goddess Dewi Sri in the Pura Banua, for the continued fertility of their rice-fields, and to take consecrated water (*tirtha*) home with them. The craftsman-caste of smiths have their own temple in a rectangular building on the west side of the Pura Agung. There you can often see processions of wives of the gamelan-, gong- and swordsmiths' castes, carrying imaginatively decorated sacrificial offerings piled high and balanced on their heads.

About 100 yards north-west of the Pura Agung stands the much smaller **Pura Batu Madeg**, dedicated to Vishnu. Approximately 25 yards east of the temple of Agung is the **Pura Kiduling Kreteg,** the temple to the god Brahma, with a row of tiered *merus*. You may not find any nectar of the gods (*amrita*), but soft drinks are on sale on some higher ground in the north-east corner of the Pura Agung, from where there is also a fine view of Besakih, the Agung volcano and the coast.

Temple festivals

When the full moon shines in the month of Kedasa, the fourth in the Balinese calendar, Besakih once again becomes the scene of impressive processions. On the day when the gods visit the Pura Besakih, tens of thousands of Balinese come here to celebrate the festival of *Batara Turun Kabeh*. This is simultaneous with the *Odalan* festival, the anniversary of the founding of the temple, which according to the Hindu calendar is celebrated every 210 days. The new year festival of *Galungan* is also celebrated here and lasts about ten days.

The great *Eka Dasa Rudra* only takes place every hundred years – the last one was in 1979. Back in 1963, there was a plan to bring the festival forward to coincide with a visit by President Sukarno, but the Agung volcano put paid to that:

the dramatic eruption was seen as a bad omen and a punishment for having monkeyed about with the divinely ordained calendar. In 1965, there was terrible butchery in which devout Hindus unleashed their hate against the godless communists, whom they blamed for the whole disaster. Finally, in 1979, the *Eka Dasa Rudra* ceremony for the appeasement of the angry Shiva and the ten other chief Balinese deities, was held without incident and with the support of the Indonesian government. President Sukarno, although himself a Moslem, was guest of honor. No cost or effort was spared: no less than 77 animals were brought for sacrifice, including a tiger, an eagle and a crocodile, as well as domestic animals and even insects. The sacrificial ceremony took place in Besakih on 27th March, 1979, and thus was the harmony between gods and men restored.

Every ten years – the last time in 1989 – the *Panca Walikrama* is held, a sacrificial festival which serves to purify the souls of Hindus.

Climbing Gunung Agung

It is true that there is a path leading up to the 10,305 ft (3142 m) summit of Gunung Agung, but this is no gentle mountain walk: to do it, you need to set off shortly after midnight, not just in order to reach the top ridge by sunrise, but so that you can be down again before sunset! The climb takes you up some 7,200 ft (2200 m) and lasts five or six hours. There is a nasty surprise towards the end: a very steep lava-field that is really tough going. Before that, the path winds through jungle and brushwood, in which – particularly on the lower slopes – it is easy to lose one's bearings. For this reason it is a good idea to hire a local guide. These are usually physically fit students, who will even carry one's rucksack. You should bring with you several litres of water, provisions, a flashlight with spare batteries, as well as warm clothes, since it is easy to underestimate the icy wind at that altitude. Once you arrive at the top, you can look down on to the floor of the

Agung crater which is 300 ft (100 m) lower than the summit ridge, and whose diameter across the top is about 500 yards. The view across the whole of eastern Bali as far as the sea is nothing short of overwhelming.

From Besakih to Amlapura

Away from the great streams of tourists, a little road leads from Rendang eastwards through superb landscape in the southern foothills of the Agung massif. Around **Muncan** there are some particularly impressive rice-terraces, and in the little village of **Padanggaji** the old tradition of the *Gambuh* dance is preserved.

In **Selat**, a mountain track branches off towards Gunung Agung. It goes through the village of **Sebudi** and ends about 4 1/2 miles (7 km) further on. From there,

Above: The view from Gunung Agung over south-eastern Bali. Right: A Lontar-scribe at work in Tenganan.

one has to continue up the mountain on foot. In the area round Selat, traces of the volcanic eruption of 1963 can still be clearly seen; some hardy plants and cultivated fruit-trees only sparsely cover the solidified streams of dark lava. It will be a long time before *sawah*, or rice-fields, flourish here again, as they did before the catastrophe.

East of Selat, one can make a little side-trip southwards to the farming village of **Iseh**. It was here, in the 1930s, that the Berlin-born artist Walter Spies, inspirer of the modern Balinese school of painting, bought a hut and called it home. He immortalised the enchanting view in his paintings: *Iseh in the Morning Light* and *Sawah Lanscape with Agung*.

There is a panorama of rice-terraces as far as the coast, from the weavers' village of **Sidemen**, which lies about a mile (2 km) down the valley, on the road to Klungkung. Here *ikat* and valuable *songket* fabrics are hand-woven, to the tradtional patterns, using silk and gold and silver thread.

You can stay overnight in stylish accommodation with a private family in Sidemen.

Back on the hilly road between Rendang and Amlapura, you should make another detour to the little village of **Putung**, for some superb views. From the tea-terrace of the Putung Bungalows your gaze sweeps over a deep, narrow valley, whose steep slopes are terraced with rice-paddies, down as far as Amuk Bay on the south-east coast. A pleasant walk takes you in just three hours from Putung, through Yehpoh and Bakung, downhill to the almost medieval-looking village of **Manggis**. Here you will find probably the classiest "homestay" in the island – a good opportunity to get a first-hand experience of the way Balinese farmers really live.

Plantations with thousands of prickly salak-palms, a bit further eastwards, tell you that you are arriving in the village of **Sibetan**. The main harvest season for these delicious but tough-skinned fruit lasts from December right into the summer. Continuing through Bebandem, Bungaya and Subagan, you finally reach Amlapura, capital town of the regency of Karangasem.

AMLAPURA

This sleepy regional capital was given the new name of Amlapura as a symbol of a fresh beginning, after the devastating eruption of Agung in 1963, which affected this region particularly badly. For centuries before, the town had been called Karangasem – the same as the old rajadom, and today's administrative district in eastern Bali.

The Raja of Karangasem was an important man to the Dutch colonial regime, because, ever since the successful Balinese conquest of neighboring Lombok in 1678, he ruled the island through viceroys from his own family. The Dutch cleverly exploited family quarrels and,

after a military intervention in 1849, appointed a Karangasem prince of the Lombok line, who was collaborating with them, to be lord of Lombok and eastern Bali. From that period date some of the Sasak villages around Amlapura, and the traditon of *Cekepung* music, a kind of vocal *gamelan* in which the singers perform alternate verses in the Balinese and Sasak languages.

Officially, the feudal age came to an end in Bali after the Second World War, with the independence of Indonesia. However, until as recently as 1969, a prince of the royal house acted as *Bupati,* or regent, of Karangasem.

Altogether there are four historic royal residences in Amlapura. However, the only one open to the public is the **Puri Agung Kaningan**, which lies to the north of the market square. It was built as a palace for the Raja Anak Agung Gede Jelantik, who held court there from 1902 until 1935 – though subject to Dutch administration. Over 100 members of the royal family still live within its walls.

The palace consists of several court-yards with *bales* and ponds fringed with trees and shrubs. Entering through a gate, one first comes to an outer court of the palace which is like a little garden with a beautiful old lychee-tree in the middle. Through a second towered gateway, guarded by two stone lions, one enters another courtyard, dominated by the **Maskerdam**. This is a reception hall for important guests; its gilded wooden towers were carved by Chinese crafts-men. One can look through its windows into the rooms inside. In the last of these stand chairs in a baroque style; they were a gift presented by the Dutch queen, Wil-helmina, to her oriental subjects in 1910. The Bale London (not open to view) con-tains pieces of antique furniture bearing the royal coat-of-arms of England.

The former **moated palace of Ujung**, 2 1/2 miles (4 km) south of Amlapura,

Above: The picturesque remains of the moated palace of Ujung. Right: One of the ponds in Tirthagangga.

was almost completely destroyed in the eruption of Mount Agung in 1963.

It is certainly worth visiting, and per-haps staying a few days at the **royal baths of Tirthagangga** ("holy water of the goddess Gangga"), 3 3/4 miles (6 km) north-west of Amlapura. It is gorgeous to splash about in the pools, set in an en-chanting landscape among rice-fields, at the foot of Mount Agung. The village children also enjoy the cool, fresh water that gushes out from demon-faced gar-goyles. For those who want to stay over-night and experience the real Bali, there are several small *losmens* to choose from. As you walk through the surrounding countryside, you can see every stage of rice-growing in the waterlogged *sawah*, or paddy-fields. Here, the traditonal Ba-linese types of rice have not yet been driven out by the high-yielding but dis-ease-prone and fertiliser-hungry varieties favored by the so-called "green Revol-ution."

From Tirthagangga it is worth walking along the path that first runs northward to

Ababi and then bends south to the gold-smiths' village of **Budakling**, in which there lives a small community of Mahayana Buddhists.

It is a stiff climb – but worth the effort – up to the crater-rim of the volcanic Seraya massif (3850 ft / 1175 m), whose northern slopes are crowned by the seldom-visited little **Pura Lempuyan** temple. As you climb, ever more magnificent views open out before you. The best place to start this day's walk is **Ngis** or **Basangalas** (reached via Abang). The Lempuyan temple is one of the six chief temples of Bali. At the New Year's festival of *Galungan* it is the scene of a great religious ceremony.

If you take the road to Singaraja, north-east from Tirthagangga, it is worth making a detour to the village of **Culik**: then through fields of peanuts (*kacang*) to the Moslem fishing-village of **Amed**. There is a little road leading from Amed around the Seraya massif, and back along the coast to Amlapura, but it is in poor condition, very winding and therefore very time-consuming. Ever since the volcanic eruption of 1963, this easternmost tip of Bali has become largely depopulated; only a few fishermen, salt-panners and coral-gatherers continue to scratch a meagre living along the black shores.

If you carry on from Culik towards the north coast, past plantations of cotton-trees (*kapok*), you come to **Cape Muntik** and the village of **Tulamben**, whose diving-waters are frequently visited by day-trippers from Balina and Sanur. On the sea-bottom, about a mile (1.5 km) offshore, lies the wreck of the *SS Liberty,* an American merchant ship, which was torpedoed in 1942 by Japanese forces based on the island. Snorkellers will also be amazed by the enormous number and variety of fish off this stretch of coast. In contrast, the hinterland is dry and studded with cactus, but it has a certain rugged attraction. However, as you continue driving north along the picturesque coast road, Bali once again shows her most beautiful face – a face that has up to now scarcely been scarred by tourism.

KLUNGKUNG
Accommodation / Restaurants

Ramayana Palace Hotel, east of the center, relatively quiet, slightly set back from the main street, simple rooms, with restaurant and garden, from Rps. 12.000; **Losmen Wishnu**, Jl. Gunung Rinjani, centrally located, near the bus-station, ask for a room on an upper floor.

The best place to eat is the Chinese restaurant **Bali Indah** in the main street, or at **Sumber Rasa** nearby, south of the main street.

SOUTH-EAST COAST

PADANGBAI
Accommodation

The accommodation we would most recommend is on the beach, east of the pier. **Rai Beach Inn**, 2-storeyed Bungalows built like rice-stores, from Rps. 15.000; **Sedani Kerthi Beach Bungalows**, similar to the above, from Rps. 8.000; **Padangbai Beach Inn**, with a view over the bay, from Rps. 8.000; **Topi Inn**, furthest to the east, from Rps. 10.000. Only in emergency: **Losmen Madya** right on the main street, from Rps. 10.000. In the town, but away from the main street, one can spend the night in a farmstead: **Homestay Dharma**, very clean, from Rps. 8.000.

Restaurants

Topi Inn, on the beach, offers the best ambiance and good fish. Among the Warungs on the beach we would mention **Pantai Ayu** because of the friendly service, but the others are worth a try. People taking the ferry often sit in the **Warung Sederhana**, because it is the best place from which to see when the ferry ticket-office opens.

Ferry connections to Lombok

As long as no ferries are cancelled, there are three departures per day to Labuhan Lembar on Lombok. You can find out the times on the quay; they seem to keep on being changed.

At the time of going to press the scheduled departure times were: 9 am, 11 am and 2 pm. Depending on the weather the crossing takes about 4 hours. Fare per person: depending on which class, between Rps. 3,500 and 5,000; motor-cycle: Rps. 4,000, jeep: Rps. 40,000.

Every 2 weeks, there is also a ferry to Surabaya (Java) and one to Ujung Padang (Sulawesi).

BALINA BEACH (BUWITAN)
Accommodation / Restaurants

Balina Beach Bungalows, Tel: 88451, large spread on the beach with restaurant, from US$ 18, also much dearer rooms ; **Puri Buitan**, Tel: 87182, from US$ 35; **Cangrin Beach Homestay**, from Rps. 20.000; **Sunrise Homestay**, from Rps. 20.000.

Scuba-diving and snorkelling

From the Balina Beach Bungalows diving-trips are organized, along the coast as well as to Nusa Penida and Pulau Menjangan. Cost: US$ 30-65, depending on duration and destination. Snorkelling trips begin at US$ 10.

CANDI DASA
Accommodation

There is an ample choice of accommodation in all price-categories.

LUXURY CLASS: **Candi Beach Cottages**, Tel: 51771 (book through the parent-hotel in Legian), Fax: 51715, situated outside the town, to the west; swimming-pool, tennis-courts; on the beach, which is less built-up than in Candi, from US$ 70; **Rama Ocean View Bungalows**, Tel: 51864, closer to Candi Dasa, spaciously laid out by the beach – which is just a narrow strip here – from US$ 60; **Taman Air** (Water-garden), Tel: 35540, inland from the center, with small fish-ponds, from US$ 45; **Puri Bagus Beach Hotel**, under palm-trees east of Candi Dasa, from US$ 60.

MID-PRICE: **Candi Dasa Beach Bungalows Two**, Tel: 35536, three-storey hotel , in the center, on the seaward side, from US$ 33; **Pondok Bamboo Seaside Cottages**, in the center, by the sea, restaurant, from Rps. 32,000; **Puri Oka**, on the beach, east of the lagoon, with swimmingpool, from Rps. 25,000.

BUDGET: among the cheapest, but still pleasant, establishments are the bungalows on the sea, west of the road-junction to Tenganan, e.g. **Pelangi** and **Taruna Homestay**, from Rps. 8,000. Also very reasonable are some places near the lagoon, e.g. the **Rama Bungalows** and **Sidhu Brata** from Rps. 15,000.

Restaurants

Many of the hotels by the sea have their own restaurants. Among the best are the **Pandan** and the **Pondok Bamboo**. On the landward side of the main road, **TJ's** has a little pond and is quite idyllic. There is a platform built out into the water, on which one sits on cushions, in the Balinese manner, and eats one's meal on the floor. Although you will be offered, among other things, Mexican food here, this is limited to guacomole and tacos.

The **Kubu Bali Restaurant**, with its open kitchen, is spectacular and particularly popular. The cooks, bathed in sweat, juggle with their pans, and now and then a sheet of flame shoots six feet in the air. Good Chinese and Indonesian food is served here. Some of the tables are placed round a secluded little pond.

Activities

The reef directly in front of Candi Dasa is no longer particularly suitable for **snorkelling**. Fishermen take snorkellers out in their *prahus* to the little off-shore islands. The **Candi Dasa Bookstore** organizes a snorkelling-tour by bemo to three different points along the coast towards Padangbai. The best place is on the blue lagoon. Rough cost per Person, depending on numbers, from Rps. 12,000.

There is really nothing that one could call an exciting **night-life**. Occasionally, dance-groups are brought in from outside to put on a show, usually in conjunction with a buffet dinner. Posters advertising these events are put up everywhere.

Candi Dasa is also a good base for walking-tours of the area. One small expedition is to climb the heights behind the town. This is worth while chiefly for the beautiful view over the lagoon and the beach. For a day's walking, taking your own food with you of course, we would recommend a round trip via Tenganan (you go through the town and up to the end of the adjoining valley) – Macang (here one can buy tea and peanuts in a Warung) – Ngis – and back to Tenganan. On this walk one passes through inhabited rain-forest, over curving rice-terraces and reaches one summit after another, which give wonderful views of the coast, Nusa Penida island and of villages like Ngis, nestling in the jungle. Essential requirements include a strong sense of direction, good physical condition and solid footwear.

Important addresses

There is no **Post Office,** but several shops sell stamps. The Permuntel **Telephone Office** is in the middle of the town near the top end of Pondok Bamboo. Several bureaux de change also cash travellers-cheques at acceptable rates.

At the **Pandawa Tour Information Center** (near Pondok Bamboo) you can book coach tours or hire jeeps, motor-cycles, scuba-diving and snorkelling equipment. In addition there are several smaller hire agencies.

The ascent of Gunung Agung

Anyone wishing to climb the mountain without a guide, is best advised to pick the route that starts near **Sebudi**, south-east of Besakih. Drive up the steep, potholed road, until the asphalt surface runs out. At the parking-place, you have to leave your car and walk. Only very tough overland vehicles can, in dry weather, drive on a bit further, as far as a temple that

is being built. The path starts climbing beyond the temple. In daylight you cannot miss it, since it climbs straight up the mountainside, turning neither to right nor left.

The climb can take up to 6 hours, assuming you are carrying equipment for a possible overnight camp in one of the few, only passably comfortable, clefts in the rock. You should only undertake the climb if the weather is forecast to be fine for several days ahead, since the sole reward you get for the considerable exertion is the view over the green contours of the island. In addition to being in excellent physical condition, with a strong circulation, it is essential to take strong mountain boots and warm, waterproof clothing in case the weather breaks. And don't forget to take plenty of drinking-water!

AMLAPURA
Accommodation / Restaurants

Hardly anyone spends the night in Amlapura, since Tirthagangga is so near. As you enter the town, near the monument on the left hand side, there are two Losmens: **Lahar Mas**, bordering the rice-fields, from Rps. 10,000; **Homestay Sidha Karya**, nearer to the center, from Rps. 8,000. Some way out of town, going towards Rendang, there is also the **Kembang Ramaja**.

For meals, the best place to go is **Lenny's**, on Jl. Gajah Mada (the continuation of the road leading to the Raja's Palace), or else to the warungs at the bus-station.

TIRTHAGANGGA
Accommodation / Restaurants

Tirtha Ayu Homestay, in the grounds of the Water Palace, has a restaurant above the pool, use of the pool included, from Rps. 20,000; **Losmen Dhangin Taman Inn**, near the Water Palace, with garden and restaurant, from Rps. 7,000; **Kusuma Jaya Inn**, situated above the town with a view over the rice-fields, rooms extremely plain, from Rps. 8,000. **Rijasa Home-stay**, on the side of the street facing the palace, simple but pleasant rooms, from Rps.7,000.

In front of the palace there are some simple warungs. At the **Taman Sari**, you can choose your fish fresh from the pool.

TULAMBEN
Accommodation

Gandu Maya Bungalows, situated very close to the wreck (100 yards), is much frequented by divers and diving-schools, from Rps. 12,000; **Paradise Palm Beach Bungalows**, nice spot with garden and fish-restaurant, from Rps.15,000; **Bali Timur Bungalows**, pretty place, from Rps.15,000.

HISTORY AND
CULTURE OF LOMBOK

The first settlers on Bali may have reached their new home by an overland route, since Bali, together with Java, formed part of the continental shelf, but seaworthy craft would always have been required to reach Lombok. The depth of the Lombok strait makes it seem unlikely that there could ever have been any land link between Lombok and the land mass of the Asian continent. For a long time it was assumed that the first settlers crossed the straits some time between 50,000 and 30,000 years ago. There have been archaeological finds on the island of Flores, which have not yet been precisely dated but may go back as far as 100,000 years, so it is conceivable that people could have been living on Lombok as well, as long ago as this. However, the earliest archaeological discoveries on Lombok date only from the Iron Age. On the mountain of Gunung Piring in southern Lombok shallow graves have been discovered, with bronze bracelets, iron tools and earthenware vessels buried alongside human remains. Traces of a megalithic culture are also detectable. On the south coast near Sepi, a four-and-a-half foot (1.5 m) high menhir is still worshipped as the *Batu Pujaan* (stone of worship). It is said to be 3,000 years old.

Recorded history also has relatively little to say about Lombok: it appears to be mentioned for the first time in the 14th century chronicle *Nagarakertagama,* the richest source of information about the East Javanese empire of Majapahit. Lombok is recorded here as a tribute-paying

Previous pages: Summit and crater-bowl of Gunung Rinjani. Fishing in the old harbor of Ampenan. Left: Going down to the river.

dependency. Otherwise, authority was in the hands of local rulers, one or other of whom would from time to time set himself up as a prince over a larger region. In the east, particularly, there was for a time a kingdom called *Selaparang,* which temporarily lent its name to the whole island. The present name of Lombok is presumably derived from the chili plant of the same name, and was given to the island by traders. The native Sasak call the island *Bumi Gora*, which means "land of dry fields."

The first Hindu influences reached the island from 1294 onward, with the rise of the East Javanese Majapahit empire. As on Bali, some of the population wished to remain apart from this new culture and religion and settled in other, less accessible and more mountainous parts of the island. It is not clear whether these native inhabitants were the "Budas" (also described as "mountain people" or "Sasak living apart from the others") mentioned by a German expedition to the Sunda straits in 1911. Just as little is known about the origins of the name "Budas" – it may go back even earlier to the Buddhist gurus and hence point to a link with the Indianised kingdoms of central Java and Sumatra. As well as the influence of the Javanese variety of Islam, there came, from the 17th century onwards, the more orthodox form of Islam practised by the Bugis and Makassars of Sulawesi.

Politically, western Lombok came under the informal influence of the Balinese rulers of Gelgel, which had emerged as a new center of Hindu power after the downfall of the Majapahit empire in 1527. The Raja's palace at Selaparang was destroyed in 1678 by the Balinese invaders, though they were initially unable to subjugate the eastern part of the island. The irrigation system of western Lombok was improved under Balinese rule so that the region around Mataram flourished economically.

From 1740 onward, western Lombok was governed by the Karangasem dynasty and in the period that followed, quarrels between the Balinese feudal overlords meant that the Sasak aristocracy was able to win new freedoms. Meanwhile, in the east of the island, Moslem Makassars from southern Sulawesi were from time to time able to gain a foothold.

In 1843, the Balinese Raja of Mataram, a descendant of the lords of Karangasem, signed a treaty of protection with Holland, which expressly excluded the subjugation or even the occupation of the island by the Dutch. Thus secured, and with the support of the Sasaks in the area which they themselves ruled, the Raja of Mataram subjugated the east of the island in 1849 and forced the peasant farmers into serfdom. Revolts against the new

Above: Lessons beneath depictions of historic deeds in the former Raja's Palace at Cakranegara. Right: A village in the poor south-east of Lombok.

feudal lords broke out in 1855, 1871 and 1891, but were ruthlessly supressed.

The Dutch used a further Sasak rebellion in 1894 as an excuse to intervene and to colonize Lombok. The first attempted occupation by the Dutch suffered many casualties because Mataram had modern weapons at his disposal, but they succeeded in pacifying the island with a second invasion. After a bitter struggle, many members of the Balinese aristocracy committed ritual suicide in the honorable ceremony of *puputan*. The raja's palace was burnt down and the rich treasure-chamber plundered. Miraculously, the only copy of the 14th century *Nagarakertagama* survived.

The new rulers proved themselves the equals of their predecessors, at least as far as the exploitation of the island was concerned, and the Sasak, who had turned to the Dutch for help, once again found themselves at the mercy of a harsh regime. The native population were forced to labor on the construction of roads and dykes, and under an administrative system employing local potentates as agents, were compelled to pay high taxes. It is true that the agricultural yield increased thanks to the infrastructure improvements, but the growth in population together with a drastic increase in the levy imposed on harvests, from a previous 50 percent (under the Balinese rajas) up to 80 percent, led to a considerable worsening in the food situation for the indigenous population. Their plight was aggravated by the Japanese occupation of the island in the Second World War. Two years after Indonesia achieved independence, Lombok was combined with Sumbawa, in 1951, to form the province of Nusa Tenggara Barat, but today has still not recovered from the effects of colonization. In years when the weather is unfavorable and harvests are poor, thousands die of starvation even now. Particularly vulnerable are those living in the dry south-east of the island.

LOMBOK SOCIETY

The ethnically Malay Sasak people form the majority of the population of Lombok. Apart from a few coastal villages that have been settled by Buginese fishermen, they inhabit all the land to the east of the area around Mataram formerly under Balinese influence. Most of them rely on agriculture as their chief source of income, yet only about half of them own cultivable land.

The land belongs either to the large hereditary landowning Sasak aristocracy or to the Indonesian government; the latter leases it to peasant farmers. The landless peasants lack capital and so do not make a very good job of farming the land that they have leased. Others simply hire themselves out as seasonal agricultural workers. However, the frequently recurring periods of drought, and problems over land-tenancy, make it impossible to scratch a living and they have no choice but to seek other sources of income. Even the majority of landowning farmers are not immune to this fate, since about 70 percent of them own less than two and a half acres (1 hectare) of land, and 40 percent own just over one acre (0.5 ha.)

To keep starvation at bay they cut firewood in the forests, even in the nature reserve on Gunung Rinjani, and sell it at the market. Many of them have to move from the country into the three-town capital of Ampenan-Mataram-Cakranegara and seek work in the few factories and craft businesses that have been set up there. A number of them try their luck as hawkers along the beaches of Senggigi.

In the west of Lombok there is a settlement of about 85,000 Balinese, who form an important political and cultural minority there. Many of the religious customs, including those to be found in the rest of Lombok, stem from them.

Some of the Balinese settlers have adapted swiftly to the new tourist industry and have successfully specialized in providing cheap accommodation and hotels in the medium price range for independent travellers.

The conditions of land tenure in Balinese west Lombok are the same as in the rest of the island, except that here it is the Balinese aristocracy who forms the top stratum of big landowners. In many of the village communities a traditional feudal form of co-operation has been preserved, whereby in times of need the landowners are obliged to provide special assistance to their tenants and bondmen. However, as the land loses its ancient mythical significance and becomes a commodity, so these traditional feudal bonds between master and serf are becoming looser.

Urban life, on the other hand, thrives in the capital in the west of the island, which has developed from the expansion of the three villages of Ampenan, Matram and Cakranegara into one town. More than ten percent of the population already live here. Apart from the Sasak and the Balinese, there are two other conspicuous ethnic minorities: the Chinese and the Arabs. Most of the latter live in a quarter called the *Kampung Arab* in the old port of Ampenan and generally pursue middle-class occupations, while the Chinese control the food and restaurant sector and the rapidly expanding number of small businesses.

It is particularly in Ampenan and Cakranegara that the number and variety of Chinese shops is very noticeable. The wealth of these descendants of former coolies, who were once brought in to the island as cheap labor by the Dutch, is now a thorn in the flesh of many Indonesians. In 1965, when everyone suspected of being a communist was ruthlessly persecuted, many Chinese fell victim to these pogroms. Numerous small communities in east Lombok were almost completely wiped out at this time. Even today there are official regulations in force, which impose strict limits on the separate cultural activities of the Chinese minority.

Above: A mosque in central Lombok.
Right: At many festivals religious and national elements are combined.

168

THE RELIGIONS OF LOMBOK

In contrast to Bali, the majority of the inhabitants of Lombok are Moslem. In the west of the island, Balinese Hindus live peacefully alongside more or less orthodox Moslems and Chinese, whose Buddhist, Confucian or Taoist faiths are not recognized by the state. A symbol of this coexistence is the temple of Lingsar, which is venerated by followers of various creeds.

Furthermore, the religion of the people of Lombok differs from that of other Islamic Indonesians in that there exists a sect of Islam which is found here and nowhere else: the *Wetu-Telu* religion. This is a hybrid religion which, beneath a veneer of partially observed Moslem precepts, clings to the old animistic beliefs and has even grafted on Hindu rituals. This religion is not recognized by the state and it is therefore only possible to make a rough estimate of the number of adherents at around 30,000. There is also a steady flow of converts to orthodox

Islam. The main centers of this Sasak faith are in the north, in Bayan and the region around Tanjung, as well as Sade and Rambitan in the south.

The religious inspiration of Islam is derived from two sources: the Koran, which is the holy word as revealed by Allah to the Prophet Mohammed, and the Hadith, a collection of sayings and deeds attributed to Mohammed. From these are derived the basic principles of the practice of the Moslem faith, or the "five pillars of Islam": 1. Belief in Allah as the only God, and in Mohammed as his last prophet; 2. prayer five times daily; 3. observance of the laws of fasting in the month of Ramadan; 4. charitable giving to the needy, and 5. the pilgrimage to Mecca.

The followers of the Wetu-Telu religion only partially fulfil these ordinances. They certainly recognize the Koran as Holy Writ, but less from a desire to do God's will than from their belief that the Koran is something invested with magic power.

169

Acoordingly, their copies of the Koran, like the Balinese *lontar* writings, remain for most of the time locked up in a small chest beneath the roof of the mosque, and are only read out on a very few high feast-days. The invocation of Allah does not take place five times, but only three times a day – the religion's name (*telu* = three) derives from the recurrence of the number three. An orthodox Moslem might find fault with the Wetu-Telu prayer, because it would sound to him more like the recitation of a mantra than a reminder of the supreme power of God.

Followers of Wetu-Telu celebrate Ramadan in a different way too: instead of fasting during daylight hours for a month, they only abstain from material pleasures for three days. The commandment to dispense charity is obeyed by making an offering of rice, as they do in Bali. A visit to the holy places of Islam on Lombok or Java replaces the pilgrim-age to Mecca. In accordance with their animistic traditions they visit the graves of their ancestors and offer sacrifices to them. The Rinjani is a sacred mountain for them and they make pilgrimages there on nights of the full moon, to spend three days by the lake and at the hot springs, from which they believe they will acquire magical powers.

The Wetu-Telu worshippers, whose faith is regarded by orthodox Moslems as an imperfect form of Islam, have always been the target of revivalist Islamic movements – for better or worse. So it was that in the purges of 1965, when they were paradoxically suspected of being a-theists, they suffered terrible persecution, and to to this day refer to it as "The year of danger to life." Orthodoxy, mainly in the form of a fundamentalist movement, began in Sesong in the east of Lombok, and has gained many new followers. One of their most effective recruitment techniques is the generous distribution of food supplies in times of widespread drought and hunger.

Above: A young mother finds shade beneath a banana-plant.

FESTIVALS AND CEREMONIES

Whereas in many parts of Bali the people are proud and pleased to welcome respectful outsiders as spectators at their festivities, it is still the case in Lombok that villagers are very unaccustomed to seeing foreign visitors at their religious celebrations. For this reason, their reaction to tourists can at times be very ambivalent. On the one hand the visitors do cause a certain sensation, but on the other the villagers wonder rather anxiously what these foreigners, with their constantly flashing camera equipment, think they are doing in the middle of the ceremonies. Then again, the law of hospitality demands that they should protect the visitor from the brazen curiosity of the local children.

However, there is a danger that strangers can cause real annoyance when their unaccustomed intrusion on the scene frightens the water-buffalo, causing them to stampede out of the village pond and flee in wild confusion across the parched rice-fields. To sum up, it is more difficult for the tourist to participate in the "real" life of Lombok, than it is in Bali, and requires the utmost restraint and sensitivity.

Lombok trails behind Bali in the total number of festivals held, and while it is true that the many religious sects provide a large variety of ceremonies, there is nothing on Lombok to compare with the professional skill of the Balinese dancers from Ubud. On Lombok, everything is rather more amateurish and primitive.

West Lombok's calendar of religious festivals basically recognizes all Balinese celebrations because the Balinese minority clings doggedly to its traditions, which are nurtured devoutly by each temple community. However, these festivals often have different names from those used on Bali and no variations of them have yet developed as tourist attractions, as they have in Bali. Especially worthy of mention is the annual *Pujawali* festival, which is celebrated in honor of the god Batara in the Kalasa Temple at Narmada. At the same time crowds of devout Hindus make the pilgrimage to the seat of the God on Gunung Rinjani, and during a ceremony called *Pekelan* they offer him golden objects such as drinking-vessels, which are cast into the crater lake. The date of this festival is determined by the *Saka* year and takes place at the time of the full moon in the fifth month, which corresponds to July or August in the Gregorian calendar.

In March or April a festival of thanksgiving for the harvest is held at the shrine on Gunung Pengson, in the course of which a water-buffalo is sacrificed. One of the most splendid Balinese temple ceremonies is to be witnessed annually at the time of the full moon in June at the Pura Meru temple in Cakrane.

The Balinese Hindus and the Sasak followers of the Wetu-Telu religion celebrate another festival together in the double temple of Lingsar. It begins in the late afternoon before the night of the full moon towards the end of November or early December, and is another festival with the name of *Pujawali*. The climax of the celebrations is a rice battle between the two groups of inhabitants. Cooked rice is packed tightly into banana-leaves which are then thrown like grenades.

Outsiders, and especially tourists, are considered fair game and the "battle" is not without an element of danger, because stones sometimes "accidentally" find their way into the ammunition. The festivities conclude with cock-fights, which only on this occasion have official approval, and the sacrifice of water-buffaloes, goats or hens.

The Wetu-Telu worshippers organize their calendar of festivals partly along the lines of the Balinese, which focuses on the principal milestones in a person's life, and partly based on the high feast-days of the Moslems.

171

Here, as in Bali, the rites and rituals following the birth of a child include the burying of the four "brothers and sisters" born at the same time: placenta, after-birth, birth-waters and blood, in a coco-nut-shell container at the front entrance of the house. There is also a ceremony to accompany the child's first hair-cut after 105 days. From the Moslems they have adopted the custom of circumcising boys between the ages of twelve and fifteen, after which they are carried round the village on a decorated trolley in shape of a lion. The expressions on the faces of the elaborately bandaged boys speak volumes. At the same age, the girls have their teeth filed, according to the Balinese custom. Once they have had their first menstruation, they are carried through the village on a wooden horse, so that everyone will know that they are now of marriageable age.

Above: Girls of marriageable age are carried through the village. Right: Musicians on their way to the festival near Senaru.

Many Sasak communities have special customs whereby teenagers who are ready for marriage get to know each other. The *Nyale* festival offers one such occasion. This takes place once a year between February and April, in Kuta. The whole night is spent catching the glowing *nyale*-worms which can be found in the water here in their thousands. The young people then cook them and eat them together.

Another opportunity for getting to know your future partner is in a domestic setting among families of higher caste. If there is more than one suitor for a girl's hand, they are all invited by the family and have to exercise their charms to win her. This courtship involves compliments and poems composed by the suitors, but touching, to say nothing of kissing, is very much frowned upon. If a girl publicly accepts a gift from a potential bridegroom, she is permitted or even obliged to marry him.

As a rule, marriages take place by arrangement between the families concerned, or they can be between cousins. It is also permissable for a suitor to abduct the bride, when she, if not her family, has indicated interest, but if this happens the couple may only return to the village when the families have agreed on a price for the bride.

The official state holidays, such as the Indonesian national holiday on 17th August, are fixed according to the international (Gregorian) calendar, and are celebrated with as much extravagance on Lombok as everywhere else. These include a number of Moslem festivals: the most important, the *Hari Raya* ("great day") lasts for at least two days and ends the month of fasting of Ramadan. This is a time for visiting relatives and catching up on all the fun one has missed, or so it seems. Huge feasts give ample opportunity for carousing. Any tourists travelling around during this period must be prepared for high prices and crowded public transport.

HINTS ON ETIQUETTE

Much of what is true for Bali also applies in Lombok. But in addition there are one or two peculiarities that one should note when dealing with the Moslem population. These people, even though they may not be orthodox in their observances, nevertheless think in basically religious terms, and therefore one should take account of this in one's own behavior. For instance, Moslems have to obey their dietary laws, which forbid them to eat pork or drink alcohol. A particularly awkward time is the fasting month of Ramadan. Moslems have to get up before dawn in order to take a final meal and say the morning prayer before the sun rises. This means that as the day wears on, they often become nervous and irritable. In these circumstances you should treat them with consideration. You should not, for instance, eat or smoke in their immediate company. If you are travelling in

the east of the island at this time of year, you should equip yourself in the evening with food for a picnic the next day, since many shops are closed during the day.

As far as clothing is concerned, one should perhaps be more fully covered than is necessary in Bali, even in a supposedly lonely area. On the beach women should wear at least a one-piece swimsuit and preferably cover up with a tee-shirt or sarong enveloping the whole body. Men should also avoid wearing anything too casual and revealing.

If travelling as a "confirmed" single person it is advisable, and, more importantly, courteous, not to argue against the married state or having children, in conversation with local people. Outspoken views of this kind will, in a traditional society like that of Lombok, only come up against incomprehension. Children and marriage are firmly rooted elements of their social structure. The same applies to any confession of an atheistic philosophy – however much it may be founded on ethical and humanistic principles.

173

AUSTERE BEAUTY

WESTERN LOMBOK
SENGGIGI AND THE GILIS
GUNUNG RINJANI
EASTERN LOMBOK
SOUTHERN LOMBOK

WESTERN LOMBOK

In order to reach Lombok from Bali by boat one may take the ferry from Padangbai, which takes between four and five hours depending on the sea conditions, or the hydrofoil from the port of Benoa, which takes approximately two hours. The voyage will take the traveler past the outriggers of the fishing fleets with their typical triangular sails. You may also catch sight of dolphins swimming near the ferry. The arrival point on Lombok is the harbor of Labuhan Lembar, whose pier lies in a sheltered bay. The little town itself is just over half a mile (1 km) further inland. From here you can take a bus or a *bemo* to the three-town capital of Ampenan-Mataram-Cakranegara, a journey of about an hour. Most people prefer to continue their journey immediately to Senggigi, which will take another half-hour or so by *bemo*. There you will find a well-developed (and continually expanding) tourist infrastructure, offering accommodation in all price-categories. As long as you are not sleeping next to a building-site, this is the one place on

Previous pages: In the markets you will find a colorful array of tropical vegetables and fruit. Left: Deserted beaches to the north of Senggigi.

Lombok which comes closest to offering everything one could wish for in a South Sea paradise. At the height of the season, in August, accommodation is admittedly hard to come by. If you are arriving in Lombok by plane, you land at the airport of Selaparang on the northern edge of the town of Mataram, from where you can get a *bemo* into the town center. If you are heading for Senggigi, you should go in a westerly direction to the *bemo* terminus on the northern edge of Ampenan. From there you can reach your destination in less than half an hour.

Ampenan

Ampenan is the oldest and most authentic of the three towns in western Lombok, which have grown together to form the capital. The rusty pillars of the jetty are a reminder that this was once a port. Today, fishermen sit on them and cast out their lines. The warehouses behind the beach are gradually decaying whilst the shoreline is adorned with a bright fleet of fishing boats, lying in the sun.

The heart of the town lies around the Jangkok river. The people here are a mixture of Sasak, Balinese, Javanese, Arab and Chinese. Those living beside the river are predominaty immigrants from Java and Sulawesi. From the bridge

BALI

Labuhan
Carik

Lokorangan

Papak

Ba
Se

Gondang ✷ Waterfall

GILI
MENO
GILI
AIR   Tanjung ✷ Krakas   Gangga

GILI
TERA-
WANGAN   Sira   Selelos

Sira   ✷ Temple   2210

Bangsal   Tembabar   Segara
Anak
Cape   Pemenang   •714
Ketinan

Rinjani

Mangsit   ✷ Tourist   969   Gunung   Reserve
Senggigi   Resort   Baun Pusuk   Punikan
1490
Batu Bolong   Sidemen

Batu Layar   Lendang   Sesaot   Peseng
Menintang   Bajur   Endut
Aik
Selaparang Airport   ✈   Temple   Bukak
Ampenan   Temple   Suranadi
Lingsar   Pancordao   Wadja
gesen
MATARAM Cakra-   Sweta
negara   Narmada   Mantang
Pagutan   Bengkel   Summer
Bajur   Palace   Pringgarata   Kopang
Prampuan   Rumak   Kediri
Bonjeruk   S
Koranji   Kuripan   Ubung
Bangsal ✷Gunung   Puyung
Pengsong   Janapriya
Temple   Gerung   385•
Sukarara   Praya   Bel
Cape   Terang   GILI   Traditional   Batunyale
Bebera   Bay   NANGGU   Weaving   Batujai
GILI   Penjanggik
POH   Pandanan   Penujak
Labuhan   Labuhan   Potteries
Poh   GILI   Lembar   716   Kawe   Mujur
Cape   GEDE
Pandanan   Taun   Sengkol
Pelangan   Ketapang   Sekotong   Jelateng   Mangkung   Pegambur   Marketplace
Bangko   Sade/
Bangko   BATUGENDENG   Patu   153   Rambitan   Awang
Surfing   •476   Jangke   Trad.
Village
Sepi   Silung   Aan   Ta
Belongas   Sep   Pengantap   Blanak   Aa
Bay
Pegantap   Kuta
Cape   Bay   Mawun   Tourist
Sara   Are   Resort
Cape   Goling
Pangga   Cape   Grupuk
Tampa   Desert ✷
Point

INDIAN

Lombok Strait

Berentang R.

Ferry Bali - Lombok

LOMBOK

0   5   10   15 km

which links Ampenan with Mataram, one can see beds of *klangkung* (water-spinach) – this is typical of the sort of "River Kwai" bridge, now out of use, which are frequently found on the west coast. Close by the harbor is the maze of small streets which make up the **Arab quarter**, the size of which has been considerably reduced by the sale of a piece of land to an oil firm.

The Chinese presence is evident from the many Chinese shops and a number of restaurants, and on the northern fringe of the town is the large **Chinese cemetery,** which is still in use. It is said that wealthy Chinese have their most valuable possessions buried along with them, even including motor-bikes. Their place of worship is the small, colorfully restored **Chinese temple** in Jalan Yos Sudarso (also known as Jalan Pabean).

Just before you reach the Chinese cemetery in the north of the town you will see a Balinese temple, **Pura Segara,** on the beach. It is only brought to life at times of temple festivals, and in fact the scenery is worthier of note than the temple itself.

Apart from a few cheap places to stay, Ampenan can boast a large market (by the *bemo* station), a cinema (*bioskop*), a Catholic hospital, and a number of antique-shops. You can obtain useful information about climbing Mount Rinjani from the **Wisma Triguna** in Jalan Koperasi.

Mataram

Mataram is the capital of Nusa Tenggara Barat, a province which includes the neighboring island of Sumbawa, as well as Lombok. Befitting its role, the town is made up principally of of imposing, modern government buildings, banks and business headquarters, and the streets are alive with government officials and local administrators, unifomed schoolchildren and students.

179

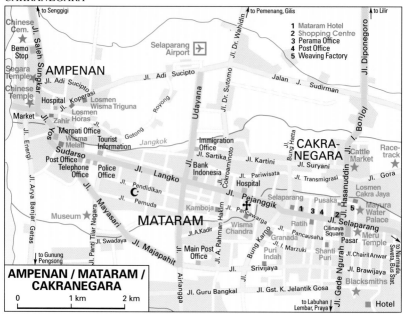

1 Mataram Hotel
2 Shopping Centre
3 Perama Office
4 Post Office
5 Weaving Factory

AMPENAN / MATARAM / CAKRANEGARA

| 0 | 1 km | 2 km |

Running from west to east through the three-town connurbation is a broad boulevard, changing its name several times along its course. The little horse-drawn carriages (*dokar* or *cidomo*) are not permitted on this thoroughfare. On the stretch that forms the border between Ampenan and Mataram are the Tourist Office, Post Office, police station, telegraph office and the office of the Merpati airline.

It is well worth wandering around the streets and alleyways of Mataram, and a visit to the **Provincial Museum of Nusa Tenggara Barat** is to be recommended. Apart from basic illustrated charts and models explaining the geography, geology, culture and history of Lombok, the more notable exhibits include textiles, domestic utensils, amulets, krisses, weapons and masks. Some of the displays are labelled in English. To reach the museum, go to the crossroads where the

Right: Horse-drawn Dokars create a rustic atmosphere in Cakranegara.

tourist office is situated, then turn south into Jalan Panji Tilar Negara. After about 500 yards (0.5 km) you will see the museum on the right hand side.

Cakranegara

The handsome, though rather sterile town of Mataram is adjoined by Cakranegara, which is quite a contrast, being more primitive and exceptionally busy. The rush-hour traffic is worse here than anywhere else in the island. Endless rows of shops and workshops line the streets, and there is also a supermarket on Cilinaya Square. Here too, the efficient and industrious Chinese make an important contribution to the town's economy.

The center of Cakra, as people like to call the town, is the crossroads of the main street, Jalan Selaparang, with Jalan Hasanuddin, which runs south and becomes Jalan Gede Ngurah. Here, also, can be found the lively market, the Pasar of Cakranegara. About four blocks further south is the blacksmiths' quarter.

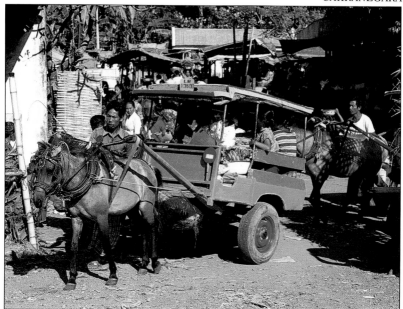

The smiths can be seen working at open furnaces, which are kept blazing with bamboo bellows. They make mainly agricultural implements and their raw material is often scrap metal from old cars.

Cakra has the Balinese settlers to thank for its two most important sights: a palace and a temple. The **Pura Meru** – the largest temple of its kind in Lombok – can be recognized from a distance by its three soaring towers (*merus*) which have given the temple its name. Built in 1720 near the market area, the temple is dedicated to the Hindu trinity of Shiva, Vishnu and Brahma; its founder, Anak Agung Made Karang of Singosari, intended it to foster peace and unity among the quarrelsome Balinese feudal lords of Lombok.

The temple, which sadly has rather fallen into disrepair, has three courtyards: in the first a wooden gong (*kulkul*) calls the devout to temple ceremonies. In the second courtyard two raised platforms serve as altars for sacrificial offerings. The innermost court has one large shrine and thirty-three small ones.

The *meru* with eleven roofs is dedicated to Shiva, that with nine roofs to Vishnu and the seven-roofed pagoda to Brahma.

Opposite, on the other side of Jalan Selaparang, stands the **Mayura Water Palace**, or at any rate as much of it as the Dutch left standing. It was built in 1744, and until the conquest of Lombok in 1894 it served as the residence of the Balinese Karangasem dynasty and their court. Its centerpiece today is a large lotus-pool, in the middle of which stands an open-sided hall. It is reached across a brick-built causeway. This apparently floating pavilion (*bale kambang*) was a courthouse for the affairs of the raja's empire as well as a place of assembly for the Hindu princes. Two fierce battles were fought in 1894 in the extensive grounds around the palace, in which the Dutch were finally victorious. Today it provides a tranquil refuge in which to escape the stress of city life. Amidst the lawns and trees fighting-cocks crow in their bamboo cages.

The palace also has a temple of its own, and one block away is a **weaving factory**, which is open to visitors. This is worth a visit, especially in the morning, which is the only time when most of the looms are in use. Apart from watching the weaving itself going on, one can see the dyeing processes – sometimes this is done before the weaving, and sometimes by hand afterwards on the finished cloth. Much of what is manufactured here is exported to Bali.

If you walk north along Jalan Hasanuddin you soon come to the **livestock market**. Before you reach it, you can turn right into Jalan Gora, which takes you the short distance to the **race-track**. Horse-racing takes place here on Sundays and holidays, and the jockeys taking part must be *under* twelve years of age; falls are not uncommon, so the young riders

wear crash-helmets and sometimes motor-bike goggles as well. In order to make the competition fair, the faster horses are handicapped; passions run high, and bitter tears are shed by the losers who have not come up to the expectations of the supporters from their home village.

Sweta

Just outside the gates of Cakra lies Sweta, the crossroads for overland traffic and the home of Lombok's largest market. Buses, minibuses, *bemos*, *dokars* and trucks leave from the bus-station for all destinations. If you want to get a comfortable seat, do not wait until the market closes around 4 pm. But it is certainly worth a visit if only because it offers all the produce and handicrafts of the island in one place, and in great abundance.

As well as every conceivable kind of fruit and vegetable, the market sells dried fish, spices, tobacco, domestic hardware, raffia and rattan articles, fabrics and even reproduction antiques.

Above: In a weaving-factory in Cakranegara. Right: Sacrificial offerings for the double temple of Lingsar.

Only occasionally will you see the incongruous figure of a smartly dressed housewife from Mataram: this is essentially a peasant market. The throngs of people, the heat and the sheer abundance of everything can be oppressive. In the half-shade of the covered bazaar, and also outside, there are numerous *warungs*, tempting you to stop for a drink and a tasty snack.

Narmada

A visit to Narmada is a more relaxing experience. Ony 7 1/2 miles (12 km) east of Cakranegara, it can be reached from any of the resorts on the west coast by the airport road (Jalan Adi Sucipto) which skirts the center of the capital. Do not forget to bring a respectable swimming costume with you. The place to go is the former **Summer Palace** of the Balinese rajas in the center of Narmada, which gets its name from a sacred river in India. The terraced site with an artificial lake at the foot of the hill is supposed to symbolize the sacred mountain of Lombok, with its crater lake. The Raja of Mataram ordered its construction – albeit a rather pale imitation of the real thing – in 1805, because he had reached an age when he could no longer climb up the Gunung Rinjani to make offerings. From that time on he made his sacrifices in the **Pura Kalasa**, which was part of the palace and where the solemn *Pujawali* ceremony is still celebrated annually. Rumour has it, however, that the old raja had another reason for building the palace: he would invite young girls to bathe in the lake and would then select the loveliest of them to be his mistress.

It was the Dutch who were responsible for the enormous irrigation pipes to the rear of the palace grounds. These were part of an island-wide infrastructure program designed to enable the tax-paying owners and tenants of agricultural land to achieve higher yields. In the long term, the colonial administrators hope that this would result in a signifiacnt improvement in their tax revenues.

The rather neglected grounds are used as a leisure park at weekends by enormous crowds of local visitors. One can sail on the lake in large boats shaped like rather kitsch swans. There is also a swimming pool with cool, clear water.

Suranadi

One of the most ancient and sacred temples of Balinese Lombok lies a few miles north-east of Narmada in the midst of an idyllic landscape. This is the **temple of sacred springs of Suranadi**. The bathing-places of the shrine are decorated with ornate reliefs, and the pool is the home of sacred eels which can be tempted from their hiding-places with hard-boiled eggs. The water itself is ice-cold.

Not far from the temple is the **Suranadi Hote**l, where, back in the 1930s Dutch colonial officials were entertained in style. The water in the hotel swimming-pool is continually replaced so that it is always refreshingly cool. The hotel has recently been enlarged with two bungalow-style buildings and is a good place to make your base for a healthy and restful walking holiday. The hilly countryside in these parts alternates between rice-fields and jungle, and quite close to the hotel is a small area of protected forest, where some of the trees are labelled for educational purposes. There are many species of birds and butterflies here, and monkeys romp through the trees.

An attractive excursion can be made to the village of **Sesaot**, 3 miles (5 km) away, where the main occupation is tree-felling. There is a river where you can bathe and have a picnic; you reach it along the main street of the village, then across a bridge and a little way on the left. The river rises in the Rinjani massif and the water is very cold.

Right: In the Balinese Pura Gaduh, part of the double temple of Lingsar.

In the village there is a simple *warung* on the main street. If you have a car and wish to return by a different route, it is possible to drive on minor roads through the hinterland, around a number of hairpin bends and through small, isolated market-towns, before rejoining the main highway that crosses the island. On the way you get an impressive view of the vast network of irrigation canals.

Lingsar

If you head westward from Suranadi, you will come, after a few miles, to the **double temple of Lingsar**, which was built in 1714 on the orders of the Raja of Lombok, I Gusti Wayan Tegeh, a member of the Balinese Karangasem dynasty. The site consists of the Balinese Hindu temple, **Pura Gaduh**, on the north side, which is linked by a flight of seventeen steps down to the Wetu-Telu temple of **Kemaliq Lingsar**. The number of steps is intended to symbolize the seventeenth day of the month of Ramadan, the day on which the Koran was presented to mankind. The construction of this temple is thought to have been a gesture of tolerance on the part of the raja, who wanted to gain the allegiance of his non-Hindu subjects.

There are four holy shrines in the Hindu temple. The two outer ones face the two sacred mountains of Bali and Lombok, Gunung Agung and Gunung Rinjani. The central double-shrine embodies the twofold link between Bali and Lombok and is a symbol of their spiritual unity. The left-hand part of the shrine is dedicated to the mighty Gaduh (representing Lombok) and the right-hand part to the deified son of Ayu Nyoman Winten, the Raja's daughter (standing for Bali). There is another shrine, richly encrusted with stones, a phenomenon which harks back to animistic traditions.

In the Wetu-Telu part of the temple there is a tiled pool dedicated to the god

Vishnu and inhabited by sacred eels. A small statue shows the god mounted on his winged steed, Garuda. This is another small reminder of the way Balinese mythology and the Wetu-Telu culture are interwoven.

Followers of other religions worship their god, or gods, here as well, a fact that is proved by the mirrors donated by Chinese merchants. Even Christians and strictly orthodox Moslems come here to offer up their prayers. The latter are also called Wetu Lima, on account of the five principal commandments of Islam (*lima* means " five").

Separate bathing-places for men and women, and a larger pond complete the temple complex.

Anyone wanting to drive from here direct to the west coast, should take the narrow country road that joins the airport road not far from Cakra. The road takes you past open cattle-pens. With a bit of luck you can watch water-buffaloes in the irrigation canals having their backs neatly shaved.

SENGGIGI AND THE "GILIS"

Senggigi is a good place to recover after the journey here from Bali. It is also an ideal starting-point for a number of excursions to explore western Lombok. There is a lot of new construction going on in Senggigi, especially around the main street. This may spoil your aesthetic enjoyment a little, as you stroll around, but the buildings so far completed show evidence of considerable sensitivity on the part of the developers.

It is easy to see why Senggigi has become so popular with tourists. There are long, white sandy beaches, punctuated by palm-covered promontories reaching out into broad sweeping bays; stretches of offshore reef, just waiting for you to explore them with your snorkel, and almost every evening a gorgeous sunset, like something out of a picture-book. Across the straits of Lombok, on Bali, the silhouette of Gunung Agung is etched with perfect clarity against the glowing red sky.

Above: The temple of Batu Bolong south of Senggigi.

Luxurious hotel complexes have now replaced some of the more basic accommodation and the trend is definitely in the direction of up-market tourism. Even the nightlife has livened up a good deal. In the ever-popular **Pondok Senggigi** the band sometimes begins testing the amplification for the evening concert, in the early afternoon. But if you are looking for peace and quiet you will find it in the extensive hotel complexes by the beach. There you can be sure to be beyond the reach of the countless hawkers who parade up and down the beach. Even in many of the more popular restaurants you have to exercise caution, otherwise the enjoyment of your meal will be spoilt by a hawker, who, with swift hand and glib tongue, will turn it into a heavy business luncheon.

There are pleasant short walks to be enjoyed along the beach in either direction. However, for longer excursions on foot one has to keep returning to the coast road. About two-thirds of a mile (1 km) to the south is a small Hindu temple built on a rocky promontory. The temple's name, **Batu Bolong**, means: "crevice in the rock carved by the sea," (*bolong* = hole, *batu* = stone). The temple is oriented towards Bali's sacred mountain, Gunung Agung. Legend has it that virgins were sacrificed here by being thrown to the sharks. There are certainly still sharks to be seen cruising expectantly round the rocks.

About 1 1/4 miles (2 km) further on one comes across an important Wetu-Telu shrine, **Batu Layar**. The burial-place of a holy man is housed in a small building here and behind it is a Moslem cemetery. There is a lovely excursion to the north of Senggigi which can be undertaken on foot or by motor-bike. The road bends and rises gently. From the top of each little hill you get a wonderful view of palm-groves beside the sea, deeply indented bays and little half-hidden settlements. The farthest you can go is to the provisonal end of the tarmac'd road, and from there you can look across to the trio of little islands lying off the coast of Lombok: Gili Air, Gili Meno and Gili Terawangan.

The islands off the north-west coast

Starting from Senggigi, there are two ways to reach the islands off the north-west coast: either directly by boat, or by driving along the highway to the little harbour at Bangsal and taking a boat from there. Each method has something to recommend it. Travelling straight there by boat – which is possible both from the main beach at Senggigi as well as from other bays, like Mangsit, further north – you can enjoy the sea at close quarters and have a chance to see many beautiful bays on the way, quite apart from having less bother with luggage.

The overland route from Senggigi to Bangsal was until very recently quite a tricky undertaking, because the coast road between the two towns was still under construction. It is possible that by the time this book is published the construction work will be completed, so that the journey to the ferry-harbor at Bangsal will be a quick and easy one. At the moment, however, one must first go back towards Ampenan from Senggigi, then at **Meninting,** the first major road that turns off, drive east to the small market town of Landang Bajur, where you pick up the main road going north. Driving along this road one soon passes through **Sidemen** where there are some small but newly built settlements and a recently constructed mosque. Sidemen is otherwise well known for its red palm sugar, which is made by boiling down palm-juice. It is usually seen on sale in markets in the form of cylindrical chunks.

Shortly after leaving Sidemen the road ascends in a series of tight bends to a pass, at the summit of which there is a simple café with a magnificent panorama

of the jungle and the islands. Here you may encounter the first Javanese monkeys who line up at frequent points along the twisting road down to the valley in the hope of retrieving tidbits from passers-by. However, you should not get too close to them. It is particularly inadvisable to fool around with the old stagers, who are keen to remain the bosses of their patch. Whether driving in your own or a rented car, you should for safety's sake hoot your horn at every corner. Not so much because of the monkeys, but to warn oncoming traffic. Leaving the forest behind, the road passes through small villages lying in the midst of paddy-fields. Finally, at **Pemenang**, you reach the turning for **Bangsal.** Once there, you have a choice between taking the regular boat service, or hiring a fishing boat. Visitors wishing to spend the night on one of the islands in the high season must arrive before midday or run the risk of being forced to sleep on the beach.

Gili Air

Gili Air, or "water island," which lies closest to Lombok, is the smallest and the most densely populated of the three islands. The majority of the 1,000 inhabitants live at the southern end of the island, facing the Lombok mainland. Most of the tourist accommodation can also be found here, as well as a diving shop. Apart from income derived from the new tourist industry, the locals earn their living from fishing, from the produce of their coconut palms and from rearing cattle and goats on a modest scale.

The palm-clad isle has a rustic charm and tempts one to many pleasant walks. The coast consists of a single, pale sandy beach, running right round the island. Although the coral-reef has in many places been destroyed by fishermen using dynamite, there remains much that is attractive to explore. In general, the best places for snorkelling are in the south (west of

the landing-stage, in the south-east and the north-east. The west coast, however, apart from a bit in the north-west, is hardly worth bothering about. Scuba-divers like to go up by boat to the north, near where a fresh water spring bubbles out of the sea floor.

Gili Meno

The middle island of the group, Gili Meno, is slightly larger than Gili Air, but has only one-third of the population. The geographical feature that lends the island its strange character is the salt-water lake in the west, which is used for the extraction of sea-salt. The palm groves on the island and a hotel with its own water-treatment plant (there is no fresh water on Gili Meno) are, however, more attractive features as far as the tourist is concerned. The other *losmens* have to obtain their water from the mainland. It is therefore

Above: Grooming the water-buffalo includes giving him a wet shave.

necessary to put a sterilisation-tablet in the water you use to clean your teeth. This is the most peaceful of the islands, not least because there is little accommodation available. The east, north and north-west coasts are the best for snorkelling.

Gili Terawangan

The largest island is Gili Terawangan, whose population of some 700 people comprises a mixture of immigrant Bugis and indigenous Sasak. It was chosen a hundred years ago by the Raja of Lombok as a penal colony for 350 Sasak rebels. During the Second World War, the Japanese built a coastal battery on the hill in the south of the island with three big gun emplacements, the remains of which can still be seen today. The hill is worth climbing anyway for the wonderful views of sunrise and sunset which it affords, for which Bali in the west and Gunung Rinjani in the east provide a picturesque backdrop. Once a jealously guarded secret for snorkellers, Gili Terangawan has now developed the amentities it offers the low-budget tourist in a thoroughly charming way. Accommodation is for the most part still simple in character and provided in little houses on stilts, with water for the *mandi* bath being pumped from goodness knows where. There is no electricity on the island and so, unless you are staying in a complex served by a generator that works, you will have the enjoyment of savoring the tropical night by candlelight or an old kerosene lamp. (Don't forget to bring oil of cloves, to ward off mosquitoes). Often at the height of the season many trendy local places compete to offer back-packing guests free samples of Indonesian food (when they have fought their way to the buffet). This is usually accompanied by lively music.

The snorkelling is good along the whole of the east coast, but care should be taken not to swim too far from the reef because the current there becomes very strong. As a rule, however, one can be carried gently along the whole reef by it and enjoy the wide variety of species of tropical fish – a good guide to these is essential. For scuba-divers there is a shop which offers spectacular dives. Giant rays, sea-turtles, sharks and giant clams are among the creatures on which to feast your eyes.

NORTHERN LOMBOK AND GUNUNG RINJANI

The road which runs along the north coast leads to Gunung Rinjani, Lombok's sacred mountain, which is the highest point on the island and the climax of any visit to Lombok. The importance of this massif and its rain forests for the island's ecology was recognized by the Dutch when they came here, and so they placed the mountain under special protection. It is the second highest in Indonesia, if one does not count the range of 15,000 ft (5,000 m) mountains of West Irian, in

New Guinea). The protected area today covers more than 230 square miles (600 sq.km), in which the clearance of forest is subject to official restrictions, in order to preserve the mountain's function as a reservoir of rain-water. The success of these measures is something you can judge at first hand on this tour.

Along the north coast

Between Pemenang and Desa Anyar, the coast road goes past paddy-fields, coconut plantations and villages on river estuaries where lagoons have now formed. Floating gardens of water spinach (*kangkung*) can sometimes be seen in the rivers, where the men of the village wash their horses and the women their laundry. The further north-east one goes, the more frequent the sight of pasture land where the occasional dusty water-buffalo graze and the earth glows red-brown through its sparse covering. The beaches are of black volcanic sand. The distances between settlements increase and the dwellings become poorer. However, there are frequent opportunties to make rewarding detours to the coast.

Shortly after **Pemenang**, where the road branches off to Bangsal and the ferry to the three "gilis," you come to a track down to the coast at **Sira**, where a white sandy beach and wonderful snorkelling waters await you. A tourist hotel is planned.

One and a quarter miles (2 km) outside **Tanjung**, to the west, (above the bay where one can snorkel) stands a **Balinese temple**, which is a good point for taking photos of the picturesque sunsets with Bali in the background. Beyond Tanjung, in **Krakas**, you can go out to sea with the fishermen to a fresh water spring which bubbles up from the ocean floor. They collect the water there for the village. It is possible to dive on the reef.

Gondang offers pleasure of a different kind. A signpost in the village points the

way to a **waterfall**. On a cross-country motor-bike it is possible to drive up to within 500 yards of it, having first forded a knee-deep stream; the climb up on foot will take a good hour from the road.

Leaving behind **Desa Anyar**, a modern village inhabited by people who have been resettled from Java, one is soon in Wetu-Telu territory on the road south to Gunung Rinjani. Today **Bayan** is the stronghold of this faith, and according to legend it was also the first early Islamic community on Lombok. A road leads from here up to **Senaru**. There is a view out across a fertile valley and soon after this one reaches a row of *losmens*, shops and restaurants nestling in the mountainside to the east of the road. There, in **Batu Kok**, provisions can be obtained for the climb up to Rinjani, and guides and porters hired. It is also possible to

Above: The boys of Gondang play Tarzan at the waterfall. Right: The hot springs of Rinjani emerge from a cleft in the crater bowl beneath Segara Anak.

rent a room for the nights before and after the expedition – the ascent of Rinjani is now an everyday occurence. On nights of the full moon in the dry season many people – native pilgrims and tourists seeking a new experience – can be seen making the trek up the mountain. If you are spending the night before the ascent in Batu Kok, below Senaru, you should make a point of walking to the waterfall at **Sendang Gila**. You can see it as soon as you reach the last restaurant, in an exposed position east of the road.

The ascent of Rinjani

The classic ascent begins and ends in Senaru. One should allow for two overnight stops on the mountain, although if you want to go further than the crater lake and the hot springs and climb the peak itself, three will be required. The path is easy to find, but it is steep and difficult. Anyone considering the climb should take into account his or her own stamina and capabilities, and give serious thought

to hiring a guide and porters – in any event it is definitely not advisable to set off alone.

At first, the path follows the marked route up to a village at the edge of the forest at a height of 2000 ft (600 m), and from here plunges into the rain-forest where the felling of trees has created clearings. (The timings that follow are for serious walkers with light baggage. The native porters are so strong and fit that they can carry 45 lbs (20 kilos) quite happily.) After what is for the most part a steep climb of between one and two hours through increasingly dense forest, one reaches the so-called Position II (Pos II) which is distinguished by a somewhat lopsided *bale*. In emergencies one can spend the night here. There is a watering-place about 200 yards away ·that sometimes has water. Waterproof clothing may be needed at this stage. At this altitude, even in the dry season, and particularly in the afternoons, mist clings to the tree-tops, or a tropical downpour will soak walkers already bathed in sweat.

Initially this presents no problems, because temperatures are still high, but after another 1 1/2 to 2 hours at the most, at Pos III you have reached an altitude of 6900 ft (2100 m) and you begin to notice the cold. Here, a simple hut on stilts which can be used as an overnight stop awaits climbers, although at the height of the season it is not large enough to accommodate everyone who might arrive. Anyone arriving here after 2 o'clock in the afternoon should stop at this point, because the next accommodation is at the lake or the hot springs. This would mean a further four hours walking, and it is not advisable to arrive in the mist and the pitch dark. Pos III is not particularly inviting because many walkers dump their rubbish here and the watering-place does not always look very appealing.

The tree-line is reached shortly after leaving Pos III. Initially the path is again very steep, but the view across to Bali is a reward for one's efforts. After two or three hours the lip of the crater is reached at 8500 ft (2600 m) and the hard toil of

the ascent is forgotten when the crater lake comes into view, with the volcano in the lake and the summit beyond. You will only get this view, of course, if you do not arrive too late in the afternoon and the peak and lake are not obscured by cloud. The descent to the lake, which is at an altitude of 6550 ft (2000 m), is very steep in many places and takes about two hours. The best place to make camp is either at the level of the lake, near where it flows over the edge, or a little further down by the hot springs. The local authorities have stocked the lake with carp (*ikan karper*) and a species called *tilapiae* (local name: *mujair*), which are often kept in fish-farms and are excellent eating. Judging by the keen local anglers that one sees, the lake is well-stocked.

The crescent-shaped **Lake Segara Anak** is about 800 ft (250 m) deep. The crater forms an oval 7 1/2 miles long and

5 miles wide (6 km x 8 km). The small volcano in the lake, known as **Gunung Baru** ("new mountain"), is about 500 ft (150 m) high and is believed to have grown in height in the last 30 years. Despite reports to the contrary, the volcano was definitely there as long as 80 years ago, because there are photos from that time which show clearly a fumarole, or vent, emitting smoke and ash. The last major eruption of Rinjani was in 1901, so it must be considered as still highly active. The summit is 12,220 ft (3726 m) high. The **White Springs** (*kokok putih*) below the cleft of the crater are sulphurous and the water emerges from the rock at a temperature of over 70° C. The islanders come to the springs to cure skin disorders and to seek physical and spiritual healing in general. Regularly each afternoon mist and clouds descend and drift across the lake through the cleft, so that the air temperature drops rapidly and it becomes cold and wet. Many walkers are then glad of the steaming hot natural baths and do not want to leave them.

Above: View across Lake Segara Anak towards Gunung Baru. Right:Young people from Sembalun Bumbung.

Very few people undertake the strenuous ascent to the summit of Rinjani. It is only worth attempting when the weather is particularly fine, and if one can manage to be at the top before the clouds come rolling in and the strong wind threatens to blow you down into the lake. To see the sun rise over Sumbawa from the peak is a memorable experience. But it is not without its perils. This is because you have to set off from the lake by midnight at the latest, and really struggle up in the moonlight. The question: "Why on earth am I doing this?" will spring to your lips more than once before you have reached the summit – or given up the enterprise. Before setting out, you should give some thought to the fact that night climbing really can be dangerous.

The plateau of Sembalun

Driving on further eastward from Bayan one reaches a crossroads at **Kali Putih** ("white river"). Here, one road turns south into the mountains and winds steeply up to the Sembalun plateau, passing, in places, through virgin rain-forest with occasional banyan-trees. Surprisingly in this apparently isolated high valley there are two large villages which are said to be among the wealthiest on the island. In **Sembalun Lawang**, there is a market with one *warung* and a modest lodging-house which you see as you enter the village. The twin village of **Sembalun Bumbung** lies on the far side of a fertile plain which is intensively cultivated and produces onions, shallots and garlick. Hence the wealth. At any time of day the sight of this pocket of civilization and fertility, so high in the mountains, comes as quite a shock; Sembalun Bumbung also offers modest accommodation.

For those who enjoy walking there is a route over the pass to the south, towards **Pesugulan**, which is also much used by the local inhabitants. It leads through forests which are the habitat of black, long-tailed monkeys. Taking you past waterfalls and warm springs it emerges in cinnamon plantations and civilization.

EASTERN LOMBOK

Eastern Lombok is undeveloped as a tourist destination, and for many it is only a region that one passes through on the way to Sumbawa and Flores; but its landscape has many facets which invite further exploration. There are beaches of both white and black sand in the northeast, rain forests, paddy-fields and open heathland in the foothills of Rinjani, and between the settlements on the coastal plain there are large expanses of flat wilderness which appear almost surreal.

The visitor wishing to explore eastern Lombok has several starting points to choose from: the best way to reach the north coast is from Batu Kok (between Bayan and Senaru, to the north of Rinjani) – as long as the last rainy season has not washed away any of the bridges.

If you are looking for more variety, you should make for Tetebatu, on the south side of the Rinjani massif. Apart from Batu Kok, it offers the best accommodation (including simple but clean little cabins), it is conveniently close to the east coast, and also provides walkers with a choice of refreshing excursions on the doorstep. Alternatively, you can base yourself right on the coast at Labuhan Lombok.

The north-east

Although *bemos* operate between Bayan and Labuhan Lombok, it is preferable, if you can, to make your own way there, using an all-terrain vehicle. The distance along the north coast, starting from Batu Kok or even from Sembalun, can easily be covered in a day, including stops by the sea to bathe, have a meal or take photographs. After Bayan, the road doubles back again into the interior of the island before reaching the coast at

Right: In east Lombok the Buginese fishermen build their houses on stilts.

Medas. Near the verdant paradise of **Obel-Obel** one can swim from black sand beaches, then the road leads once more into the interior and through an ever changing landscape with river-beds which are usually dried up in summer but which fill up plentifully again in the rainy season. The deposits of debris and boulders and the damaged roads and broken bridges bear eloquent witness to the force of the rivers in flood. One such wrecked bridge is likely to be encountered near Obel-Obel.

Near **Belanting**, just after a steep, blind double bend, there is a simple restaurant, where you can also fill up with gasoline.

In **Labuhan Pandan** it is possible to negotiate with the fishermen for a boat-trip to the offshore islands. These isles are uninhabited and their attraction lies in their beautiful sandy beaches and the good opportunites they offer for snorkelling. On **Gili Sulat** there are mangrove swamps. You have to bring your own provisions and water.

Beyond Labuhan Pandan, opposite the little island of **Gili Pentangan**, there is a beach where, in 1991, the first signs of impending tourist development could be observed.

From here on, there is a continual alternation of fertile oases with barren, stony land. Shortly before reaching Labuhan Lombok one can see a small grove of tall trees – the last remaining, isolated stand of giant tropical hardwood trees outside the Rinjani conservation area.

From Labuhan Lombok to Tetebatu

Labuhan Lombok, on the east coast, lies on a sheltered bay and is an important ferry terminal for boats to Sumbawa. The landing-stage for the Sumbawa ferries is located outside the village, on a spit of land. In the center there is a market with several *warungs*. There are also two very simple *losmens*. A large number of Bu-

ginese have settled around the bay and make their living from fishing, or are employed in the construction of large wooden cargo boats. Some of their houses, built on piles, are painted in a variety of eye-catching colors. But sadly very few of these are left.

Labuhan Lombok is connected with the 3-town capital, Ampenan-Mataram-Cakranegara, by the much-improved east-west highway. Going west, one passes through a barren, steppe-like, or even desert landscape, which reminds one of a smaller version of Arizona, and the similarity is heightened by the sight of herds of cattle.

The first settlements of any size are **Pringabaya** and **Aik Mel**. From both villages there are roads leading to **Pegusulan** on Gunung Rinjani. From there you can make a lovely trek up to the plateau of Sembalun. Beyond Pringgabaya, the face of the landscape changes. The road is now bordered by irrigated paddy-fields, and the further one drives towards **Masbagik** along the main road to the west, the more frequently one sees tobacco plantations and the typical platform-like tables on which the harvested tobacco leaves are dried.

Near Masbagik, a well-surfaced road turns off to the south-east and runs through Selong, the district capital, to **Labuhan Haji,** which was formerly an important mercantile port and is traditionally the harbour from which pilgrims from Lombok depart on their journey to the holy city of Mecca.

Back once again on the main highway, there is a turning at **Pomotong** for Tetebatu and the north. One or two of the villages south of Tetebatu are noted for their hand-made products, and the two neighboring settlements of **Loyok** and **Kotaraja** specialize in woven articles which one can buy either at the market in Kotaraja or in a shop in Loyok. The village of **Rungkang**, only about half a mile east of Loyok, is famous for its black earthenware pottery.

The village of **Tetebatu** lies at the foot of the Rinjani massif, at an altitude of

195

nearly 2000 ft (600 m), between paddy-fields and fish-ponds. On the far side of the village, some thinned out mountain forest remains, and is inhabited by the comical black long-tailed monkeys. It is noticeably cooler and perhaps just for that reason provides a welcome change. There are two alternatives for accommodation: one is a guest-house dating from the 1920s and built by the Dutch colonial administration. It has since been extended with additional bungalows. The other choice is a group of relatively new cottages in the rice-fields on the east side of the road, before you reach the center of the village.

From Tetebatu it is possible to reach a number of waterfalls on foot, the largest being about 7 1/2 miles (12 km) away. One of the smaller waterfalls is also well worth seeing: walking towards it you cross rice-fields, tracts of surviving rain-

Above: Foreigners still cause quite a sensation here. Right: In the south it is not every village that has a pond like this.

forest and areas where the forest has been cleared by burning. Here and there, this rural landscape is dotted with small villages. Near the waterfall, the dense jungle is populated by gray-brown Javanese monkeys. It is essential to consult the map in the guest-house before setting out, as it is easy to lose your bearings. Alternatively, little village boys offer their services as guides.

SOUTHERN LOMBOK

Worthwhile excursions in the southern part of Lombok include those to the Batugendeng peninsula in the south-west and to Kuta and the surrounding area on the south coast. There you will encounter, as a rule, a simpler form of tourist infrastructure, if there is any at all, and most trips into the wild are only possible on foot, or in an all-terrain vehicle (e.g. a jeep or Enduro). It is usually necessary to bring your own food and water. The following suggested routes both start from Cakranegara.

The Batugendeng peninsula

If one sets out early enough in the morning, on the journey from Cakranegara to the Batugendeng peninsula, it is worth making a small detour over the mountain of Gunung Pengson. To do this, leave the main road south of Cakranegara and drive in the direction of **Pagutan**. It was in the temple here that in 1894 a rare copy of the *Nagarakertagama* was discovered and preserved by a Dutch ethnologist. The epic was written in Old Javanese in 1365 by the court poet and histrorian Prapanca, and describes, in the form of a poetical eulogy to the rulers of the time, life in the kingdom of king Hayam Wuruk (1350 – 1389) and the life and deeds of his great-grandfather Kertanagara (1268 – 1292). The epic, the original name of which was *Desa Warnana* ("description of the country"), was composed on the orders of the statesman Gajah Mada and represents the most important indigenous source concerning the Javanese Majapahit empire.

Gunung Pengson is a small mountain, less than 6 miles (10 km) south of Cakranegara. There is a **temple** here with white shrines and an altar with an egg-shaped stone cemented into its surface. The steps leading up to it are besieged by a horde of monkeys. The most attractive feature is the view across the rice-paddies to Gunung Rinjani, which is usually free of cloud until 10 o'clock in the morning. In the evening the peak of Gunung Agung on Bali provides a wonderful backdrop in the west.

The most important feature of the **Batugendeng peninsula** is its offshore reef, wonderful for snorkelling and diving, and the many small islands have similar reefs. Here too are the last stretches of lowland jungle of Nusa Tenggara Barat, where deer and wild boar still roam in large numbers. Many species of seabird nest in the rocky cliffs of the peninsula. Around the coast, cliffs alternate with bays and sandy beaches, but places to sit in the shade are pretty rare. The islands usually have sandy beaches all round.

A surfaced road leads from **Labuhan Lembar**, where the Bali-Lombok ferry docks, southward to the Moslem village of **Sekotong**, which one reaches after a switchback of steep hills for 6 miles (10 km). Sekotong lies some way from the coast; from here one can go either in an all-terrain vehicle (preferably an Enduro), or on foot (remembering to take water and food) to Sepi and Belongas in the south (see below), or you can drive along the increasingly rough road to **Taun** in the west.

As far as Taun the road is generally passable in a normal car, but not really any further than that, unless major road-building has taken place since this book went to press. On the way one passes beaches of black sand and small settlements with large fish-ponds (*tambak*). In Taun itself there is a white sand beach, and bungalows can be rented on the off-

Above: A friendly smile for the camera.
Right: Market-day in Sengkol.

shore island of **Gili Nanggu**, which is reached either by a charter-boat from Labuhan Lembar or from the beaches of the peninsula.

About 3 3/4 miles (6 km) further west you come across a group of houses on the beach, where fishermen and lime-burners live. The place is called **Ketapang**, and from there a boat leaves every morning (except Fridays) for Koranji Bangsal, which lies on the coast south of Gunung Pengson. You should allow three hours for the trip. Boats also leave for the largest offshore island, **Gili Gede**, from Ketapang or from its neighbor to the west, **Pelangan**. The island has a ship-building yard, where Buginese are employed building heavy wooden outriggers of up to 200 tons, to order. Each ship takes up to two years to complete and the work is done without any drawings – the master shipwright manages to keep the whole plan in his head.

Pelangan is the end of the line for trucks, but further west there is still a string of small villages. **Labuhan Poh** is said to have the most beautiful beach for miles around, and the last place you come to, at the western tip of the peninsula, is **Bangko Bangko.** This has recently become known as a paradise for surfers, who arrive in numerous motor-boats from Labuhan Lembar. Already some huts have sprung up, where you can spend the night. A little way inland the forest begins. It is teeming with wild game and is a favorite spot for wealthy city-dwellers to go hunting.

Trips by motor-bike from Sekotong to the south should only be undertaken in the dry season, otherwise the terrain is almost impassable, since the track leads through the beds of several streams.

After some 6 miles (10 km) along this track, past small settlements where there are pitiful attempts at cultivation on steep terraces, you reach **Sepi**, an unremarkable fishing-village. From here you can get an outrigger to take you to the white,

sandy beach of **Belongas.** Scuba-divers tell stories of seeing sea-turtles, and sharks of up to 7 feet (2 m) long around the reef. This is largely intact and the visibility for snorkelling is good.

The village of **Pengantap**, with its two offshore islands, lies 5 miles (8 km) away to the east. This is one of the last few places where Budas, a small group of the aboriginal inhabitants of Lombok, still live today, and they worship at the nearby stone shrine.

If you climb the steep hill behind the village you will get a good view over the whole area. The landscape becomes more monotonous and after another 11 miles (18 km) you reach **Silung Blanak**, after passing through a few impoverished hamlets on the way. From **Patu Jangke,** a small market town, the road is once more asphalted. Silung Blanak lies on a broad bay with a white sandy beach and a few *warungs*.

The surfaced road then takes you through Mangkung and Praya and back to the capital.

Southwards to Kuta

The next expedition takes us to Kuta on the south coast of Lombok. Kuta, and its neighboring coastal villages are the ideal place for anyone who seeks nothing more than miles of white, sandy beaches shaded by palm-trees, who will be enchanted by a sea in every shade of turquoise, and who most of all can do without the noisy and expensive tourist racket. But if you are one of those people, you had better hurry. It may not be like that for much longer. Certainly the building plots that have been staked out and the growing number of property deals give an idea of what is to come.

The road from Cakranegara is on the whole well-surfaced and passes through Kediri towards Praya, the chief town of the Central Lombok district.

From **Puyung**, famed for its attractive rattan goods and regular stick-fighting contests, there is a worthwhile detour to be made to **Sukarara**. This is a typical Sasak village whose beautiful textile-weaving has made it a favorite stopping point for package-tours. The locals have adapted to this with alacrity – the women now charge a fee to pose for photographs, and it ain't peanuts! One tends to be pestered by touts as well. However, you should not let this put you off paying a visit to the place.

The atmosphere in the weaving workshops is friendly though reserved. Almost every household has at least one simple loom at which a woman will work for weeks and months to produce a single large cloth called a *purbasari,* which is worn at festivals like a sarong. Woven sashes, belts (*sabuk*) and even tablecloths can be purchased.

Returning to the main road, another 3 3/4 miles (6 km) brings you to **Penujak**. Here you can look at, and buy, red ceramics made in the time-honoured way and with traditional patterns; or you can just watch the skilled potters at work. There are containers in the shape of animals, and simple bulbous vessels up to three feet (1 m) high.

The village of **Sengkol** is a special attraction on Thursdays, which is market-day, when the men and women from the surrounding Sasak settlements come to buy and sell, many wearing their traditional costume. The women wear a black sarong and a short black blouse which leaves the navel exposed. The only adornment is a brightly coloured hand-woven belt. Many wares which the visitor may already have seen in their places of origin are offered for sale here, and anyone who has already experienced the amazing market at Sweta, may not consider the Sengkol market anything to write home about.

About 3 3/4 miles (6 km) before reaching Kuta you cannot fail to notice the little village of **Sade/Rambitan** perched

Right: The beaches of Kuta offer lots of sun, and miles of white sand – and you hardly have to share them with anyone.

on a flat-topped hill. This Wetu-Telu community is just made for tourism, in the best sense, and even before you reach the concrete footpath up to the village gates, you will be met by children offering to guide you round. Some of them are really smart and have learnt by heart an entire conducted tour in English. Needless to say, an elementary souvenir trade has developed, and you can buy woven articles, which you can watch being produced on the spot by women at simple wooden looms. Although the children's continuous presence as guides can get a bit tiresome, they do allow the visitor to get a little glimpse of the social structure of a Sasak village. The houses of prayer of the Wetu-Telu Moslems are typically built in the shape of a mosque.

Beaches around Kuta

Kuta itself is nothing more than a collection of houses near the sea, and its attraction lies in its beaches which stretch away in both directions. Once a year the *Nyale* festival takes place here. There have been frequent rumors that work is about to start on the construction of large hotel complexes, but at present there are just a few places offering basic accommodation, and one or two simple restaurants dotted along the beaches. Even at the height of the season you get the impression that this whole stretch of coast is sunk in a lethargic sleep.

If you enjoy rough tracks and enchanting scenery, you should take the exhilarating motor-bike ride westward to the village of **Mawun**. To reach the most beautiful vantage-points you need to follow the 6-mile (10 km) stretch of track along the coast from Kuta, which is tough going in parts, rather than the faster road (despite being nearly a mile longer) through Pegambur. There is a beautiful beach to be found at **Are Goling**, before you get to Mawun, but it means taking an almost impassable detour down to the

coast. There is also an island off the beach to which it is possible to wade at low tide. Mawun, too, has a beach of beautiful white sand.

If you select Kuta as your base for further journeys of discovery, there are many opportunities if you head to the east. Quite close by is **Tanjung Aan**, with its magnificent bay and a peninsula jutting out into the sea; from its highest point one gets a superb view of the surrounding area. Surfers drive a bit further on to **Grupuk**. They are predominantly Australians, and the place where they ride over the breakers they have named **Desert Point**.

Further to the east lies **Awang**. However, it can only be reached by a very poor road, which branches off at Aan, before the turn-off for the coast and Tanjung Aan. A kind of sea-weed is cultivated in the Bay of Awang, which is used in the production of gelatine.

On the other side of the bay lies **Batu Nampar**. It is a place where immigrant Buginese and Maduran settlers now outnumber the native Sasaks. Many of their houses, which are built on stilts, are decorated with brightly colored geometrical designs. Near the village there are extensive salt-pans.

To reach Batu Nampar you must either drive over extremely rough tracks, or else charter a boat from Awang. There is, however, a third possibility, which is to drive in a wide loop through Mujur and Sukaraja. Except in the rainy season, this route takes you through arid, bone-dry tracts of land. Like Sade, **Sukaraja** is a kind of Sasak showplace for tourists.

The peninsula in the south-east has now been opened up to traffic with a new highway as far as **Ekas**. There are rumors that the entire peninsula is soon to be given the necessary infrastructure to enable it to handle tourism.

For the moment, however, the best way to travel round it is in a charter-boat from Tanjung Luar or some other village on the coast. The walk from Ekas to the caves of **Tanjung Ringgit**, on the eastern tip of the island, takes a whole day.

AMPENAN / MATARAM
CAKRANEGARA

Accommodation

LUXURY CLASS: **Hotel Granada**, Jl. Bung Karno, Cakranegara, Tel: 22275, Fax: 23856, with swimming-pool and restaurant, from Rps. 50,000;
MID-PRICE: **Puri Indah**, Jl. Sriwijaya, Tel: 27633, with swimming-pool and restaurant, from Rps. 20,000;
Wisma Melati, Jl. Yos Sudarso 4, Ampenan, Tel: 23780, relatively quiet and close to all main facilities, from Rps. 29,000;
Selaparang Hotel, Jl. Pejanggik 40-42, Cakranegara, Tel: 22670, with restaurant, from Rps. 20,000;
Mataram Hotel, Jl. Pejanggik 105, Cakranegara, Tel: 23411, with restaurant, from Rps. 18,000.
BUDGET: **Hotel Shanti Puri**, Jl. Maktal 15, Cakranegara, Tel: 22649, owned by a Balinese family, possible to hire Jeeps and motor-cycles, with restaurant, from Rps. 6,000; **Wisma Chandra**, Jl. Pancawarga 55, Mataram, Tel: 23979, from Rps. 9,000; **Ratih**, Jl. Pejanggik 127, Cakranegara, Tel: 21096, with restaurant and hire of Jeeps and Motor-cycles, from Rps. 7,000; **Hotel Zahir**, Jl. Koperasi 9, Ampenan, Tel: 22403, rooms with small verandahs around a courtyard, motor-cycles available for hire, from Rps. 5.000; **Losmen Horas**, Jl. Koperasi 65, Ampenan, Tel: 21695, clean and well-run, from Rps. 6.000; **Losmen Wisma Triguna**, Jl. Koperasi Pelembak, Ampenan, Tel: 21705, with garden, the place to meet back-packers interested in climbing Mount Rinjani; possible to hire sleeping-bags, cooking-utensils, etc., tours to Rinjani organized, rooms from Rps. 8,000.

Restaurants

AMPENAN: Pabean and **Cirebon**, Jl. Pabean 111 und 113, Indonesian and Chinese cooking, the Cirebon is particularly popular; **Arafat**, Jl. Pabean 64, Indonesian food, cheap and good; **Setia**, Jl. Pabean 129, **Depot Mina**, Jl. Yos Sudarso 102, and **Timur Tengah**, Jl. Koperasi 22, basic and good value.
MATARAM: Garden House Restaurant, on the south side of Jl. Penjanggik by the Pusat Pertokoan (Shopping Center), Indonesian, Chinese and international, ice-cream (e.g. durian flavor) is the great speciality here, nice atmosphere; **Al Azhar**, Pusat Pertokoan, serves *Ayam taliwang*, a chicken speciality from West Sumbawa; **Deny Bersaudara**, Jl. Rumah Sakit Islam 6, Tel: 23619, fresh Gourami fish and Sasak specialities; other recommended restaurants in and around the Cilinaya Center: **Pattaya**, fish, Indonesian and Chinese; **Shanti Puri**, Indonesian, Chinese and international; **Dirga-**
hayu, mainly Indonesian; **Muksin Taliwang**, Sasak specialities.
CAKRANEGARA: Flamboyan, Jl. Pejanggik 101, delicious fish dishes, Chinese; **Madya**, Jl. Hasanuddin 7, Sasak cooking and specialities from Sumbawa; **Sekawan Depot Es**, Jl. Selaparang, seafood, Chinese.

Important addresses

The **Tourist Office,** Dinas Pariwisata, is on the border between Ampenan and Mataram, Jl. Langko 70, Tel: 21866/21730.
Opposite is the **Telephone Office** of *Permuntel* (International calls and fax available).
The **Head Post Office** with a counter for poste restante mail is in Mataram, near the junction of Jl. Srivijaya and Jl. A. Rahman Hakim. Opening hours: Mon–Thu and Sat 8 am–2 pm, Fri 8 am–11 am.
In the continuation of Jl. Langko in Ampenan, you will find the **Merpati Airline office**.
Bus and transport information is obtainable at the **Perama office** in Jl. Pejanggik 66, Tel: 22764/23368.

Activities

Provincial Museum of Nusa Tenggara Barat: Tue – Thu 8 am–2 pm, Fri 8 am – 11 am, Sat, Sun 8 am – 12 noon. Entrance: 200 Rps.
For **shopping**, the best streets are Jl. Yos Sudarso (Dina, Jaya Bahagia, Rora, Renza) and Jl. Saleh Sungkar (Sudirman, Lombok Today, Heri). Their side-streets in Ampenan are good for genuine and reproduction antiques.
In Cakra it is worth visiting Jl. Selaparang and Cilinaya Square and their side-streets, where you will find textiles and many other local handicrafts.
A number of **textile factories** can be visited, e.g.: Balimurti, Slamet Riyadi on Jl. Tenun near the Mayura water palace, Rinjani Hand Woven, Jl. Pejanggik 44/46, where it joins Jl. Selaparang, Sari Kusuma, Jl. Selaparang 45, in Cakranegara and Putra Khatina, Jl. Ismail Marzuki 5, in Mataram.

SURANADI
Accommodation / Restaurant

Suranadi Hotel, Jl. Raya Suranadi, P.O. Box 10, Mataram 83000, Tel: 23686, very restful, with swimming-pool and tennis-court, US$ 12 to 30. The restaurant offers Indonesian, Chinese and international dishes.

SENGGIGI
Accommodation

In Senggigi, there is a wide choice of accommodation in every price-category. However, in the high season it is advisable to book in advance.

LUXURY CLASS: **Senggigi Beach Hotel**, P.O. Box 2 Mataram, Tel: 23112/23430; the complex offers every conceivable facility from a pharmacy to a bureau de change, centrally located on the sea, the restaurant and bar have a South Seas atmosphere, from US$ 65;

Ida Beach Cottages, P.O. Box 51 Mataram, Tel: 21013/21353, on the slope beyond the main road with a view over the bay, many extras, from US$ 45; **Pacific Beach Hotel**, P.O. Box 36 Mataram, Kerandangan, Tel: 22342, on the beach, a little way from the center, with swimming-pool and restaurant, from US$ 30; **Lombok Intan Laguna**, P.O. Box 50 Mataram, Tel: 23659, very luxurious, from US$ 45; **Graha Beach Hotel**, Tel: 25331/23782, very central, right on the beach, with restaurant, water-sport facilities, from US$ 45;

Bunga Beach Cottages, Mangsit, on the sea a long way from the center, from Rps. 80,000; **Sheraton Senggigi Beach Hotel**, Tel: 27721, Fax: 27730, right on the beach opposite the Ida Beach Cottages.

MID-PRICE: **Mascot Cottages**, Tel: 23865, very central, reliable, from US$ 26; **Lina Cottages**, right on the beach, central, with good, popular restaurant, from Rps. 25,000; **Windy Cottages**, Mangsit, away from the center right on the sea, with an airy restaurant, from Rps. 15,000; **Batu Bolong Cottages**, Tel: 24598, huts on both sides of the road, as you come into town, from Rps. 23,000.

BUDGET: **Pondok Senggigi**, Tel: 22876, on the landward side of the road, central, with a popular restaurant, occasional open-air concerts, popular with long-range trekkers, from Rps. 8,000; **Pondok Sederhana**, on the landward side, simple rooms, from Rps. 5,000; **Pondok Shinta Cottages**, a short walk from the center, rooms from Rps. 10,000.

Santai Beach Inn, Mangsit, a long way out of town, on the beach, is run by an Englishwoman in an informal style, and is very popular with alternative travellers. It has a vegetarian restaurant, and rooms from Rps. 10,000.

Restaurants

Apart from the hotel restaurants, there are relatively few restaurants in town. The **Sunshine** in the center is very popular. It serves good fish dishes.

The **Dynasty**, Tel: 24619, at the edge of town has good Chinese food, but is too far out to be popular. Near the road to the Senggigi Beach Hotel there are some very cheap *warungs* serving traditional Indonesian dishes.

Activities

Senggigi's infrastructure is chiefly geared to beach holidays and water-sports activities. The hotels in the luxury category also offer tennis, badminton,

table-tennis and fitness equipment. There are popular day excursions by prahu boat to the three Gili islands to the north-west. In the evenings, dance performances take place occasionally in the Senggigi Beach Hotel, or there is live music in the Pondok Senggigi.

Important addresses

Next to the Sunshine you can find a **Tourist Office**, a *Permuntel*-**Telephone office** and a mailbox. **Jeeps** and **Motor-cycles** can be hired either from Surga Rent Car & Motorbike between Ampenan and Senggigi, north of the Asri Beach Cottages, or on the main street in Senggigi near the turning off to the Senggigi Beach Hotel.

GILI AIR / MENO / TERAWANGAN
Accommodation

LUXURY CLASS: **Indra Cemara**, Gili Meno, with its own water-purification plant, rooms from US$ 40.

All remaining accommodation on the islands are simple *losmens*. These, however, often turn out to be charming places to stay. On Gili Air, the **Hans Bungalows** (northern end) and **Gili Indah** (southern end) are very popular. On Gili Meno, the **Kontiki** (in the south-east) and the **Blue Coral Losmen** (in the north-east) are recommended, and on Gili Terawangan, the **Karin Homestay** (northern end) and the **Rainbow Cottages** (south-east).

If you are looking for some action, stay in Terawangan near the jetty. Prices for a double room begin at around Rps. 10.000. The restaurants are mostly quite basic, relatively cheap and serve the usual range of delicious local dishes.

TETEBATU
Accomodation / Restaurants

Wisma Soedjono, with restaurant and swimming-pool, from Rps. 11.000; **Diwi Enjeni**, very much simpler, but with a restaurant and a lovely view, from Rps. 5.000.

KUTA
Accommodation

To date, there is only a choice of simple and inexpensive accommodation, always with a small restaurant attached: **Losmen Mata Hari**, in the village, from Rps. 10,000; the following go from west to east: **Rambutan**, from Rps. 7,500; **Segara Anak**, from Rps. 8,000; **Pondok Sekar Kuning**, rooms on the upper floor, with a beautiful view, from Rps. 10,000; **Anda**, has places to sit in the shade and a good restaurant, from Rps. 9,000; **Cockatoo Cottages**, from Rps. 15,000.

BALINESE CUISINE

As one travels around Bali one will come across many dishes which are typical of the whole of Indonesia. Balinese specialities, on the other hand, are unfortunately much more difficult to obtain, since in many cases they are only served at major festivals and require hours of work to prepare. Nevertheless, there are a number of restaurants which will make these dishes to order. In the tourist centers international cuisine has become established and you will be served everything from Italian pasta, or American steak, to rich German cream-cakes.

The most important form of food for the Balinese, as almost everywhere in Asia, is rice. They give it a different name for every stage of its growth or

Previous pages: Parasols protect the throne of the gods. A Kecak dance being performed. Above: A wayside Warung in Asak. Right: Vegetables and spices are at the heart of Indonesian cooking.

method of preparation, and the Balinese name will often differ from the Indonesian. *Padi* is the general name for rice when it is still on the stalk. Once it has been threshed, it is given the same name in High Balinese as in Indonesian: *beras*. In everyday Balinese, however, this word is shortened to *baas*. But when it is boiled, rice becomes *nasi*. Among the varieties of regular white rice, the better-tasting *beras Bali* (Bali rice) is becoming increasingly hard to find. But there are many other types, including *ketan*, a sticky rice, *ketan injin* (black rice) which is often eaten as a dessert, and *beras barak* (red rice). For the festival of *Kuningan* (*kuning* = yellow) white rice is dyed yellow with turmeric. Rice is eaten in a variety of ways: either as *nasi jakau* (boiled rice), but preferably as *nasi kukus* (*kukus* = steamed) or as *nasi goreng* (*goreng* = fried). The rice is freshly prepared every day and kept in a pot in the kitchen. Whenever one of the family gets hungry, they just go and take some. Consequently, rice is mostly eaten cold.

Rice that has been cooked slowly in little parcels made of banana-leaves, is called *ketipat*. It makes a good midday meal for the men to take with them to the fields, or the children to school.

You can have a solid breakfast of *nasi goreng* or *mie goreng* (*mie/bakmi*e = noodles), mixed with egg, meat or seafood, as well as tomatoes, gherkins and of course spices and chili. However, the main component of a meal is always rice or noodles.

Other typical Indonesian dishes include: *Nasi campur* (*campur* = mixed), steamed rice with vegetables, meat, pickles and *krupuk*, which are crisps made from fish-flakes or shrimp paste; *cap cai*, a vegetable dish similar to the Chinese chop suey; *soto*, a soup to which thickened coconut-milk (*santen*) is added; *sop*, a meat and vegetable stew; *gado-gado*, a vegetable salad with peanut sauce; and, of course, *sate*, a mini-kebab made from chicken (*ayam*) beef, lamb, pork (only in the non-Moslem regions) or fish; especially delicious is the *sate Bali*, made from ground pork, spices and coconut; *tahu* is a soya-bean pudding and *tempeh* a kind of cake made from fermented soya-beans. Most dishes are automatically served with *nasi putih* (white rice). A typical Balinese dish is *babi* or *be guling*, a sucking-pig, and *betutu bebek*, a stuffed duck which is wrapped in banana-leaves and cooked slowly for several hours. What gives traditional Balinese food its special quality is the way it is cooked over a wood fire in a simple brick fire-place.

When it comes to vegetables, the western visitor will find much that is familiar, such as different kinds of cabbage, aubergine, tomato, cucumber and gherkin, but also unfamiliar vegetables such as *kangkung*, a kind of water-spinach, sweet potato, bread-fruit (*timbal*), the flower and stalk of the banana-plant, *nangka* or jackfruit and papaya, both of which can also be eaten uncooked, as fruit.

In the preparation of all kinds of food, a good deal of spice is used. So you will see almost every known kind of spice in the markets of Bali and Lombok. A hot, spicy sauce, used in many dishes, is called *sambal.* The basic mixture is made up of shallots (*bawang*), garlic (*bawang putih/kesuna*) ginger (*jahe*), cumin (*kunyit*), galanga-root (*cekuh/isen*), shrimppaste (*trasi/ sera*), cardamom (*kepulaga*) and chili (*tabia*). Other ingredients are pepper (*merica/mica*), lemon-grass (*serai/ sereh*), tamarind (*asam/celagi*), salt (*garam/uyah*), nutmeg (*pala*), palmsugar (*gula merah/gula barak*), coriander (*ketumber/ketumbah*), cinnamon (*kayu manis*), cloves (*cenkeh*), monosodium glutamate (MSG/*pitsin*) and lime (*lemo*).

The Balinese also have some delicious desserts to offer: bananas can be baked, fried or deep-fried in batter. Other delicious sweets are made from rice. *Lontong* is a sticky rice, tasting a little like semolina, and boiled in plantain or bananaleaves. Another pudding made from rice is *ketan*. It is cooked in coconut-milk and syrup. *Bubur santen* is a sort of rice porridge cooked in palm-sugar and coconut-milk. Something you can have either as a dessert or for breakfast is black rice with coconut-milk. This delicious dish is even better if a fruit salad is served with it. Things to nibble between meals include coconut or peanut biscuits, nuts, rice-cakes, banana-flakes, potato crisps and a lot more. Ice-cream, too, comes in many varieties, usually made with fesh fruit, such as durian ice-cream. Something very unusual, which is virtually unknown in the western hemisphere, is *rujak*. This is fresh fruit covered in a piquant sauce made from palm-sugar, chili and *sera* (shrimp-paste).

The choice of fruit is enormous. In addition to familiar fruit such as grapes (*anggur*), pineapple (*nenas*), citrus-fruit (*jeruk*) and bananas (*pisang/biu*), there are many which are little-known or completely unknown in the west. Even bananas come in a greater variety of shapes and sizes than one would ever guess from the standardized product one sees in supermarkets. And each one has a particular name. The *biu batu* is one which always takes Europeans by surprise, because it has a number of kernels or stones; the word *batu* means "stone." The *biu udang* (shrimp-banana) is red, the *biu susu* (milk-banana) is only as large as a finger and is especially delicious. The *biu kate* is of normal size but grows on a dwarf plant. The *biu gadang* remains green, even when ripe, the *biu mas* is a deep golden color and the *biu raja* is the variety which most closely resembles the product exported to Europe from the Americas. A particular favorite dish is fried bananas (*gogodoh biu*), but the fruit are also processed into chips or flour. The banana plant is so versatile that even the stalk is eaten, and the leaves are used as

plates or wrapping-paper. Other delicious fruit include the mango-plum, the guava (*jambu biji*), the cape-gooseberry or starfruit (*belimbing*), the pomegranate (*delima*) the custard-apple (*jambu air*), the water-melon (*semangka air),* the papaya, the mangosteen (*manggis*) and the mango (*mangga*). The sapodillo (*sawo*) looks like a small potato but tastes like a ripe pear. The *rambutan* (from *rambut,* meaning "hair") is small and round and covered in long, thick hair. The *sirsak* is a spiny fruit from which a refreshing drink, like lemonade, is made, The *salak* is a pear-shaped fruit with firm flesh, which tastes rather like a mixture of pear and gooseberry. It has a beautiful glowing brown skin which feels like snakeskin. For this reason it is sometimes also called snakefruit.

The jackfruit (*nangka*) is a large spiny fruit weighing several pounds, and made up of numerous small segments which are sold separately. The durian is a fruit about which opinions differ sharply. It is similar to the jackfruit but its spines (in Indonesian: *duri*) are sharper, and it does not grow so large. It is the only fruit eaten by tigers. Its flesh has a creamy consistency. It is divided into many segments and has twelve kernels. These are the size of chestnuts, and like chestnuts they can be roasted and eaten. They give off a smell which westerners find rather repulsive, especially when the fruit has been lying around for a while. The taste is even harder to describe: a mixture of strawberry, gooseberry, pear and camembert cheese! Even if you cannot get used to the taste of the fruit on its own, you should nevertheless sample the durian ice-cream in the *Garden House and Ice Creme Palace* in Mataram, on Lombok. You should always avoid combining the durian with alcohol, as this can lead to serious illness.

Then, of course, there is the coconut (*kelapa/nyuh*) which, like rice, has a different name for every stage of its growth.

Right: Coconuts are split open to dry out in the sun.

There are something like 300 named species of the family *Cocos nucifera*. Twelve kinds can be found on Bali, which are differentiated by the color of the nut and the size of the tree.

The young "baby" coconuts are called *bungsil*. When they are a little older, but still not edible they are *bungkak*. The young mature nut is called *kuwud*. This is the best stage to drink the coconut fluid (*yeh kuwud*). When it is fully ripe, which is the condition in which they are sold in Europe, their name is *nyuh*. Now you can scrape out the flesh and make coconut-milk, oil or copra. However in Bali, the flesh of the fully ripened nut is considered to be of a lower quality than the *kuwud,* which is softer. The liquid in a young nut is also sweeter and richer. At this stage, the outer skin is still green. When it has become yellow, the Balinese say it is past its best.

The palm-trees standing close to habitation are harvested regularly, to prevent the nuts simply dropping down and thus constituting a danger to life and property.

For the same reason, the Balinese are careful not to park their cars under a coconut palm overnight. From these palms several different drinks can be obtained. As well as the thirst-quenching *yeh kuwud*, there are two alcoholic drinks: *tuak* and *arak*. *Tuak* is a beer made from the juice of the palm flower. It is frothy and mild. In the morning, immediately after being tapped, it is still very sweet, and is called *manis*, but by the evening and for the next three days, it makes a good strong beer (*tuak wayah*). The British who settled elsewhere in South-East Asia called it "Toddy," but this name is not known in Bali. *Arak* is distilled from *tuak* and has a powerful, pungent taste. This palm liquor is also used in traditional medicine. Many Balinese avoid it altogether, while others add spices to it, to make a drink called *mabasa*.

A third alcoholic drink found in Bali is not made from the palm, but is a sweet rice wine called *brem*. However, the best way to quench your thirst is with the locally brewed beer called *bir bintang*.

BALINESE DANCES

It is important for the typical Balinese village to have not only a virtuoso gamelan orchestra but also a good dance group. Like the gamelan musicians the dancers are, as a rule, amateurs. They learn to perform a number of specific dances such as the *legong*, *arja* or *pendet*, rather than dancing in general. Those dancers who have a particular talent for a certain dance are selected by a committee of experts. As much attention is paid to their health, the symmetry of their limbs and their facial characteristics as to their potential skill in a given type of dance. This means that girls are selected for the *legong* dance when they are as young as five, and their career is already over by the time they reach puberty. If there are two village girls who look very much alike, they are both certain to be chosen.

Above: The Barong is the good spirit of the village. Right: In Peliatan some new dance-steps are being tried out.

The dances are learnt purely by imitation, not in a mirror, as they would be in a ballet-school. The teacher stands behind the pupil and helps by putting the wrist in the right position, for example, correcting the way a hand is held, or pushing the knee one way or the other. Along the way the pupil gets a feeling for the movements and after a while can perform them unaided. At the same time as learning the basic steps, simple sequences and general arm movements, the young dancers develop the flexibility of each individual muscle, through regular exercises, so that they become almost "rubber-jointed."

Balinese dancing, like most dancing of South-east Asia, is somewhat static. Leg- and footwork plays a secondary role compared to gesture and mime. Unlike classical European ballet, the movements of Balinese dance are not designed to free the dancer from the force of gravity. This earthbound quality is epitomized in the *Kebyar Duduk*, a sedentary dance in which the legs are not used at all.

However, it is true that there are some dances, for example the *Baris*, in which it is important, as in classical ballet, to extend the line of the body with bent legs and knees pointed outwards. Whereas in Javanese dancing all emotions are expressed through carefully controlled gestures of the arm and hand, while the face remains immobile, in Balinese dance every movement of indiviual parts of the body "speaks" to the audience. The eyes and eyebrows are continually in motion, from side to side, and up and down, and although the face remains impersonal, the entire body is alive, expressing the whole gamut of emotions. Sudden changes of direction, and precise, jerky steps create a tension which is lacking in Javanese dance. The Javanese, on the other hand, would claim that the Balinese are too exuberant and lack refinement.

The dance is intended to be entertaining for performers and spectators alike, as well as for the gods, while it frightens off evil spirits. The dancer appears literally to glide into another world, and into a state of consciousness which knows no fatigue and which sometimes leads to a trance.

It is possible to divide Balinese dances into three broad categories: 1. dances of animistic and ancient Indonesian origin, chiefly group dances and sacred cult dances, often of an exorcising nature (*tari wali*); 2. dances of Hindu origin, which are also called sacrificial dances (*tari bebali*) and usually tell stories from the Hindu epics, and 3. display dances (*tari balih-balihan*), which are not only performed in temple precincts and royal courts, but also on stage in front of a paying audience.

Arja (balih-balihan)

In this comic folk-opera the performers speak as well as sing. As in the *wayang kulit* shadow-puppet plays, the speeches of the leading players are trans-

lated into common language by clowns. The plots are drawn from Chinese love-stories as well as from the *Mahabharata* (see p. 224) and the *Panji* cycle. The latter is a series of adventure tales about Panji Raden of Koriban, an extensive collection from the heyday of the Javanese Majapahit dynasty. Panji had rejected the hand of the beautiful Rangkesari without even seeing her, but when they did finally meet, he was consumed with love for her. But the wind carried her off to a distant kingdom. Setting out in search of her, Panji encounters many adventures, until they are finally reunited.

Baris (wali)

The *Baris* is a war-dance from the pre-Hindu period, when the rulers of Bali were continually feuding with each other. It used to be danced as a way of asking the gods for their help and their blessing in the forthcoming battle. The word *baris* literally means "line" or "row;" it originally meant the battle-line of the warriors, and later came to refer to the warriors themselves.

This very masculine dance takes many different forms, whose names derive from the weapons that are carried. Only the *Baris Kekupa*, or Butterfly *Baris*, is danced by young girls. The stage represents the scene of warlike deeds. At first the dancer's movements are hesitant, cautious, as if entering unknown territory. Then he stretches himself up to his full height, and stands motionless, only his arms trembling with pent-up strength. Then without warning he spins round on one leg, with audacity and arrogance glinting in his eyes.

The *Baris*-dancer must have the ability to conjure up a tremendous range of facial expressions: a look of wonderment when faced by an invisible world of magic, astonishment and rage at his enemies, as well as pleasure, tenderness and love. The *Baris* lies at the foundation of all other male dances, and every prince once had to know how to dance it. The dance can be performed by a group as well as by a solo dancer. The stylized imitations of the warrior in battle are followed by the gamelan orchestra, and not the other way around.

Barong (wali)

The *Barong* or *Kris* dance portrays the eternal struggle between Good and Evil; whose forces must in the end be balanced. The power of Good resides in the Barong, a fabled creature with shaggy fur, an elaborately carved mask and a red beard, in which all his strength is concentrated. This protector of mankind is danced by two men hidden under a fur pelt. His opponent is the witch Rangda, who embodies the destructive principle of the death-goddess Durga. She draws

Right: The magic power of the Barong protects the kris-dancers from injury in their trance-state.

her might from black magic and rules over the powers of darkness.

Her entrance through the gates of the temple is first announced by the ghostly appearance of her hands with their excessively long fingernails. The next things to become visible are the long tongue of flame hanging out and the entrails hanging round her neck. The two figures encounter one another and fight. When the Barong looks like being defeated, the *kris* dancers, who have already put themselves into a trance, come to his assistance.

By means of a magic spell Rangda manages to make them turn their swords on themselves. The Barong is unable to lift the curse, and only becomes weaker. The men dancing in a trance really do thrust their *krisses* against their chests, but without actually getting wounded. In order to waken them from their trance, the priest sprinkles them with holy water, in which the Barong has previously dipped his beard. The drama ends with a sacrifice to the evil spirits.

Gambuh (bebali)

The *Gambuh* is one of Bali's oldest dances, and is known as "the mother of all Balinese dances." The movements are slow and stylized. The performers sing in Kawi, the language of medieval Java. The clowns who, in other types of dance-drama, act as interpreters, scarcely appear here, which means that the choreography must be watched carefully. Mysterious-sounding melodies are played on three-foot-long flutes and two-stringed violins. Except in Batuan, Gambuh groups are hadly to be found anywhere.

Jauk (bebali)

The *Jauk* is a masked dance, whose theme once again is the conflict of good and evil demons. The good *jauks* wear white masks, the evil ones, brown; they

all have goggle-eyes and long, shaggy hair. Out of the confrontation of the two groups of demons has developed a solo dance, which is very similar to the *Baris* solo. The musicians have to take their lead from the dancer's movements, which are not linked to any particular story-line, but are, for the most part, freely improvised.

Joged (balih-balihan)

The *Joged* has many variants, but the common factor in all of them is the participation of the audience. A female dancer, or several of them in turn, begin to perform steps from the Legong. After a short while they start making eyes at a particular young man in the audience and lure him out to dance with them. Since many Balinese have mastered the basic dance-steps, this usually produces an artistically creditable ensemble performance. If the chosen male happens to be a tourist, the locals are hugely amused by his grotesque movements.

Kebyar (balih-balihan)

The Kebyar Legong is a relatively modern invention, having been first danced in 1914. It is always performed by two girls. In this case the emphasis is more on the music than on their interpretation. This new approach to dance spread like lightning across the island and indeed the word *kebyar* means "lightning." The dance combines the tender, delicate movement of *Legong* with the heroic posing of the *Baris*.

In the 1920s, one name came to the fore, which today is inseparably linked with the *Kebyar*: I Ketut Marya (Mario). He developed the *Kebyar Duduk* (*duduk* means "sitting"), in which the dancer squats on the floor for most of the time, with his legs crossed and a fan in his hand, moving his arms, hands and backside in imitation of the music. To achieve perfection in this dance, the performer learns to play all the instruments, and absorbs the acoustic characteristics of each one. He can express their different

215

sounds and moods with the supple movements of his body and the expressiveness of his mime and eye-movements. It is almost as if he himself becomes a sensitive musical instrument In the *Kebyar Trompong* or *Trompong Duduk* the dance is complemented by the playing of a *trompong*, an instrument with a long row of horizontal gongs. Mario was an exceptionally fine exponent of this form of the dance, coaxing sounds from the instrument with theatrical, expressive movements. His balletic gestures with the sticks reinforced the musicality of the performance.

Sanghyang (wali)

Sanghyang means something like "worthy of adoration," and relates to the divine spirit which for a while comes down to earth and expresses itself through the medium of trance. The *San-*

Above: The dances of Bali are far more static than classical European ballet.

ghyang Dedari is always danced by a virgin, and the *Sanghyang Jaran* by a young man or a priest. In the latter version the dancer "rides" on a hobby-horse around and though a bed of burning coconut shells. All *Sanghyang* dances are intended to protect a village from the forces of darkness and are performed in times of general peril and hardship, in order to ward off disaster.

Kecak (balih-balihan)

The origins of the *Kecak* lie in the *Sanghyang* trance-dances, in which the young girls or boys are put into a trance by a choir repeating a syncopated chant that sounds like "chackachacka." It is performed in a manner which is virtually unchanged from the dance that was first developed by Walter Spies for the film *Island of Demons*. At least 50 men, wearing only a *poleng*, or black-and-white chequered sarong, sit in several rows around an oil lamp. With their "chacka-chacka" chant they create a carpet of sound which is meant to resemble that of a gamelan band; in doing so they weave as many as seven different rythms in and out of each other. They only move the upper half of their bodies, rocking back and forth, stretching up their arms and hands and letting them drop again. Because there are so many of them, the men's movements give the effect of a heaving sea with spray from a wave suddenly breaking. Against this background a story from the *Ramayana* (see p. 223) is acted out. It ends with the freeing of Sita from the clutches of the wicked Ravana with the help of the beloved Hanuman and his troop of monkeys. Half the circle of male singers represents the army of monkeys and the other half Ravana's army, or sometimes the serpent, which the arrow aimed at Rama turns into. Earlier, the flight of Ravana, as he carries Sita off to his kingdom in Sri Lanka, is accompanied by a sharp hissing from the choir.

Legong (bebali)

It is said that the *Legong* is the most charming of all Bali's dances. At all events the best known is the *Legong Kraton*, which originally might only be danced by princesses. Today it is performed by three girls: two of them (also called *Legong*) represent members of a royal house, while the third, the *Condong*, plays the part of a servant-girl. It is she who begins the piece with a ten-minute introductory dance. At the end of her solo her eyes light on two fans and she picks them up. Then she turns to the two *Legong* who have appeared on the stage and hands each of them a fan.

The most frequently performed story concerns Princess Rangkesari, who wanders into the forest, where she is found and carried off by King Lasem. Rangkesari rejects the king's advances by hitting him with her fan. When her brother, the Prince of Daha, learns of her imprison-

ment, he threatens war if she is not released. The king decides on war. On his way to the battle he is warned of his impending defeat by a crow, played by the *Condong* in gold wings. The king nonetheless continues on to the battlefield, and the dance ends with his death.

The *Legong* present the story in pantomime, slipping from role into another. Sometimes they act as a double image of one person, which you can recognize by the absolute synchronization of their movements. Then they separate again and play the parts of different people. Swathed in golden cloaks and wearing crowns of chased gold and frangipani flowers, the young dancing-girls make an extremely attractive picture.

Pendet (bebali)

This dance was originally used in the offering of sacrificial gifts to the gods, and could be danced by anyone, without special training. Today the *Pendet* is performed by trained girl dancers as a dance of welcome at the beginning of a *Legong* performance, after which they scatter handfuls of flowers into the audience.

Topeng (bebali)

Topeng, whose name means "pressed against the face," is a masked dance. All the characters wear masks, but the servants and clowns leave the lower half of their face uncovered, so that they are able to speak. There are usually three or four dancers, who, with the aid of different masks, each play a number of roles: the comic or the serious man, the young man or the old. There are even long-nosed tourists and Dutch colonial types. The *Topeng Tua* is particularly popular; this is a solo performance, which shows the typical behavior and appearance of an old man. A variant of this represents an old soldier in retirement, touchingly trying to recapture his lost youth.

217

THE MUSIC AND DANCE OF LOMBOK

Within the music and performing arts of Lombok, which are still, unlike the west, deeply rooted in religious ceremony, a development is taking place which can best be described as a clash of cultures. Three different forces are at work on the mature and overlapping traditions of music and dance: Islamic orthodoxy, modern popular music and the Indonesian government.

The musical elements of Lombok's cultural heritage are a mixture of indigenous Sasak ritual, Javanese and Balinese cultural influences and religious ideals drawn from Islam. Within this multi-layered mixture the rather orthodox Islamic religious teachers do not like anything which is reminiscent of the "heathen" tendencies of the Wetu-Telu

Above: During a comic dance interlude between stick-fights, a sarong is presented to the winner.

devotees and other Sasak traditionalists. Thus the Imams strongly disapprove, for instance, of unambiguous flirtation-dances such as the *Gandrung*, because they present a threat to the decorous separation of men and women.

Foreign observers may be surprised at the apparently trivial details which come in for criticism by the religious establishment. Thus, orthodox Moslems disapprove of the instrumentation of the traditional gamelan music, because the bronze instruments, often called "the voices of the ancestors," date back to animistic times. This has already led to many gamelan orchestras in east Lombok either breaking up or changing over to iron metallophones, or even going back to "Islamic" *rebana* drums. But Balinese music has remained untouched by these influences.

The most recent and probably the most successful opposition to the old customs and dances is the music that blares out from the modern-day audio-visual media. As in every part of the world, young people are captivated by the technical perfection of pop music hits and lose interest in tradititonal music. The only force which resists this trend, and works to preserve the old traditions – often using the same media to do so – is the Indonesian government. In the cultural sphere at least, it holds firm to its motto of "Unity through Diversity," and recognizes the attraction which these ancient and exotic cultural forms hold for foreign visitors, and their importance in the tourist economy. However, the battle is not yet won.

Quite a number of dances have been preserved, and these differ considerably from those of Bali. As you travel across the island, you are most likely to come across procession-dances. In the region round Lingsar the rather martial-looking *Batek Baris* is still performed. Dancers dressed in old Dutch uniforms and armed with wooden rifles, drill in rank and file to the harsh commands of an angry or at any rate very serious-looking commanding officer. They lead a procession which includes *Telek* dancing-girls and the rest of the village. Their route takes them from the village to a sacred spring. In the context of village festivals, female Telek dancers often play male roles. In the gamelan orchestra that accompanies them, you will notice an instrument that is unique to Lombok: called a *preret,* it is a woodwind instrument that rather resembles an oboe.

In central Lombok, the festivals marking the significant stages of life are accompanied by a *Gamelan Tawa-Tawa.* This music is notable for the sound of cymbals fixed to lances, and provides the perfect background for processions and parades. Also attached to the lances are tassels which dance in time to the music. In the same region it is common to see a procession with a Barong monster. In the monster's "body" kettle-gongs are beaten. This type of orchestra, called a *Gamelan Barong Tengkok,* usually accompanies a wedding procession, in which the happy couple are carried around on wooden horses.

From an earlier age a whole series of war-dances can be traced. In one of these, called *Tari Oncer,* and which can be seen in eastern and central Lombok, two dancers approach each other with drum-like instruments and dance around each other in dramatic poses. This symbolic contest is not based on any particular story. The *Paresean,* or stick-fight, though thinly disguised as a dance, can get pretty violent, and blood quite often flows.

For romance one turns to the *Gandrung.* Here a girl dances in the middle of a circle and sings a song full of longing and melancholy. After she has danced alone for a while, she gives one of the men a little slap with her fan and challenges him to dance with her. He then gives her a small sum of money and follows her movements in an improvised dance which covers a whole range of expression from the eccentric, through clumsy comedy to suggestive eroticism. This delightful performance nearly always gets a storm of applause from the audience.

There are also dance performances in a theater which last a whole evening. Like the *Arja* opera in Bali, they tend to be basd on the *Panji* cycle of stories. A specifically Moslem achievement in this field is the *Kemidi Rudat.* (The word *kemidi* is derived from the English "comedy"). This is based on the Arabian *Tales of a Thousand and One Nights.* In Bayan, in northern Lombok, you will be struck by the unusual, old Turkish costumes worn by the actors. It appears that this custom was started by an islander returning from a pilgrimage to Mecca at the beginning of this century. There he was so impressed by the Ottoman *Kaaba* hats as well as the fezzes and turbans, that he brought some back with him and introduced them to Lombok.

BALINESE GAMELAN

In the days of the Majapahit empire, Bali was entirely dedicated to the courtly art of the Javanese gamelan. This music was slow, restrained and melancholy. *Gamelan* is an ancient Javanese word for an orchestra, and is used all over Indonesia today. However, the Balinese call their orchestras *Gongs*, as for instance in *Gong Gede*, the "Great Orchestra" of the rajas which dominated the Balinese musical scene until well into the 20th century. In the colonial period, the art of the courts changed. The splendor of the princely houses faded in the 1930s, and with it the great gamelans disappeared.

The instruments were either mothballed, or sold to village communities and their music clubs. The latter often had the bronze instruments melted down and new ones made, which had greater appeal to

Above: The big gong signals the end of the piece. Right: Every village worthy of the name, has its own gamelan orchestra.

the popular audience. Thus the change to popular gamelan-music was complete: the style became louder, faster and more cheerful, and was played with greater passion. Since then, there has been continuous experimentation, encouraged by state support of festivals. In 1938, a competition between five regions was won by a gamelan from Peliatan, led by A.A. Gede Mandera, and playing music which "tenderly caressed the skin like the rays of the sun," as Colin McPhee described it in his book *A House in Bali.*

Often a gamelan will consist of two sets of instruments, one tuned to the 5-note scale (*slendro*) and the other to the 7-note scale (*pelog*). But even with the 7-note scale the five notes of the *slendro* system are especially important and are more frequently played. They correspond roughly to the notes C, D, F, G and A in the European diatonic scale. The individual instruments of a gamelan are tuned with each other at the time they are made. The one exception is the *rebab*, a stringed instrument which is thought to be the forerunner of our violin. Different gamelans are tuned to their own particular pitch and therefore cannot play together. In an orchestra most of the instruments perform in pairs. Each pair is tuned in such a way as to produce a slight dissonance. And even single instruments, which have a range of more than one "octave" are not conventionally tuned, but the high notes are slightly sharper than the corresponding low notes. This produces a multi-layered and more attractive sound. A great range and depth of sound is provided by the indiviual drums, gongs and cymbals; and instruments with a high-pitched sound are struck more frequently than the low-pitched ones.

Balinese music is characterized by sudden changes, syncopations, unexpected bursts of rapid and accurate playing, crescendos and diminuendos, from a sound like a hurricane to a barely audible murmur, and by highly elaborate coun-

terpoint based on simple melodies. The straight 4/4 beat which they normally use can quickly be split in to a multiple rhythm. The mode of playing follows the principle of the *kotekan*, to complementary and interweaving parts: *sansih* and *polos*. They are played as fast as possible by two musicians, who together produce the melodic configuration. In this way a tempo is achieved which is twice as fast as either musician would be capable of playing on his own.

Basically, the instruments can be divided into four groups: one plays the melody, a second decorates this melody, a third accentuates the composition, and the fourth leads the rest of the orchestra, controlling tempo and dynamics.

The instrumentation consists mainly of metallophones, xylophones and drums. The keys of the metallophone generate a sound not only because they are made of metal, but because of the bamboo pipes placed below them, which act as resonators. The whole thing is encased in wood, which is elaborately carved and painted. They are repainted for big occasions; red and gold are considered particularly festive colors.

The larger instruments, with just five notes, are the *jublag* and the *jegog,* which are both played rather slowly. The smaller *jublag* plays the basic melody, while the larger *jegog* amplifies the important notes of the *pokok*, and punctuates longer phrases.

The smaller instruments of the second group are the *gangsas,* which decorate the basic melody. They have two 5-tone scales, and exist in various different sizes. The smaller they are, the faster they are played. The player wields the mallet with his right hand, and the left hand, a fraction of a second later, damps down the sound, while the right hand is already striking the next note. The *riyong* is a long wooden frame, holding a a row of horizontal gongs. Four people sit behind it to play it. The gongs have a protruding knob in the center, which is where the player most often hits them. By touching the edge they can obtain other effects.

The *trompong* is similar to the *riyong*, and paraphrases the melody in the same way, but it is played by only one instrumentalist. It is the only instrument on which a solo is sometimes played, or a melody improvised.

In the third group there are a series of hanging gongs, none smaller than 2 feet (75 cm) in diameter. The fullest tone comes from the largest gong, which is struck at the beginning and end of each piece of music. The other gongs mark accents and divisions in the composition as a whole. Individual smaller, horizontal gongs (*kempli*) are necessary to hold the whole piece together and maintain a steady tempo.

However, the most important instrument is the drum. Again, there are two of these, one of which plays the lead part. The *kendang* is a drum with skins on both ends, both of which are played. Different sounds can be produced, depending on whether the player uses the palm of his hand, the knuckles or the fingertips, whether he muffles the sound or not, and whether he hits the middle or the edge of the drum. Sometimes the drummer also uses a drumstick. A player does not graduate to the drum until he has mastered all the other instruments. He holds the whole performance together and introduces changes of tempo or pauses. He uses his head and movements of his hand to communicate with the other musicians and the dancers, who have to take their cue from the drummer for the basic elements of the melody and any accentuations of it. If the ensemble works well, a whole elaborate polyphony can be built up, without confusing the dancers.

The musicians start at a very early age – sometimes as young as four; and are almost exclusively male, though Ubud boasts a fine all-woman gamelan. The complexity of this music has fascinated many western composers, but the Balinese find our music much too simple.

Above: The Kendang sets the rhythm and gives the cue for changes of tempo.

WAYANG KULIT

Wayang kulit is the shadow-play of colorful leather puppets, which are decoratively cut and perforated, so as to create memorable silhouettes. The puppet-master is the *dalang*, whose voice and agile fingers endow them with souls and personalities. He needs a white linen screen (*kelir*), a coconut-oil lamp (*damar*) which gives off a flickering light, musicians and assistants. The bulk of the audience sits in front of the screen, but a few people go round the other side to admire the color and movement of the puppets and to follow the activities of the *dalang* and the musicians with rapt attention. The orchestra consists of two large and to small *gender*, or metallophones, whose keys, like those of the *gangsa,* are suspended over bamboo resonators, but which are played with two mallets and are damped almost instantaneously. The musicians pay very close attention to the movements of the *dalang* with his puppets, so that they can illustrate the action musically, underline certain points and, when there is a fight, give an acoustic counterpart to every blow.

At the beginning of the performance the *dalang* knocks on a big wooden chest (*kropak*) with a wooden or horn clapper, held between the toes of his right foot. This is to bring the puppets, who are in the chest, to life. He then selects from his large supply anything from 30 to 60 puppets, which, with the help of his assistants, he places in the soft banana-stem (*gedebong*) along the bottom edge of the screen. The figures are of two principal types, easily distinguishable from each other: *alus* and *kasar*. The first group are sensitive and even-tempered, the second vulgar and irascible. The first are considered good, the second, bad. The good protagonists come in from the right side of the screen, the bad from the left. The more important a character's role is in the play, the closer he stands to the *kayonan*, or Tree of Life, which is represented by a large, finely etched leaf. The *kayonan* is brought on at the beginning and end of every performance, and in every important scene. From time to time it also serves to represent the forces of nature, such as fire, wind and water. On these occasions the *kayonan* is flapped about violently, and moved closer to or further from the screen, so that its sharply defined contours alternate with blurred shadows. An excited wagging of the figures creates a mysterious, disturbing mood. In addition there are the courtiers (*panasar*), two loyal servants and two ne'er-do-wells, who have fat stomachs and jaws which move, so that you can actually see them speaking. They have the task of translating the speeches of the king's sons and the gods into ordinary Balinese, for these characters only express themselves in Kawi, the ancient, Sanskrit-based language of the theater, of poetry and religion. They use 47 different couplets from the *Ramayana* and the *Mahabharata.* Those two Hindu epics are the main source of moral guidance, which ensures that in the struggle between Good and Evil, the latters does not prevail.

Probably the best-loved theme, and one which is presented in many different dramatic forms, is the epic of *Ramayana.* It is set in the kingdom of Kosala, near the Himalayas, which is ruled by King Dasarata. When he expresses his intention of abdicating in favor of his son Rama, his second wife Kekayai, who is the mother of Barata, insists that Dasarata keep his promise of granting her two wishes. She demands that her son Barata be crowned king, and that Rama be exiled for 14 years. Rama respects his father's promise and, with his wife Sita and favorite brother Laksmana, he withdraws to the solitude of the forest. After a time, the demon-king Ravana notices the beautiful Sita and vows to have her. He sends his minister disguised as a golden hind, to lure Rama and Laksmana deeper into the

forest, leaving Sita alone. Rawana then comes to her, and carries her off.

As they fly high through the air towards Ravana's kingdom in Sri Lanka, the brave bird Jatayu attempts to rescue Sita, but in the ensuing struggle he is mortally wounded, and only just succeeds in getting back to tell Rama of the encounter. On their journey to Ravana's domain, the brothers meet the monkey-king Sugriva. He promises to help them liberate Sita if they in turn agree to support him in winning back his rightful position as monarch in the Realm of the Apes. After this is accomplished, Sugriva sends his warlord, Hanuman, with his troops of monkeys, to help Rama. Hanuman personally brings news to Sita of her impending rescue, then orders his troops to build a causeway from the southern tip of India across to Sri Lanka, so that Rama and his allies can reach the island. After a

Above: The Dalang at work. Right: The skill of the Dalang breathes life and personality into the shadow-puppets.

terrible battle in which Ravana is fatally wounded by one of Rama's arrows, Rama and Sita are finally united again. Upon their return to Kosala with Laksmana, Barata gladly hands over the reins of monarchy to Rama, since in spite of his mother's ambitious plans for him, Barata had only been exercising power provisionally in Rama's absence.

In the second epic, the *Mahabharata,* which also originates from India, the story concerns a feud between two families of the Bharata people, who both claim the right to rule the kingdom of Hastinapura. The occupant of the throne, Dhritarashtra, fathers a hundred sons, the Kauravas. His brother Pandu is granted five sons of divine descent, the Pandavas: Yudhistira, the eldest, is the son of Yama, the god of death; Bhima is the son of the wind-god Vayu; Arjuna is descended from Indra, king of the gods, and then there are the twin brothers Sahdeva and Nakula. Pandu acts as regent, ruling the kingdom on behalf of his brother Dhritarashtra, who is blind. Upon his death,

Pandu's eldest son, Yudhistira, is to rule in his place, but the Kaurava brothers are not at all happy about this arrangement. They plot against the five Pandavas and force them to flee with their mother, Kunti, and to wander through the country living as beggars. On their way they learn from a Brahman that the Princess Draupadi is to be allowed to take a husband of her own choosing. The rival suitors hold an archery contest and Arjuna, who is an incomparable bowman, is the winner, thus gaining the hand of Draupadi in marriage. Returning home, he tells his mother of his good fortune. However, she commands her sons together to seek Draupadi's favours. In this way, she becomes the consort of all five Pandava brothers.

After a temporary truce in their quarrel, the Kauravas enlist the help of Prince Sukani, who is an accomplished cheat, and lure Yudhistira into gambling away not only his whole kingdom, but also himself, his brothers and Princess Draupadi, in a game played with loaded dice.

Thus were the Pandavas sent into exile for twelve years and were then obliged to live another year unrecognised among their own people. At the end of this time, the Pandavas return with the intention of reclaiming their rights to the kingdom. However, this claim is rejected by the Kauravas. Thereupon the battle of Kurukshetra breaks out, and for eighteen whole days the sky is darkened by the arrows of the opposing sides.

During their exile, the Pandavas had gained the friendship of Krishna, whose sister Subhadra had married Arjuna. Krishna does not wish to take an active part in the battle, but acts as Arjuna's charioteer. When Arjuna refuses to wield his weapons in this murderous fraternal war, Krishna reminds him of his duty as a warrior, and at the same time extols the immortality of the soul. This passage of the epic, called the *Bhagavadgita*, is held to be India's most important didactic poem. The Pandavas are victorious, but their triumph is overshadowed by grief, since Arjuna and Bhima lose their sons.

ART AND CRAFTSMANSHIP

Until the 1930s all creative activity in Bali, which could in any way be described as art, was of a sacred character. Virtually every artistic or handcraft skill was put to the service of decorating or beautifying the temples or adorning religious festivals. The fact of being an artist did not, however, release an individual from his normal social and economic obligations. Indeed, no distinction was made between ordinary manual work on the one hand, and the most elevated form of art on the other. The decorative construction of a tower of gifts on the head, the delicate weaving of a rice-goddess from palm-leaves or the exuberant painting of a cremation-coffin – each had to be done with the same degree of care and imagination. Accordingly, there was no word in the Balinese language corresponding to our concept of "art."

Whenever a temple festival was due, everyone in the village would contribute to its success to the best of their ability. In doing so, anyone who displayed a particular talent was naturally held in high esteem, and would be invited on the next occasion to put their skill to the service of the gods. After a day's work in the rice-fields, people would gather to produce cult-objects and sacrificial offerings in the traditional manner. It is therefore not surprising that no individual artists are known to us by name, from the period prior to 1930; and in any case it was not the contribution of the individual which was at the heart of the creative process, but rather the ritual value of the object in question. Even today, though circumstances have changed, in many places people prefer to work in groups rather than as an individual artist, set apart from the community. Thus, for a long time, the purpose was not one of original and sub-jective creativity, but the successful imitation of favorite tried and tested motifs.

There is something else which distinguishes the creative activity of Bali: much of what is produced is never intended for posterity, but is only meant for one brief religious occasion. The woven palm-leaf is the very next day crushed and dried up, the flamboyantly decorated coffin goes up in flames in a few spectacular moments, and even the temple demons, carved in sandstone or tufa are usually eroded by wind and rain within a decade, and are reduced to toothless and faceless sad-sacks. The continuous requirement for temple decorations of all kinds demands the permanent involvement of everyone, and thus a large number of talents are kept active in whatever manual skills are required; this ensures that the flow of artistic tradition remains uninterrupted from generation to generation. With time, even the simplest object becomes refined, and this is how the impression has been gained that every Balinese is an artist.

However, this picture of a democratic, egalitarian art needs to be corrected, inasmuch as it did not only belong to village culture; there existed recognised centers of artistic activity. These were the feudal courts of the rajas. Here, there was a definite concentration of particularly gifted painters, sculptors or wood-carvers, most of whom belonged to the higher castes. Their work can be distinguished from that of village art, in that it often drew its inspiration directly from the ancient scriptures, and was therefore more academic than the primitive fantasies of the villagers. Their technique was also often much finer, though this does not mean that their content was any more sensitive or refined. One only has to think of the obscene ceiling-paintings of the Kerta Gosa in Klungkung.

It was this courtly art which suffered the most drastic eclipse with the Dutch conquest of 1908. Having been deprived

Right: The "Bumble-Bee Dance" of Anak Agung Gede Sobrat.

of their power, the rajas also lost their financial resources, so that their ability to promote the fine arts was severely limited or disappeared altogether.

The boom in painting

The revival in the 1930s can claim many originators. Firstly, the Dutch colonial administration made a great effort to preserve Balinese culture, on the one hand by funding the restoration of culturally important buildings, and on the other by trying, with considerable success, to shield the island from western tourists and Christian missionaries. Secondly, some of the influential aristocratic families of Bali, like the Sukawatis in Ubud, began once again to support artistic activity. From a European point of view, it is particularly interesting to note the impact of the wealthy, international, art-loving dropouts, who introduced their western ideas and techniques to the Balinese artists. In the first wave one should mention in particular the German painter

and musician, Walter Spies and the Dutch painter Rudolf Bonnet. Spies settled in Bali in 1927 and soon moved to Ubud, where, in a very short time, he became the much-visited and much-consulted interpreter of Balinese culture to the western world. It is, to a great extent, his image of Bali which has determined western perceptions of the island. Bonnet, who was equally fascinated by Bali, was concerned about the possible damage which might be done by outside influences. These two men, together with Cokorda Gede Agung Sukawati, were responsible for the founding of the *Pita Maha* school of painting, in which about 125 Balinese artists have worked. Among them was a personality who in many respects stands out from other native artists: Gusti Nyoman Lempad. Even before the arrival of Spies, he had already made a name for himself as a designer, builder and sculptor of temple gates, as a carver of *barong* masks and as a constructor and decorator of burial-towers. He now became famous the world over as a portrayer of the physical and spiritual world of his native island. He produced his last work shortly before his hundredth birthday, and died, laden with honors, in 1978 at the Methuselah-like age of 122.

A second influential art-school can be attributed to Arie Smit, another Dutchman, who stayed on in Bali after the Second World War. In the then rather impoverished town of Penestanan, Smit gathered around him a group of young people and let them paint according to their own inclinations and ideas. These *Young Artists* differ from the painters of the *Pita Maha* school principally in their choice of subjects. The peasant children painted from their solid experience of every day life in the country, things that affected their own lives, whereas the *Pita Maha* painters for the most part remained wedded to the the traditional themes and methods of portrayal – myths, epics etc.

With the rapid growth of tourism after 1965, the output of Bali's painters increased to unprecedented levels. As well as traditional styles of painting, such as were still practised in Kamasan, near Klungkung, you will now see every conceivable form of artistic expression. There also seems to be no limit to the reproduceability, in huge quantities, of similar examples of every style. Ubud has always been the center of this almost industrialised art production. But it is also possible here to get a very good general idea of Balinese art as a whole. Before touring round the innumerable artists' studios, it is a good idea to visit two museums: the Puri Lukisan Museum in the center of Ubud, and the Neka Museum in Campuan.

In both of these one gets a good overview of Balinese art and Bali's interpretation of western painting. Once you know what to look for, your studio ramble will be more valuable.

Right: Rough hands are often capable of shaping delicate objects.

The wood-carvers with the Art Deco touch

Just as in the field of painting there was a turning-point around the year 1930, so it was with the art of wood-carving. Up to that time, wood-carvers mainly produced tableau-like reliefs and religious figures, which were destined either for temples or the palaces of the rajas. In these princely residences it is still possible today to admire finely chiseled door-panels and supporting beams.

The story goes that the contemporary Balinese style of wood-sculpture can be traced back to a work which Walter Spies commissioned from a local carver. He asked the man to carve two figures from one fairly long piece of wood. But instead of two, he only carved one figure, with an exaggeratedly long body and thin limbs. The artist made the excuse that the soul of the piece of wood did not permit any other design. The figure appealed to Walter Spies straight away, not least because it reminded him of the Art Deco style, which at the time was much in vogue. It became the prototype of a new style of Balinese art. In Mas, Kemenuh and Sumampan near Batuan, good but expensive figures can be found.

Thanks to the thriving tourist economy, wood-carving began to blossom again. It started with carvings of banana-plants in light wood; then came anthropomorphic frogs and other kitsch creatures. No doubt these will be replaced by other big sellers in due course. Whole villages in the area between Ubud and Sebatu are kept busy mass-producing cutesy items of this kind.

A subject which was once shrouded in a certain shy secrecy, has recently found its way into the mass market: these are the grotesque masks, of which it used to be believed that anyone putting one over his face would lose himself a little, if not entirely, in the figure which the mask represented.

It is still the case that in special dances or dramas, only the *topeng* masks from the best carvers are used. These come from Mas or Singapadu.

Gold- and silversmiths

The traditional center of the gold- and silversmiths' art is still today found in Kamasan, south of Klungkung. It is from here that the priests order valuable ritual objects in precious metals for their temples. There has been no decline in the number of religious ceremonies, and it is for that reason that this branch of craftsmanship is still very much alive. Their main products are sacrificial bowls, betel-nut containers and adornments. The town of Celuk is where silver jewelry, in particular, is produced for the tourist market. If you want something made especially for you, head for the side-streets and take a drawing with you. For a small down-payment these masters of the jeweller's art will accept your commission and complete it promptly.

Shopping

Anyone wishing to get an overall impression of what other types of handicrafts are on the market, should visit the tourist centers of Kuta and Sanur, or make enquiries at the art centers in and around Denpasar. The market in Sukawati is a good place to make comparisons on quality and price.

Apart from textiles, the best buys are *wayang kulit* puppets (either cut from leather, or stuffed), waxed parasols, bags and baskets woven from rattan or palm-leaves (often imported from Lombok), wind-clappers (useful as bird-scarers in the garden), pottery jars from Ubung (near Denpasar) and terra-cotta figurines from Pejatan (Tabanan). You may also be interested in antiques, such as *krisses* or furniture. If you are thinking of buying anything made from bamboo, you should bear in mind that this material cannot tolerate the dryness you get in central-heated homes in temperate latitudes, and is very liable to split.

IKAT AND DOUBLE-IKAT

Looking at Balinese clothes and fabrics, the eye is delighted by their variety of color and the often sumptuous materials – you would never suppose that the Balinese consider them "impure." But it is true, and because of this, they even avoid walking under washing that is hanging out to dry. Indeed, the more conservative Balinese will never enter a two-storeyed house, because you never know what there might be upstairs.

In spite of this ritual impurity associated with clothes, the Balinese devote much time and imagination to the task of making them and adorning them, using a variety of traditional techniques. Three types of fabric are produced on the island. Each one has a particular significance in the social hierarchy.

Above: Threads are dyed by hand in the Nyantri technique. Right: Threads are untied and stretched on a frame before being steeped in the dye.

Firstly, there is the *songket*. It is a brocade material which is never woven to a greater width than 30 inches (75 cm) and is shot through with gold or silver threads. These threads are introduced in such a way as to make a contrasting pattern on the cloth. The motifs are usually flowers, birds or animals.

At one time, *songket* was only worn by Brahmans or the nobility. Nowadays it is worn by anyone who has a fairly high position in society, or for special ceremonies. One piece of the cloth can cost as much as several hundred thousand rupiahs.

Next comes the *kain prada*, a cotton fabric, on which a pattern is applied after weaving, with gold-leaf or gold paint. This is mainly worn for family ceremonies such as tooth-filing or weddings, as well as at dance performances.

If *batik* is considered the "national textile" of Indonesia as a whole, then the equivalent for Bali is *ikat*, or *endek*, as it is more commonly known on the island. The word *ikat* comes from the Malay lan-

guage and means something like "knotting" or "tying". In this process, the threads are dyed in bunches before weaving, so that a blurred pattern emerges. This can be done in one of three styles: a) the warp-*ikat,* in which only the warp-threads are dyed, while the weft remains uncolored; b) the weft-*ikat,* in which the process is reversed; and c) the double-*ikat,* in which both the warp and the weft are dyed before weaving. For those who need clarification, the warp is the lengthways thread, and the weft is woven across, over and under the warp.

In Bali, it is chiefly the weft-*ikat* that is produced. The weft-threads are stretched horizontally over a frame in precisely counted hanks and tied with strips of plastic in such a way that a pattern emerges. The hanks are dyed, washed and dried. If the material is to be multi-colored – some factories use as many as six dyes, others only one – plastic strips of various colors are used for tying, and are gradually cut away during the dyeing process. In Bali, and also in Lombok,

where the Balinese have introduced this technique, an additonal process is employed, called *nyantri* or *coletan* – a kind of crowning glory of *ikat.* It consists of applying additional colors by hand, using a brush-like instrument. The dried threads are wound on to specially marked spools, and used as weft-threads so that during the weaving a slightly fuzzy pattern once again emerges. The finer a pattern has to be, the more labour-intensive and expensive is the *ikat,* because fewer threads can be bunched together. On the other hand, the process can be simplified, by using a frame of half the usual width. The threads are turned in the middle and and stretched back double on themselves. In this way a mirror-image of the pattern is created.

Far more complicated and time-consuming, however, is the making of the double *ikat.* There are only a few places in Bali where it is done, and the material is called *geringsing,* "cloth of flame". The villages which make this *ikat* are Bali-Aga villages, and probably the most

famous of these is Tenganan, also known as *Tenganan Pegeringsingan*, after the fabrics that are woven there.

The complexity lies in the fact that that the previously dyed warp- and weft-threads must be woven together in such a way that a recognisable pattern emerges. For this reason the weavers will often restrict themselves to geometrical designs, which are easier to produce.

All over Bali, the *geringsing* has a ritual significance. It is used at ceremonies or to heal sickness. In Tenganan itself, fragments of Indian double-*ikat* are used for this purpose, since they are supposed to have the same magical powers as *geringsing*. But it is also worn as part of everyday clothing. The men wear it as a sarong, while the woman wrap it round their torso and bosom, when it is called an *anteng*.

In Bali, the *kamben sarung* is the name of the garment traditionally worn by men around their hips. The two ends are sewn together to make a sort of tube. What the women wear is not really a sarong at all but is a *kamben lembaran*, known as a *kamben* for short. Its ends are left open. *Kamben* is the Balinese word for a piece of material which in the rest of Indonesia is called a *kain*. This *kamben* is also worn by men, who let the longer end hang in folds at the front. In order to allow more freedom of movement for the legs, when dancing or playing sport of some kind, this "tail" can be pulled back between the legs and tucked into the waist of the sarong. The women always tie their *kamben* in a simple way, slung around the hips without any embellishment.

Men usually wear a shirt over their sarong, except on ceremonial occasions, when, like the women, they wear a cloth over their chest, or a kind of sarong which reaches from the chest to the legs. For everyday purposes the women wear the *kebaya*, which is a tight-fitting, long-sleeved jacket, closed over the chest with a broad ribbon.

Above: Examples of modern Batiks.
Right: Master-craftsman Soerono at work.

ENCOUNTER WITH A BATIK ARTIST

We had thought that Mr Soerono would be one of those "typical" Balinese painters, who sit in their open-sided studio-pavilions, surrounded by their pupils, composing delightful pictures in the traditional style: pictures with scenes from mythology and everyday life, in which the magical world of demons, ghosts and witches, is often drawn into the reality of the modern world with its towns and traffic; pictures which are filled to the very edges with careful portrayals of plants, animals and people, in pastel shades; and which, in their detailed, stylised representation, are reminiscent of the narrative illustrations of medieval Europe.

We found Mr Soerono's studio a few hundred yards outside Kuta, a little way off the busy road to Denpasar. A large wooden sign points the way for us: a grassy front-garden, a little ochre-colored house, and next to it an open workshop, smothered in red flowering bougainvillea. Inside, on a rough wooden table against the back wall, pictures and batiks are piled higgledy-piggledy. We are in for a surprise. This is no tradtional Balinese painter's studio; the style is western, the colors strong, the pictures are full of energy, even drama ; they are at once passionate and sensitive. And yet it is clearly not European painting.

We do not notice the artist until he is right beside us, a small, wiry, boyish figure, barefoot, wearing a tattered T-shirt and a silk sarong. He welcomes us with a smile, the courteous but inscrutable smile of an oriental sage. We strike up a conversation, and when he sees that we are genuinely interested in his work and have time to spare, he willingly tells us about himself.

He is a Javanese by birth, 64 years old, who came to Bali as a child, and later, as a schoolboy, studied for two years with

the Dutch painter, Velthuysen. His subjects are many and various: rice-growers at harvest-time, river scenes, portraits of women, young and old. They are impressive; realistic but also impressionistic. Tender, sensitively drawn batiks, a classic head of a girl in profile, which makes one think of Picasso, a powerful and dramatic vision of demons from the legends of his people; and, again and again, self-portraits imbued with a passionate grief – he lost his family in the Second World War – or of the artist at his easel, refusing with a violent gesture an offer of money from Death. He interprets this for us: "If I were to sell myself for money, it would mean my death as an artist." Yet he knows exactly what his pictures are worth. For one of his Batik pictures costs US$ 75, a sum which a teacher in Bali would have to work three weeks to earn.

"Would you like to see how a batik is made?" Soerono asks suddenly. "Have you got time?" And he takes us into the house to fetch the material. Here, too, there is a table laden with pictures, which are suffering from damp, a figure of a Buddha and all manner of junk. On the left-hand wall hang two pictures: Christ on the cross and a large head of Buddha, both in brownish-black tones, with bright highlights, in the style of a woodcut. Underneath them, hanging horizontally, is an electric guitar. The versatile Mr Soerono sits down with the instrument and plays the German christmas-carol, *Silent Night*, followed by a Balinese dance. His ear-ring glints, and the wide bronze band around his right ankle glows like gold. The time is passing, but what do we care?

However, Soerono has not forgotten the batik. He leads us into a shady backyard behind his studio, surrounded by a hedge and bordering on a field of ripening rice. Here, he draws up two bamboo chairs for us, under the projecting tin roof. With a practised hand he stretches a piece of cotton cloth over a frame. Then with rapid, sure strokes he uses a piece of chalk to draw on it. Soon a Balinese temple is created, and a setting sun, whose last rays fall through the crown of a palm-tree, and on to a young girl carrying sacrificial gifts to the temple on her proudly erect head. At her feet, a pot-bellied pig trots out from the lush, tropical undergrowth. Soerono pauses briefly, pulls a small gas-stove towards him, then with hot, melted wax, goes over the drawing, in brisk, unhesitating sweeps, and spreads wax with a broad brush over the areas which are not to receive the dye. While his buxom girl assistant stirs the dye, he explains the next steps in the process. Then he seems to forget us. In a kind of ecstasy, he dances like a boxer back and forth between the bowls of dye, dips a corner of the cloth into the red, another into the green, a third into the yellow, leaps up, holds the fabric up to the

light and dips it in again, first into a dye, then into water, examines it once more, hangs it over a washing-line, squeezes it between his fingers, squirts some dye on a particular spot, takes it down from the line, dips it again...

His feet dance on the soft earth floor, his bare, wiry torso glistens, his expression is remote, full of concentration, while his hands work away for a good hour with a wondrous sureness which bespeaks a lifetime of practice.

From time to time, at the end of one of the stages in the work, he stops, emerges from his rapt concentration, and, as a way of calming himself, he strokes the little gray monkey that is chained up there. He tells us that he occasionally takes on pupils for a few weeks, tourists from Japan, Australia and America, and some Germans and Dutch. He regrets never having met Picasso – and the fact that he has ten children, all dependent on him. Two of his daughters are Catholic, and two Protestant, but that doesn't worry him, he is all for liberty and tolerance; he himself is devoted to Buddha – and here he kisses the bronze pendant that he wears round his neck. He lives here alone, he tells us, because he too needs his freedom, in order to work. Sometimes he gets up in the night to paint, if an idea comes to him; and sometimes he makes ten batiks one after another, and then sleeps for two whole days. In the afternoon he often goes to the beach and throws javelins. Soerono's hands are black with dye and acid. The batik is now ready and his assistant washes out the wax with hot soda-water. While drinking a cup a coffee, we wait for the cloth to dry in the sun. The master's creation is an impression of Bali that has a thrilling intensity: in the blood-red glow of the setting sun, the young girl carries her sacrificial offerings with unwavering steps through the ghostly, threatening shadows of evening, towards the dark silhouette of the temple.

Right: This fighting-cock is his owner's pride and joy.

COCK-FIGHTING

In the mind of the devout Hindus of Bali, the world is full of demons. They are responsible for disaster, grief and sickness. In order to keep them at a distance, innumerable small gift-offerings are laid out every day at all key points of the threatened area. Sometimes, however, the demons seem to require a sacrifice of blood. On these occasions, even today, animals are sacrificed at important temple festivals and purification ceremonies. When, for example, at one of these festivals, the quarrel between Barong and Rangda is ended, a member of the congregation, in a trance-like state, bites the head off a live chick. The blood of the creature moistens the ground and thus is meant to mollify the malevolent forces of the spirit-world. It is in this context of a religious sacrifice that cock-fighting has its origins. It was and is a fixed element in temple festivals, but certainly goes back to pre-Hindu times. Long before the Dutch arrived on the scene, cock-fighting in its secular form had emerged from religious ritual. It is true that even in its worldly version, the cock-fight did not begin without a short religious ceremony, but the important thing, both for the owners of the cocks, and the spectators, was to see their "own" roosters in an exciting fight. Although the Dutch colonial rulers were to a great extent prepared to see Balinese cultural individuality preserved, they nevertheless found cock-fighting so barbaric that they banned it – as they did the notorious burning of widows. However, cock-fighting continued to thrive under cover, and after Indonesia's independence it was once again legalised. But in 1981, the government in Jakarta made the decision that henceforth cock-fighting should only be permitted in its religiously inspired form. The reasons for this were principally social, and had less to do with the bloodythirsty nature of the fighting, than with the dire economic effects of the passion for betting which is enflamed by the sport. One only has to ob-

serve the hectic activity surrounding these fights to understand clearly what was upsetting the government.

Before a fight is held, the owners of the cocks, or their ringside agents, inspect the fighting-birds and reach the contradictory opinion that each of their birds is going to win. Only then do they agree to a fight. Since experts are at work here, they are each unshakeably convinced of a favorable outcome for their contender, and bet correspondingly large sums on their victory. This is the first phase of the betting negotiations. The two owners also offer an equally large sum for the other's rooster. This sum has a lower limit and is announced publicly as a point of reference for subsequent bets. The organisers of the contest receive a 10 to 25 percent share of the turnover. So whatever happens, they cannot lose.

Above: A fighting-cock spends a large part of his life in a basket-cage. Right: The quality of the cocks is always the object of speculation.

In the second round of betting, the spectators take part. First come the professional punters and tipsters, according to whose judgement one or other of the cockerels emerges as favorite. Then everyone starts in with shouts and gestures, haggling with their betting-partners over acceptable odds. When two punters have reached agreement over odds, they briefly touch heads, then turn to another betting-partner. The owners of the competing birds often place further bets with the public, using front-men, because these bets are not subject to any deduction payable to the organisers. The wagers mount ever higher, the more so since the professionals make their living from this activity. The simple farmer who wants to keep up, runs a high risk. It is reported that at many contests the starting bet for one fight is as high as 100,000 rupiahs. The owner of a fighting-cock often has to borrow a sum of that magnitude from members of his family or clan. It is not unheard-of for a peasant farmer to gamble away more than a whole year's income on a single fight. Or that an entire village is plunged into penury because their favorite rooster let them down in the moment of truth.

In view of the fact that this sport has become a matter of life and death, it is no surprise to learn that the cock-fighting business has been invaded by all sorts of skullduggery. Cases have been discovered where owners of birds have deliberately had their metal spurs fitted too loosely, then been seen to place moderately high bets on them, while using front-men to put very high bets on the opposing cock, in the absolute certainty of cleaning up. At one time, the outcome of a fight would determine whether whole families went into slavery, or could afford to buy another field. The passion for betting was so universal that it was said even to have turned rajas into paupers.

It must have been examples like these that the Indonesian government had in

mind when they issued their prohibition. Even so, you cannot walk through any town or village in Bali today, without seeing a row of cages at the roadside, from which fighting-cocks observe the parade of passers-by. Every male Balinese worth his salt is the proud owner of at least one of these feathered trouble-makers. And just so the bird doesn't get bored, he is allowed to watch the activity of the village. But chasing hens is another matter altogether. The job of the cock is to fight, not to flirt! To this end he is pampered, massaged and fed with a specially prepared diet.

Whenever the men of the village gather for drink and a chat, they swop experiences, make predictions for future fights, and allow their prized possesions to test their strength against each other. After about a year and a half, they get down to serious business. The natural instinct of the creature to assert itself against any male member of the same species, is enhanced with the deadly weapon of a spur attached to the foot.

It is from this spur that cock-fighting gets its Balinese name: the razor-sharp piece of metal can be up to 6 inches (15cm) long and is called a *taji.* Hence the word *tajen* for the fight itself. Each contest lasts a maximum of five rounds. However, as a rule, two or three direct hits with the artificial spur are enough; and the wounded cock sinks into the dust of the arena, which is called a *wantilan.* Only if both birds can still stay on their feet after five hard-fought rounds, is the match declared a draw. A cock which has survived unbeaten in four contests earns himself retirement as a superannuated champion. He is given permission to strut around the village with as much dignity as his injuries will allow, and only has to take care not to get tangled up in the spokes of someone's motor-cycle. And what about the ban on cock-fighting? It is still in force, and for this reason fights of more than three rounds may only be held on temple-festival days – with no betting. Apart from that, the 11th commandment applies: Thou shalt not get caught!

STICK-FIGHTING IN LOMBOK

Narmada is one of the centers of the sport of stick-fighting called *perisean,* or sometimes *peresehan.* On frequent days demonstration-fights are held in the open sports-hall, just on the right as you go in. You will see two youthful fighters advancing on each other, dressed in the traditional sarong, with a head-cloth, a roll of padded material around their hips, a stick and a shield. Their elegant, balletic duel is accompanied by a small gamelan band. Although the blows are extremely violent, the spectators are relieved to see that they are always aimed at the shield. It looks most spectacular, and the clatter of stick on shield makes a hellish din, but no-one gets hurt.

If you want to see a "genuine" stick-fight, you have to ask around, and Narmada is the best place to start. In the grounds of the palace (on the street side) fights are sometimes held on Sundays. It is still a fairly well-kept secret that in Puyung stick-fighting goes on nearly all the time, even during the week. The fighting arena is on a football field, tucked away at the end of the village. The fights begin at 4 pm, and gates open half-an-hour earlier. The spectators squat on the ground around a roped-off square, about 10 yards to 15 yards square (100 -200 sq. m). On one side sits a gamelan orchestra under an awning, playing the audience in as they arrive. Later, during the fight, the crescendo and diminuendo of the music accompanies the action like a well-written film-score, underlining the dramatic moments. In addition, a vocalist comments on what is happening, in a mixture of recitative and song, and often in a very bawdy manner, which always provokes the large crowd to gales of helpless laughter.

Right: In the final phase of a fight the action grows ever more frantic and violent.

By around 4 o'clock the arena is full. Under the supervision of the organisers, the two seconds, called *pekembar,* start selecting the first pair of contestants. In the two corners facing the gamelan orchestra they look for likely contenders. They do this while performing a provocative and almost feminine kind of dance, in which they shimmy with their hips and make their eyes roll and glint. When a second sees a likely-looking contender, he prods him out with his stick. Meanwhile, the other second points to his chosen champion. The two men who have been selected now consider, with advice from the spectators, whether they will accept the other as an opponent. The *pekembar* themselves also check to see that the two fighters are of roughly equal strength. If an opponent is accepted, the seconds strike each other's shields. The contestants are now equipped with weapons and prepared for the fight.

The shield is woven from bamboo and rattan and covered with buffalo-hide. The stick is also made of rattan. Thin string is wound round each end, so that one end can be held firmly in the hand, while the other can cause no stab-wounds with its otherwise sharp point. Injuries are also prevented by the headgear and the padded material wound round the kidneys. But to make sure the protective padding really does its job, a lucky-charm amulet is often woven into it, or some reassuring motto printed on it.

At last the referee gives the signal for the fight to begin. With considerable elegance the two contenders skip and dance towards each other. This is their way of getting into a fighting mood and shaking off their nervousness. Each man wants to let his opponent see he is not impressed by him. The first blows are usually fended off. Then they start hitting their mark. The moment the human fighting-cocks get wedged close together, the referee separates them. The first trickles of blood appear on their naked torsos.

Whichever of the two is so inclined, will endeavour to save face by transforming the winces of pain into a little capering dance. Sometimes his second will playfully join in with prancing steps. For some moments all the tension and danger seem to have gone out of the fight, and the universe is in harmony. Then comes the next round. Now that the gloves are off, so to speak, the fight takes a more violent turn. Three to five rounds is the usual duration. The chief and assistant referees keep a score of the hits. Blows to the head rate the highest. The man who receives three head-blows suffers not only pain but a premature defeat. If the fight lasts for the agreed number of rounds, the result is decided by the referees on the basis of the number of blows, the loss of a stick, and the number of times the contestants are thrown on the ground.

If both fighters are equally strong, it is possible to declare the match a draw. But more often the fight is stopped before the end, because one of the contestants is bleeding from a gaping wound. A medical auxiliary looks after him. When the result is announced, a prize is awarded to the victor either by a dancer or by one of the seconds, after a little dance interlude. In Puyung the prize is usually a sarong. Then other fights follow.

When darkness falls over the arena, at about six o'clock, the best fighters of the day make a final appearance. The atmosphere among the spectators reaches a peak of excitement.

This rough, tough contact-sport appears to be, and is today, played by amateurs for fun, as the mood takes them; but in former times it was intended to get warriors battle-fit. It was also customary to hold *perisean* contests after the harvest, on the rice-field during the dry season, because they believed that the sacrifice of blood would provoke the heavens into dropping their much-needed rains.

In many villages it is still said today that no man, who refuses to take part in a stick-fight, has any chance of taking a bride home with him.

Nelles Maps ...the maps that get you going.

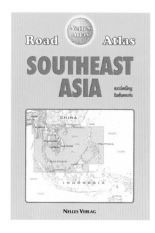

Nelles Maps

- Afghanistan
- Australia
- Bangkok
- Burma
- Caribbean Islands 1 /
  Bermuda, Bahamas,
  Greater Antilles
- Caribbean Islands 2 /
  Lesser Antilles
- China 1 /
  North-Eastern China
- China 2 /
  Northern China
- China 3 /
  Central China
- China 4 /
  Southern China
- Crete
- Egypt
- Hawaiian Islands
- Hawaiian Islands 1 / Kauai
- Hawaiian Islands 2 /
  Honolulu, Oahu
- Hawaiian Islands 3 /
  Maui, Molokai, Lanai
- Hawaiian Islands 4 / Hawaii
- Himalaya
- Hong Kong
- Indian Subcontinent
- India 1 / Northern India
- India 2 / Western India
- India 3 / Eastern India
- India 4 / Southern India
- India 5 / North-Eastern India
- Indonesia
- Indonesia 1 / Sumatra
- Indonesia 2 /
  Java + Nusa Tenggara
- Indonesia 3 / Bali
- Indonesia 4 / Kalimantan
- Indonesia 5 / Java + Bali
- Indonesia 6 / Sulawesi
- Indonesia 7 /
  Irian Jaya + Maluku
- Jakarta
- Japan
- Kenya
- Korea
- Malaysia
- West Malaysia
- Manila
- Mexico
- Nepal
- New Zealand
- Pakistan
- Philippines
- Singapore
- South East Asia
- Sri Lanka
- Taiwan
- Thailand
- Vietnam, Laos
  Cambodia

GUIDELINES

Travel preparations 242
   Climate 242
   Travel seasons 242
   Clothing 242
   Entry documents 242
   Currency 243
   Health precautions 243

Travelling to and within Bali and Lombok 244
   Getting there 244
   Travelling from Bali to Lombok 244
   Travelling around Bali 244
   Travelling around Lombok 245
   Departure 245

Practical tips 245
   Accommodation 245
   Alcohol 245
   Bookshops 245
   Business hours 245
   Crime and drugs 246
   Customs restrictions 246
   Eating and drinking 246
   Electricity 246
   Festivals and holidays 246
   Language 247
   Pharmacies 247
   Photography 248
   Post, telephone and fax 248
   Time zones 248
   Weights and measures 248

Addresses 248
   Consulates in Bali 248
   Tourist offices outside Indonesia 248

Statistics and other useful information 249
   Population and administration

Language guide 250
Authors and photographers 251
Index 252

TRAVEL PREPARATIONS

Climate

Being close to the equator, Bali and Lombok enjoy a warm climate all year round. Daytime temperatures vary little from season to season, remaining in the range of 27° to 30°near the coast. At nights there is only a slight drop in temperature. Even in the "coldest" month, July, it only goes down to 16°– 21°. But at higher altitudes it can feel distinctly cool.

There are two seasons: the rainy season, which runs from November to April, and the dry season for the rest of the year. In the mountain regions of Bali it can rain on 160 to 210 days of the year, with a total precipitation of 118 inches (3000 mm). In the south it rains on 100 to 140 days, giving 79 inches (2000mm), while in the dryer north there are only 50 to 80 rainy days a year, with a precipitation of less than 40 inches (1000mm). Thus the rainfall is anything from 3 times to 5 times heavier than in Europe.

But even in the rainy season the rain tends to fall in short, heavy showers, rather than continuously over a longer period of time. Nevertheless, rainfall of 24 inches (600mm) in a single day is not uncommon. Even in the dry season there can sometimes be short, heavy showers, usually in the late afternoon. Very occasionally there are tornadoes. Lombok is, on the whole, rather warmer and dryer than Bali.

Travel seasons

As it is particularly hot and humid in the rainy season, the recommended time to visit Bali is in the dry season, from May to October. This is especially the case if you plan to go walking in the mountains. Even if you are not comfortable in the heat, you need not worry: by the sea there is a gentle but steady breeze which gets stronger towards evening, and takes the edge of the heat.

Clothing

If you plan to stay on the coast, all you need are light, airy summer clothes. If you have to meet officials, or when you are visiting temples, it is important to wear a long-sleeved shirt or blouse, and long trousers. If you are heading for the mountains, you will need strong footwear, warm clothing and ventilated waterproof gear. If you plan to go motorcycling we suggest you bring your own helmet and something to protect your kidneys. The helmets issued by the rental companies may meet legal requirements but are pretty useless. Motor-cyclists and pillion-riders should wear strong jeans, unless you want to get your calves burnt by the hot exhaust-pipe.

On the subject of light clothing, unless you are a very large size, there is no need to bring a lot with you. There is no shortage of such things in Bali. Quite the reverse: there is a wider range of fashionable leisure clothes for sale at lower prices than back home.

Entry documents

To enter Indonesia citizens of the following 30 countries only require a passport valid for 6 months, with one unstamped page and a return or onward air ticket: Australia, Austria, Belgium, Brunei, Canada, Denmark, Finland, France, Germany, Great Britain, Greece, Iceland, Ireland, Italy, Japan, Liechtenstein, Luxemburg, Malaysia, Malta, Netherlands, New Zealand, Norway, Philippines, Sweden, Switzerland, Singapore, South Korea, Spain, Thailand and the USA.

On arrival you are given a tourist visa which entitles you to stay for 60 days and no more. The visa can only be extended in case of illness or if you are involved in legal proceedings. In all other cases you must leave the country and re-enter. This is usually achieved by flying to Singapore or Thailand. Citizens of countries not listed above must apply for a visa at the Indonesian embassy or consulate in their own country.

Currency

The Indonesian unit of currency is the rupiah which circulates in the following denominations: notes of 100, 500, 1,000, 5,000 and 10,000 rupiahs; coins of 1, 5, 10, 25, 50 and 100 rupiahs. Its value is linked to the US$ and fluctuates in relation to other currencies in step with the dollar. Prices in hotels and tourist centers are often quoted in US$, though paid in rupiahs.

It is forbidden to bring more than Rps 50,000 in or out of the country. However, there is no limit to the amount of foreign currency you can bring in. The safest way to carry money is in travellers-cheques denominated in US dollars, Australian dollars, pounds sterling or Deutschmarks. These can be exchanged for rupiahs at banks and officially approved money-changers.

Eurocheques are pretty useless in these parts. Outside the tourist centers and large towns only cash is accepted and there is usually no way of changing money. Anyway, you get the best exchange rates in the tourist centers, although the rates in hotels are the least good. Money-changers give the quickest service and offer rates comparable with the banks.

Banks are open on weekdays from 8 a.m. until 12 noon, and on Saturday from 8a.m. until 11a.m., while exchange bureaus are often open in the afternoon. Recently, credit-cards have become accepted in most hotels, larger souvenir shops, the better restaurants and by art dealers. Sometimes this is the only way of getting hold of some cash in a hurry.

When changing money, make sure you always get a selection of smaller denomination notes, because *bemo-* and taxi-drivers, and *warungs* are not usually able to give you change for a 10,000 rupiah note. Sometimes you may encounter problems out in the countryside if you try to pay with worn-out banknotes.

Health precautions

Long before leaving for Bali you should consult a doctor, or better still an institute of tropical medicine or a quarantine authority. They will be able to tell you what precautions are necessary. You should particularly ask about innoculation against typhus, cholera and hepatitis A and B, as well as anti-malaria tablets. You should definitely be injected against tetanus and polio. As regards malaria, enquire about any new, resistant bacilli that have been discovered. Since all anti-malaria medications have side-effects, you should pay particular attention to minimizing the risk of getting bitten by a mosquito. This is done by always sleeping under a mosquito-net, wearing a garment that covers most of your body, and treating any uncovered parts such as wrists and ankles with a mosquito-repellant. Oil of cloves seems to be pretty effective.

You should always wear shoes, or at least sandals, as a protection against hook-worms and other parasites that live in the ground.

Get your doctor to put together a little travelling pharmacy for you. It should include an antiseptic for all sorts of small wounds, since even a scratched mosquito-bite can become seriously inflamed in the tropics. You should also take with you some medication for diarrhoea and for various degrees of infection.

The best safeguard is simply to use your common sense in extreme heat or when eating and drinking. Give your body time to get acclimatized to the new conditions; find some shade in the midday heat; take plenty of fluids in the form of non-alcoholic drinks; to start with, eat in moderation, and at all times only eat things that have been well-cooked; peel your own fruit; avoid being served drinks containing ice-cubes of dubious origin. (There is state-produced ice which is perfectly usable). Avoid restaurants and accommodation whose standards of hygiene do not impress you. Water that you use to clean your teeth should always be sterilized first with a product like Micropur, to get rid of any bacteria.

It is advisable to take out travel health insurance which covers the cost of getting you home in an emergency. It is true that both in Lombok and Bali there are hospitals in the capital towns, but they are not up to the standard that westerners have come to expect.

Therefore in emergencies you should – if possible – get yourself taken to Singapore. This is where you will find the nearest first-class hospitals in the region, with western-trained specialists, such as at the **American Hospital**, Tel: 3451516. Also recommended is the **Pertamina Hospital** in Jakarta, Jl. Kyai Maja, Kebayoran Baru, Tel: 021/707214. Hospital costs have to be paid in cash, but these are much lower than in the west, and will be reimbursed by a private travel insurance company.

TRAVELLING TO AND WITHIN BALI AND LOMBOK

Arrival

Most travelers arrive in Bali by air. Many airlines land at Denpasar's Ngurah Rai airport, which is south of the capital and of Kuta. These include: Air France, Alitalia, American Airlines, British Airways, Cathay Pacific, Delta Airlines, Garuda, Gulf Air, Iberia, KLM, Lauda Air, Lufthansa, Quantas, SAS, Singapore Airlines, Swiss Air, Thai Airways and TWA.

If you are flying with the Indonesian airline, Garuda, you should enquire about current reduced fare offers on internal flights (e.g. to Mataram on Lombok). Many airlines offer reduced-price packages which include stopovers in Singapore. Independent travelers, who are visiting Java before going on to Bali, can fly to Bali in a small aircraft operated by Merpati Airlines. Or you can take the ferry from Ketapang to Gilimanuk (q.v.). The overland busses which connect all the major towns in Java with Bali also use this ferry to cross to the island.

Travelling from Bali to Lombok

Merpati, a subsidiary of Garuda, operates up to seven flights a day both ways, between Denpasar and the capital of Lombok, Mataram. The half-hour flight costs Rps.45,000

In addition, it is possible to go there by ferry from Padangbai (q.v.) or with the faster hydrofoil from Benoa Port to Labuhan Lembar. In Kuta (q.v.) you can book bus-trips to Senggigi or to the boat-pier where you leave for the three islands to the north-west of Lombok

Travelling around Bali

A very practical and inexpensive way of getting around the island is by minibus or *bemo*. These public transport vehicles connect almost all the villages with each other. There are also bus routes along the main highways. In the tourist centers and in the capital there are plenty of taxis on the streets.These are also affordable but it is as well to negotiate the fare in advance.

In all the tourist centers you can hire small jeeps and motor-cycles. You have to show an international driver's license. If you do not possess a license to ride a motor-cycle, you can obtain one valid for six weeks in Bali only. They are issued in Denpasar in the space of a morning. There is a brief oral examination. It is basically impossible to fail, because there are eager touts who look after the necessary. Every motor-bike hire company knows what is required.

Every year there are a number of serious accidents in Bali, usually involving inexperienced motor-cyclists. So, if you have to use a motor-bike, exercise extreme caution. And remember that traffic drives on the left.

Travelling within Lombok

In addition to the means of transport mentioned above, Lombok also offers a large number of small horse-drawn carriages called *dokars.* A trip in one of these does not cost much and is a unique experience. Sometimes you have to get out when you reach a small hill, because the load is too much for the delicate little horses.

Departure

On departure you have to present the tourist visa which you completed when you arrived. Remember to confirm your return flight in good time, and at the same time ask what the current level of airport tax is, as you will have to pay this when you leave.

PRACTICAL TIPS

Accommodation

In Bali and Lombok you will find accommodation in all price-categories, and in the tourist centers there is abundant choice. Away from the main centers there is generally only simple accommodation or rooms in private houses which the village headman (*kepala desa*) will organize for you in return for a small fee. The simple lodgings are called *losmens,* and are often run as family businesses. Many are idyllically located amidst tropical vegetation. Washing facilities are restricted to a *mandi,* which is what the locals use: this is a basin of water with a ladle to scoop it out and splash it over yourself. You should never wash directly in the basin, still less step into it. That way it is kept clean and hygienic. The toilets are usually the standing or squatting kind, sometimes with no paper, and with only a small water-tap.

You may not always find an intact mosquito-net, which is why you should always carry your own with you. You should also bring your own light-bulb of a decent wattage, since your are quite likely to find nothing stronger than a 15-watt bulb in the room. Although the Balinese are generally very careful about cleanliness, you nevertheless come across cockroaches and other insects from time to time. Also, most houses have their complement of geckos, which do a useful job by eating insects but do leave little messages around, so it is advisable to keep delicate clothing in covered shelves or in protective bags.

Alcohol

Alcoholic drinks are obtainable in all tourist centers. But imported brands are very expensive in comparison with the west. On Lombok it is difficult to buy alcoholic drinks during the fasting month of Ramadan, and in remote districts at any time.

Bookshops

In the capitals and the tourist centers there are a number of bookshops where you can usually find an extensive range of new titles and standard works on Bali and Lombok. Very often these bookshops also do a lively second-hand trade, and you can pick up a useful range of holiday reading in English, German, Japanese, Dutch, French, and sometimes, Spanish and Italian.

Business hours

In the tourist centers the shops often remain open right through from 9am to 9pm or even 10pm. However, if trade is a bit slow they may decide on a long lunch-break, in which case you will not find them open again until 4pm. Official institutions may say they are open until 3pm or even 5pm, but to be on the safe side you should always visit them in the morning. Don't expect to find the required official at his desk on a Friday.

Crime and drugs

Crimes of violence are very rare on the islands compared to any western country.

Nevertheless, the real or imagined wealth of tourists does lead to crime against property. Therefore, particularly in the tourist strongholds, you must always keep a close eye on your valuables, especially in rooms which cannot easily be watched or locked.

Muggings are rare, so you can have adequate security by wearing a money belt or a bag across your chest. From time to time you will be warned of thieves, who may get out of a *bemo*, taking your camera case or other items of luggage with them.They often do this with the help of a partner who is there to distract you.

On Lombok, *bemo*-drivers sometimes try to increase the fare retrospectively, lending emphasis to their proposal by pointing out that you have no idea where you are. In this situation it is helpful to mention the police, in order to get back on the "right road."

Keep well away from any kind of illegal drugs, because the penalties, even for foreigners, are extremely severe.

Customs restrictions

It is forbidden to import into Indonesia: weapons, drugs, any media with pornographic content, any material in the Indonesian language that has been printed in China or any other foreign country, and Chinese medicinal products. You should leave your video cassettes at home, as these will be subjected to a wearisome examination for pornographic content.

You are allowed to bring in up to 2 litres of alcoholic drink, plus 200 cigarettes, 50 cigars or 100 grams of tobacco. In order to protect the islands' endangered animal species, these may not be exported. This also means you may not take out a sea-turtle shell or any product made from this material. National antiquities are also protected by law, and so you may not export any genuine antique articles.

Eating and drinking

Indonesian food is in general easily digestible, though certain dishes are heavily spiced. You very quickly get used to the hot, spicy flavors and later on, back home, you will find the food seems very bland in comparison. The spices also serve the purpose of preventing food from going bad in the heat.

In order that your eating enjoyment is not followed by remorse, you should avoid certain dishes, especially at the beginning of your holiday. These include: salads, fruit that is unwashed or not washed in sterilized water, freshly squeezed fruit-juice, home-made ice-cream, meat that has gone cold, raw seafood, cold sauces etc. Where drinking is concerned, you should always go for industrially bottled lemonades and other such drinks. Drinks with fresh fruit added may taste delicious but should only be drunk in moderation.

Electricity

In the outlying districts of Bali and all over Lombok the mains power is 110 volt or 50 Hz. In the towns and tourist centers they have now switched over to 220 volt/50Hz.

Festivals and holidays

Since the calendar of local festivals is not only filled with events, but their dates are different every year, you should, at the beginning of your stay, go to the tourist office in Denpasar or Mataram and obtain a list of festivals. In the better hotels you can also get a list of forthcoming events. If you have good contacts among the local hotel or restaurant staff, it is possible to find out about purely local festivals, which are not announced officially and which are well worth visiting.

As in the west, Sunday is the day of rest. But on Friday, which is the Moslems' principal day of prayer, and also on Saturday, different business hours apply. National holidays, such as Independence

Day on 17th August, are on fixed days in the western calendar.

The cycle of festivals in Bali is determined both by constant and variable factors: the calendar and the vicissitudes of life. Firstly, the calendar: there is not just one, but at least four. For the whole of Indonesia two calendars apply: the Gregorian or western calendar, which governs national holidays as well as the weekly rest-day for offices (Sunday), and the Islamic lunar calendar, which determines the Moslem festivals, the fast of Ramadan and the date of the pilgrimage to Mecca. These dates vary from year to year in the Gregorian calendar.

In Bali two further calendars are added to these: the South Indian Saka calendar and the pre-Islamic Javanese Wuku calendar. The Saka calendar is a lunar calendar with 12 months, each having 29 or 30 days. A month runs from new moon to new moon. Every three or four years, unlike the Moslem lunar calendar, an extra month is put in, to bring it approximately back into step with the Gregorian calendar and also with the sequence of seasons in the northern hemisphere (since it was originally intended for use in India). Thus it happens that in this calendar the New Year festival of *Nyepi* almost always falls in a period shortly after 20th March. Many of the temple festivals which are held regularly, like the *Odalan*, are fixed in accordance with the Saka calendar, in mid-month at the time of the full moon. However, in temples of the underworld, the *Odalan* festival is usually held at the time of the new moon. (There are also *Odalan* festivals which follow the Wuku calendar.)

The much more complicated Wuku calendar is referred to when a favorable date is sought for island-wide temple festivals and all sorts of other celebrations and ceremonies, including those which govern the course of one's life, like birth, marriage and death. This calendar covers a period of 210 days. Each period is inde-

pendent of the seasons and of the phases of the moon, and is repeated continuously without alteration. It comprises a series of concurrently running ten-day weeks, nine-day weeks etc. right down to 210 "one-day weeks." The most important are the 30 seven-day weeks, the 42 five-day weeks and the 70 three-day weeks. From the latter, the market days are determined – one every three days.

The occasions when the last day of a seven-day week coincides with the last day of a five-day week, are considered to be especially propitious for festivals. These are the so-called *Tumpek* days. Since the average Balinese can easily get lost in all this, when it come to fixing the date of a family festival he will turn to a priest, to whom the fixing of the dates of major festivals is also entrusted.

Language

In the tourist centers one can get by perfectly well with English. However, if you are making expeditions into the hinterland, it is recommended that you learn a few important phrases of Bahasia Indonesia (See Language Guide p.250).

Pharmacies

Pharmacies selling western medical preparations can be found in all the tourist centers (and even in the shopping arcades of the luxury hotels) as well as in the big towns. It is always useful to have with you the instruction-leaflet of any medication you take regularly, so that you can identify an equivalent preparation that may be sold here under a different name.

Photography

Taking photographs of bridges and military installations is strictly forbidden. Even when taking a souvenir photo at the airport you must be careful that there are no military aircraft to be seen. Apart from this, you should show a great deal of discretion when photographing temples or

Balinese people. Children and men are generally quite happy to be snapped. But with older people and women you should always ask their permission first.

In the tourist centers you can buy perfectly good film at prices only a little higher than you would pay at home. And you can have adequate prints made very quickly.

Post, telephone and fax

In Bali there are four Post Offices, *Kantor Pos*, which are suitable addresses to give as Poste Restante (mail to be collected): Kuta, Denpasar, Ubud and Singaraja. The Post Office in Denpasar is in the Renon district and is difficult to get to by public transport.

In Lombok, the Post Office at Mataram is the only Poste Restante address. On the envelope your surname must always be underlined or written in capitals. Important letters should always be sent by registered mail.

Air-mail letters take at least a week to reach Europe or the USA. Coming the other way they take even longer, because of local delivery. Parcels are accepted up to a weight of 22 lbs (10 kg).

The state telephone company is called **Permuntel**. Through their offices in the tourist centers you get astonishingly clear connections overseas, after waiting about half and hour. To make a call to Bali from abroad, first dial the international code for Indonesia and then 361 for Bali. Within Indonesia the code for Bali is 0361 and for Lombok it is 0364.

Most Permuntel offices are also equipped with fax machines. To send one page to Europe costs about US$ 6. You can also have faxes sent to you for which there is only a small charge.

Time zones

Bali belongs to the western time-zone of Indonesia and is 7 hours ahead of GMT and 6 hours ahead of Central European Time. However, Lombok is in the central time-zone of Indonesia and is one hour ahead of Bali. This information does not take account of the introduction of Summer Time in many countries.

Weights and measures

The metric system is used in Bali and Lombok.

ADDRESSES
Consulates in Bali

Australia: Jl. Raya Sanur 146, P.O.Box 243, Denpasar, Tel: 35092/3, Fax: 31990. (Also for NZ and Canada).

Denmark and Norway: Jl. Serma Gede 5, Sanglah, Denpasar, Tel: 35098.

Finland and Sweden: Jl. Segara Ayu, Sanur, Tel: 87152/88090.

France: Jl. Sekar Waru 3, Blanjiong, Sanur Kauh, Tel: 80228/88407.

Germany: Jl. Pantai Karang 17, Sanur, Tel: 88535, Fax: 88826.

Italy: Jalan Padanggalak, Sanur, Tel: 88372/88777.

Japan: Jl. Mohammad Yamin 9, Renon, Denpasar, Tel: 34808, Fax: 31308.

Netherlands: Jalan Imam Bonjol 599, Denpasar, Tel: 51094/51497, Fax: 52777.

Switzerland: Jl. Legian Kelod, Kuta, Tel/Fax: 51735.

USA: Jl. Segara Ayu 5, Sanur, Tel: 80228/88478, Fax: 87760.

(At present there is no British Consulate in Bali, but British citizens' affairs are handled by the Australian Consulate).

Tourist offices outside Indonesia

Australia: Garuda Indonesia office, 4 Bligh St., P.O. Box 3836, Sydney 2000.

Germany: Wiesenhüttenstr. 17, 60329 Frankfurt, Tel: 069-233677/8.

Japan: Asia Transport Co., 2nd Floor, Sankaido Building, 1-9-13 Akasaka, Minato-Ku, Tokio, Tel: 5853588 /5821331.

Singapore: 15-07 Ocean Building, 10 Collyer Quay, Singapore, Tel: 5342837/ 5341795.

USA: 3457 Wilshire Blvd., Los Angeles, CA 90010, Tel: 0231-387-2078.

(At the time of going to press, Indonesia has no official tourist office in London, but a number of tour operators organize packages to Bali, as does the state airline, Garuda).

STATISTICS AND OTHER USEFUL INFORMATION

Population and government

Indonesia has around 185 million inhabitants, which makes it the fifth most populous nation in the world. Over 85 percent of Indonesians follow the Islamic faith. As well as Islam, other monotheistic religions are recognized as state religions. These include Christianity and the Balinese form of Hinduism.

The official language of the country is Bahasa Indonesia, which has evolved from the language of commerce spoken by the Malay traders all over South-East Asia. However, only about 12 per cent of the population speak Bahasa Indonesia as their mother tongue. The rest are obliged to learn it from their first year at school.

The population of Bali is about 3 million, with a density of 200 inhabitants per sq. mile (540 per sq. km). This means that of all the thousands of islands in the archipelago, it has the second highest population-density, exceeded only by Java.

Lombok is in third place. About 10 per cent of Bali's population live in the provincial capital of Denpasar, in the more populous south. In the larger towns, traders from Arab countries, India and China have established communities. The Chinese minority, in particular, have in the past been the victims of frequent bloody pogroms.

You come across European business-people, artists and drop-outs in the tourist centers. On the coast, Bugi people from Sulawesi have settled in isolated fishing-villages since the 16th century. In contrast to the rest of Indonesia, the overwhelming majority of Balinese are Hindu.

Lombok has 2.5 million inhabitants and so is almost as densely populated as Bali. The great majority of the population belongs to the Sasak race. In the west of the island there is a large Balinese minority. They represent about 5 percent of the island's population. In Lombok, too, there are Arab, Indian and Chinese communities in the towns, and Buginese minorities on the coast. The majority of the population is Moslem.

The Republic of Indonesia was formerly a leading member of the group of non-aligned nations, and today the military stills plays a decisive role in government. The republic is made up of 24 provinces, two special autonomous districts and the capital district, around Jakarta.

The province of Bali is divided into eight *Kabupaten* (regencies) plus the capital district of Denpasar. The *Kabupaten* correspond roughly to the historic principalities or rajadoms which grew up in the pre-colonial era: Badung, Bangli, Buleleng, Gyanyar, Jembrana, Karangasem, Klungkung and Tabanan.

Below the level of Regencies are administrative units called *Kecamatan* (which might be translated as counties or boroughs). Below these again are the *Desa*, either villages or districts in towns. Finally, the villages and districts are divided into the smallest administrative units of all, the *Banjar*.

Lombok is part of the province of Nusa Tenggara Barat. It is divided into three *Kabupaten:* Lombok Barat (west), Lombok Tengah (central) and Lombok Timur (east), plus the capital, Mataram.

LANGUAGE GUIDE

Good morning	*selamat pagi*
Good afternoon	*selamat siang*
Good evening	*selamat sore*
See you later . . .	*sampai bertemu lagi*
What's your name?(m)	*apa nama tuan?*
What's your name? (fem.) :	
. . . .	*apa nama nyonya?*
My name is	*nama saya...*
I am staying at	*saya tinggal di..*
Where is the...?	*(di) mana...?*
How far is the...?	
. . . .	*berapa jauhnya?*
How do I get to...?	
. . . .	*bagaimana saya ke...?*
How much is that? . . .	*berapa harga?*
Can I see the menu, please?	
. . . . .	*saya mau lihat daftar makana.*
I'd like something to drink	
. . . .	*saya mau mimim*
The bill, please! . . .	*saya mau bayar.*
I'm staying here...days	
. . . .	*saya tinggal disini...hari*
What is that?	*apa ini / apa itu?*
What time is it?	*jam berapa?*
I	*saya*
you	*kamu*
we	*kita*
we (excluding person addressed)	
. . . .	*kami*
O.K	*baik*
yes	*ya*
no	*tidak*
big	*besar*
small	*kecil*
now	*sekarang*
today	*hari ini*
afternoon	*siang*
night	*malam*
week	*minggu*
month	*bulan*
year	*tahun*
clean	*bersih*
dirty	*kotor*
hot	*panas*
cold	*dingin*
please	*tolong*
thank you	*terima kasih*

less	*kurang*
more	*lebih banyak*
come	*datang*
go	*pergi*
price	*harga*
shop	*toko*
medicine	*obat*
market	*pasar*
room	*kamar*
vegetables	*sayuran*
water	*air*
tea	*teh*
milk	*susu*
sugar	*gula*
salt	*garam*
butter	*mentega*
food	*makanan*
breakfast	*makanan pagi*
1	*satu*
2	*dua*
3	*tiga*
4	*empat*
5	*lima*
6	*enam*
7	*tujuh*
8	*delapan*
9	*sembilan*
10	*sepuluh*
11	*sebelas*
12	*duabelas*
20	*duapuluh*
30	*tigapuluh*
40	*empatpuluh*
50	*limapuluh*
60	*enampuluh*
70	*tujuhpuluh*
80	*delapanpuluh*
90	*sembilanpuluh*
100	*seratus*
1,000	*seribu*
10,000	*sepuluhribu*

Pronunciation

ai	like "eye"
au	like "ow" in "cow"
c	like "ch" in "chin"
j	as in English "jet"etc.
h	at end of word is a soft,
. . . .	hissing sound.

AUTHORS

Bernd F. Gruschwitz, editor and one of the principal authors of *Nelles Bali/Lombok Guide*, is a historian and student of English literature whose home is in Bremen, Germany. His early travels took him round Europe, the Mediterranean and North America, but more recently he has discovered a love for southern and south-east Asia. Since then, he has travelled as often as possible in India, Thailand and Indonesia. Like an amateur scholar of the Victorian age he has immersed himself in the history, philosphy and ethnology of these countries and brought them to life by seeing the places for himself.

Thus, in Bali and Lombok he has explored the remotest corners on foot and motor-bike. And he has brought back proof in the form of numerous photographs taken for this book. Following his succesful travel-book about Teneriffe, this is the second island guide, which he has been instrumental in producing.

Dorothee Krause is studying textiles and their technology. In the course of this, her interest was awakened particularly in the Indian and Indonesian techniques of textile weaving and dyeing. This took her to Tenganan, Mataram Cakranegara and Sukarara to find out more on the spot. Also, being herself a dancer of ballet and jazz, she was immediately fascinated by the unfamilar Balinese dances. At night she went to festivals and performances and during the day watched the dancers rehearsing. She was equally enchanted by the gamelan music and has since tried to play it herself.

Barbara Müller studied the Romance languages and is a freelance journalist, writing chiefly on social and religious topics. In the course of her work she has made several visits to Africa, Latin-America and Asia, including Bali.

Berthold Schwarz, a freelance author and photographer, studied geography and ethnology. Since 1975 he has been travelling professionally and privately in Africa, Asia and the Far East, and since 1984 he has been leading treks and study-trips. One of his favorite destinations is Bali. However, he is equally at home in other countries, as witness the *Nelles Morocco Guide*, of which he was the editor.

PHOTOGRAPHERS

Fischer, Peter   66
Gruschwitz, Bernd F.   9, 16, 17, 18, 19, 30, 33, 34, 41, 42, 43, 44, 45, 48, 49, 69, 87, 88, 89, 90, 95, 97, 104, 105, 112, 115, 122/123, 131, 132, 134, 135, 137, 142, 147, 151, 154, 155, 156, 160/161, 162/163, 166, 167, 168, 170, 172, 174/175, 176, 181, 186, 188, 191, 192, 195, 196, 197, 199, 208, 209, 213, 216, 218, 222, 224, 235, 239
Hellige, Wolfgang   1, 38, 46, 82, 94, 204/205, 221, 229, cover
Höbel, Robert   206/207
Kohl, Günther   2, 68, 96, 98, 120
Koninklijk Instituut voor de Tropen, Amsterdam   22, 26, 28L, 28R
Koninklijk Instituut voor Taal-, Land- en Volkenkunde, Leiden   24, 25, 27
Krause, Dorothee   10/11, 32, 36, 37, 76, 86, 102, 140/141, 150, 164, 173, 182, 190, 193, 198, 201, 230, 231
Maeritz, Kay   52/53
Müller, Barbara   232R, 233
Pausegrau, Erhard   14, 51, 56, 61, 73, 107, 116, 117, 124, 212
Rex, Peter   12/13, 20, 35, 39, 54/55, 80/81, 101, 110/111, 130, 153, 169, 211, 215, 220, 227, 237
Schaefer, Albrecht G.   91, 103, 148, 157, 236
Scheibner, Johann   99, 146
Schmerheim, Sigrid   185, 225
Schwarz, Heiner   183
Steinhardt, Jochen   67, 70, 118, 232L
Tetzner, Marina   60

A

Ababi 157
Abang 136
Agama Hindu Dharma 38-41
Agung Anom, Raja 92
Aik Mel 195
Airlangga, King 23, 98, 106
Air Sanih, springs 131
Allah 169, 170
Amed 157
Amlapura 155-156
Ampenan 167, 168, **177-179**, 180
  Arab quarter 179
  Chinese cemetery 179
  Chinese temple 179
  Pura Segara, temple 179
Amuk Bay 155
Anak Agung Panji, Raja 129
Anak Wungsu, King 105
Ancestors 37, 39, 45, 128, 152, 218
Animism 39, 60, 169, 170, 213
Apuan 91
Arabs 168, 177, 179
Arak 211
Are Goling 200
Arjuna, Prince 86
Art and craftsmanship 226-229
Asahduren 118
Awang 201

B

Badung
  see Denpasar
Badung, Regency **83-87**
Badung, Raja of 61
Bahasa Indonesia 33, 49, 59, 65, 133
Bajar 130
Bakung 69
Balangan 71
Bales 37, 150
Bali 21-159
Bali Aga 21, 132, 150, 231
Bali Arts Festival 60
Balina Beach 149
Bali Straits 114, 120
Bandung Conference 29
Bangkiangsidem 104
Bangko Bangko 198
Bangli 97
  Budaya Art Center 107
  Pura Kehen, temple 106, 107
  Puri Denpasar 106
Bangli, Regency 83, **106-107**
Bangsal 187, 189
Banjar 129-130
Banjar association 34-35
Banyuatis 132
Basanggalas 157

Batara Bayu, wind-god 62
Batik 66, 73, 96, **233-234**
Batuan 94-95, 214, 228
Batubulan 59, 60, 91, 92
Batugendeng, peninsula 196, **197-199**
Batu Kok 190, 194
Batu Nampar 201
Batur 134
Batu Renggong, King 24
Batur, Lake 134, 135, 136
Batuyung 104
Baum, Vicki 72
Bayan 169, 190, 193, 194, 219
Bayubiru 116
Bedugul 128, 133
Bedulu 98, 99
Belangsinga 96
Belanting 194
Belayu 87
Belega 96
Belimbingsari 115
Belo, Jane 72
Belongas 198, 199
Benoa Bay 59, 71
Benoa Port 177
Besakih, temple complex 44, 143, 149, **151-153**
  Pura Batu Madeg 152
  Pura Kiduling Kreteg 152
  Pura Penataran Agung 152
  Temple festivals 152, 153
Blahbatu 95, 96
Bona 96
Bonnet, Rudolf 94, 101, 103, 227
Borobudur 22
Brahma, god 34, 40, 61, 86, 152, 181
Brahmans 22, 32, 41, 95, 106, 146
Bratan 128
Bratan, Lake 85, 91, 128, **132-133**
Buahan 136
Bualu 71
Budakling 157
Buddhism 22, 98, 147, 152, 165, 169
Bugis 71, 114, 116, 165, 167, 188, 195, 201
Bukit Badung, peninsula 24, 57, **68-71**, 85
Bukit Dharma, sacred hill 23, 98
Bukit Jambul 151
Buleleng, east **130-132**
Buleleng, Regency 113, 125
Buleleng, west **119-120**
  Air Panas, Banyuwedang 119
  Bay of Gondol 119
  Makam Jayaprana, burial temple 120
  Pura Agung Pulaki, temple 119
Buyan, Lake 132, 133

C

Cakranegara 167, 168, 171, 177, **180-182**, 196, 197, 199
  Cilinaya Square 180
  Mayura, water palace 181
  Pasar, market 180
  Pura Meru, temple 181
  Race-course 182
  Livestock market 182
  Blacksmiths' quarter 180, 181
Candi Dasa 143, 148, 149
Candikuning 133
Canggu 65
Caste system 32-33, 37, 60, 125
Cekik 21, **114-115**, 119
Celuk 65, 92, 229
Celukanbawang 119, 125
Cengiling 69
  Pura Balangan, cave-temple 69
  Pura Konco, temple 69
Ceningan, island 74
Central Bali, eastern 91-107
Central Bali, western 83-91
Chinese 59, 71, 128, 143, 168, 177, 179, 180
Christians 44, 62, 115, 128, 185
Cock-fighting 34, 37, 45, 100, 171, 182, **235-37**
Cokorda Gede Agung Sukawati, Prince 102, 227
Cokorda Gede Raka Sukawati, Prince 101
Communists 29, 59, 153, 168
Cremation 47, 48, 147
Culik 157

D

Dalang, puppet-master 42, 223
Dance 31, 41, 45, 60, 70, 88, 96, 100, 101, 229
  Arja dance 212
  Baris dance 213
  Baring Ladung dance 75
  Batek Baris dance 218
  Dances, Balinese 212-217
  Dance in Lombok 218-219
  Gambuh dance 94, 214
  Gandrung dance 218, 219
  Gumbuh dance 154
  Jauk, mask-dance 214
  Joged dance 215
  Kebyar Duduk dance 212, 215
  Kebyar Legong dance 215
  Kebyar Trompong dance 216
  Kecak dance 216
  Kris dance 214
  Legong dance 212, 217
  Pendet dance 212, 217
  Rejang dance 151
  Sanghyang Dedari dance 216

Sanghyang Jaran dance
Butterfly Baris dance 213
Tari Balih Balihan dance 213
Tari Bebali dance 213
Tari Oncer dance 219
Tari Wali dance 213
Topeng dance 217
Trance dance 92, 213, 214, 216
Trompong Duduk dance 216
Trompong dance 88
Danghyang Markandeya 44
Demons 36, 37, 40, 45, 74, 76, 83, 113, 214, 233, 234, 235
Dencarik 130
Denpasar 57-62, 83, 87, 95, 113, 120, 125, 229
An-Nur Masjid, mosque 59
Bali Museum 61
Batara Guru Statue 61
Gereja Katolik St. Joseph 62
Jalan Diponegoro 59, 62
Kereneng-Bemo-Terminal 62
Kumbasari Shopping Centre 61
Pasar Badung, market 61
Pasar Malam 61
Pekambingan market 62
Pemecutan Palace Hotel 62
Puputan Square 60, 61, 62
Pura Jagatnata, temple 61
Pura Kesiman, temple 62
Pura Maospahit, temple 62
Pura Pemecutan, temple 57, 62
Rajas' Palace 62
Raya Masjid, Mosque 59
State College of Dance 60
Werdi Budaya Art Center 60, 62
Desa Anyar 189, 190
Dewa Anak Agung Manggis, Raja 96
Dewi Danu, sea-goddess 70, 133, 134
Dewi Lakshmi, goddess 40
Dewi Sri, rice-goddess 36, 45, 69, 74, 83, 86, 130, 152
Dewi Uma, goddess 40
Dharma 39
Di Made, Raja 91
Dlodbrawah 116
Dongson culture 21, 99
Drake, Sir Francis 24
Dukuh 73
Durga, goddess of death 34, 40, 98, 103, 214
Dutch 24, 25, 26, 27, 28, 44, 59, 60, 62, 87, 88, 96, 115, 125, 128, 131, 146, 147, 155, 166, 168, 181, 183, 189, 235

E

Economy, Bali and Lombok 19
Ekas 201

Etiquette in Bali 49-51
Etiquette in Lombok 173

F

Fauna of Bali 119
Fauna, Bali and Lombok 18
Festivals
Festivals, Bali 44-48
Festivals, Lombok 171-172
Kuningan Festival 208
Nyale Festival 172, 200
Odalan Festival 44, 45,152
Pujawali Festival 171
Usaba Festival 76
Flora, Bali and Lombok **16-17**
Flores 165

G

Gamelan 35, 45, 60, 92, 102, 107, 116, 147, 152, 155, 214, 216, 218, 219, **220-222**, 238
Gastronomy 62, **208-211**
Gelgel 24, 143, 147, 148, 165
Mosque 148
Pura Dasar, temple 148
Pura Nataran Jero Agung, temple 148
Geography, Bali and Lombok **15-16**
Gianyar 96-97
Gianyar, Regency 83, **91-106**
Buddhist temple 97
Pura Dalem of Sidan, temple 97
Pura Puseh Sidan, temple 97
Gili Air, island 187-188
Gili Gede, island 198
Gilimanuk 113, 114, 119, 120
Gili Meno, island 187, 188
Gili Nanggu, island 198
Gili Pentangan, island 194
Gili Sulat, island 194
Gili Terawangan, island 187, **188-189**
Gitgit 128
Goa Gajah, caves 23, 98
Goa Lawah, caves 18, 143, 149
Gods 31, 37, 38, 40, 42, 43, 57, 213, 226
Gondang 189
Grupuk 201
Gumicik 92
Gunung Abang, mountain 134
Gunung Agung, volcano 15, 31, 38, 44, 143, 151, 152, **153-154**, 184, 186, 197
Gunung Baru, volcano 192
Gunung Batukau, volcano 83, 90, 91
Gunung Batur, volcano 83, 104, 106, 131, **133-136**

Gunung Catur, volcano 57, 83, 133
Gunung Ingas, mountain 69
Gunung Kawi, mountain 23, 105
Gunung Lesong, mountain 132
Gunung Pengson, mountain 171, 197, 198
Gunung Piring, mountain 165
Gunung Rinjani, volcano 16, 167, 170, 171, 183, 184, 188, 189, **190-194**, 195, 197
Gunung Seraya, volcanic massif 143, 157
Gunung Tapak, mountain 132
Gusti Ketut Jilantik, prince 26

H

Hanuman, ape-god 87, 217, 224
Hatta, Mohammed 29
Hayam Wuruk, King 197
Hinduism 21, 22, 24, 38, 39, 40, 41, 60, 106, 128, 137, 165, 169, 171
History and Culture, Bali **21-29**
History and Culture, Lombok **165-173**

I

Ibn Battuta 128
I Gusti Nyoman Lempad, artist 227
Ikat 61, 96, 148, 151, 154, **230-232**
Double-Ikat 230, 231, 232
Endek 230
Geringsing 231, 232
Kain 232
Kain Prada 230
Kamben Lembaran 232
Kamben Sarung 232
Songket 230
Tenganan Pageringsingan 231
I Ketut Marya, dancer 88, 215, 216
I Made Budi, artist 95
Independence, Indonesian 29, 44, 125, 155, 166, 235
India 22, 32, 33, 38, 42, 43, 225
Indra, god 106, 150, 151
I Ngedon, artist 94
I Patera, artist 94
Irrigation 35, 36, 88, 165, 184
Iseh 154
Islam 24, 44, 59, 73, 113, 117, 128, 165, 169, 170, 173, 185

J

Jagaraga 26, 27, 131
Jangkok, river 177

Japanese 29, 72, 87, 128, 166, 188
Jatiluwih 91
Java 15, 21, 22, 24, 25, 39, 70, 113, 114, 115, 125, 134, 165, 170, 179
Java Man 21
Jembrana, province **113-118**
Jimbaran 68
  Pura Ulun Siwi, temple 69
  Teluk Jimbaran, beach 69
Jumpai 148
Jungut Batu 74, 75

K

Kalibukbuk 129
Kali, goddess 40
Kali Putih 193
Kamasan, artists' village 147, 228, 229
Kapal 83
  Pura Puseh, temple 83
  Pura Sada, temple 85
Kap Ngis 125
Karangasem, town 27, 96, 166
Karangasem, Regency 143, 148, 151, 155
Karangasem Dynasty 181, 184
Karma Pala 40
Kauravas 224, 225
Kay It, painter 88
Kebon Iwa, demon 96
Kediri 90, 199
Kedisan 136
Keliki 104
Kemenuh 96, 228
Keramas 96
Ketapang 198
Kintamani 134
Klating Beach 89
Klotok Beach 148
Klungkung 24, 27, 28, 96, **143-145**, 148, 228, 229
  Bale Kambang, pavilion 147
  Kerta Gosa, law-courts 146, 147, 226
  Market 146
  Pemadal Agung, gate 147
  Taman Gili 146
Klungkung, Regency 143, 149
Koranji Bangsal 198
Kotaraja 195
Krakas 189
Krambitan, artists' village **88-89**
Kris 25, 28, 61, 180, 214, 229
Krishna, god 99, 225
Ksatriya caste 85
Kubutambahan 131
Kusamba 74, 75, 143, 149
Kuta (Bali) 38, 49, 57, 59, **62-68**, 125, 229

Jalan Pantai Kuta 66, 67, 68
Pasar Senggol Night Market 67
Poppies Lane 67
Kuta (Lombok) 172, 196, 199, 200, 201
Kutri 23

L

Labuhan Haji 195
Labuhan Lahang 120
Labuhan Lembar 177, 198
Labuhan Lombok 194, 195
Labuhan Pandan 194
Labuhan Poh 198
Lange, Mads 26, 27
Lebih 96, 97
Legian 65-68
  Jalan Legian 65, 66, 68
  New Goa 67
Le Mayeur, Adrien Jean 72
Lembongan, island **74-75**, 143
  Lembongan, Hindu village 75
  Sea-temple 75
  Rumah Goa, cave-house 75
Lendang Bajur 187
Lingsar 169, 171, **184-185**
  Double temple 184
  Kemaliq Lingsar 184
  Pura Gaduh 184
Lombok 165-239
Lombok, northern **189-194**
Lombok, eastern **194-196**
Lombok, southern **196-201**
Lombok, western 165, **177-185**
Lombok Strait 15, 18, 165
Lovina Beach 129-130
Loyok 195, 196
Lukluk 83

M

Madura 59
Mahabharata 41, 99, 146, 152, 213, 223, 224
Majapahit Empire 23, 24, 100, 143, 150, 165, 197, 220
Majapahit style 85, 92
Manggis 155
Mangkung 199
Mangsit, bay 187
Marga 87
Mas 228, 229
Masbagik 195
Mas, wood-carvers' village 95
Masks 35, 61, 69, 92, 94, 95, 101, 180, 217, 227, 228, 229
Mataram 165, 166, 167, 168, 177, **179-180**, 210
  Provincial Museum 180
  Selaparang, airport 177
Mataram, Javanese empire 23

Mawun 200, 201
McPhee, Colin 220
Mead, Margaret 72
Medahan 96
Medas 194
Medewi 118
Megaliths 21, 165
Mendoyo 117, 118
Mengwi 85, 87
  Bale Murdha, pavilion 86
  Bale Pawedan, pavilion 86
  Pura Taman Ayun, temple 85-86
Mengwi Dynasty 69
Meninting 187
Menjangan Island 119
Mesigit 73
Military Coup of 1965 26
Mohammed, Prophet 169
Moslems 59, 75, 218
Mujur 201
Muncan 154
Munduk 132
Muntik, Cape 157
Music 117, 151, 215
  Arja, folk-opera 213
  Gangsa, musical instrument 221, 223
  Gender, metallophone 223
  Gongs 222
  Kendang, drum 222
  Kotekan 221
  Panji-cycle 213, 219
  Polos 221
  Rebab, stringed instrument 220
  Riyong, musical instrument 222
  Sangsih 221
  Slendro system 220
  Trompong, musical instrument 222
Music of Lombok 218-219

N

Narmada 171, **183-184**, 238
  Pura Kalasa, temple 171, 183
  Summer palace 183
Negara 115-117, 120
  Heroes' Cemetery 115
  Loloan Timur 116
  Pengambengan, fishing-port 116
  White Mosque 115
New Order, Policy of the 29
Ngis 157
Ngurah Rai, airport 71, 125
Nusa Dua 57, 68, 69, 71, 74, 125
Nusa Penida, island 15, 18, 72, 74, **75-76**, 143, 149
  Batukandik 76
  Batumadeg 76
  Bukit Mundi, mountain 75
  Goa Karangsari, caves 76
  Karang 76

Mentigi, harbour 76
Pura Batu Medau, temple 76
Pura Dalem Penataran Ped, temple 75
Sampalan, chief town 76
Sebuluh 76
Suwana 76
Toyapakeh, market town 75
Nusa Tenggara Barat, Regency 16, 166, 179, 197
Nyitdah 90

O

Obel-Obel 194
Opium 17, 133

P

Padangbai 149, 177
Padanggaji 154
Padang-Padang 71
Pagutan 197
Pakerisan, river 97, 105, 106
Palasari 115
Pamesan 90
Pandavas 224, 225
Pasut Beach 89
Patu Jangke 199
Pecatu 69
Pegambur 200
Pejatan 229
Pejeng 23, **99-100**
  Archaeological Museum 100
  Mooon of Pejeng 99
  Penataran Sasih, temple 21
  Pura Kebo Edan, temple 100
  Pura Penataran Sasih, temple 100
  Pura Pusering Jagat, temple 100
Pekutatan 118
Pelangan 198
Peliatan 100, 102, 103, 220
Pemaron 129
Pemenang 187, 189
Penarukan 88
Penelokan 97, 104, 105, 133, 134, 135
Pengantap 199
Pengastulan 118, 132
Penggragoan 113
Penujak 200
Penulisan 134
Perisean see Stick-fighting
Pesugulan 193, 195
Petulu 18, 104
Pisang 104
Pomotong 195
Prambanan 22
Prapat Agung, peninsula 119, 120, 125
Praya 199
Priests 41-42

Pringgabaya 195
Ptolemy, Claudius 21
Pujung 104
Pulau Kambing, island 149
Pulau Menjangan, island 119
Punggang 91
Pupuan 118
Puputan, ritual suicide 60
Pura Beji, temple 130, 131
Pura Dalem, temple 131
Pura Gede Perancak, temple 117
Pura Lempuyan, temple 157
Pura Luhur Batukau, temple 90, 91
Pura Meduwe Karang, temple 131
Pura Panarajon, hill temple 134
Pura Pucak, temple 133
Pura Rambut Siwi, temple 117, 118
Pura Sakenan, temple 74
Pura Tegeh Koripan, mountain temple 134, 135
Pura Ulun Siwi, temple 85
Purajati 135
Putung 149, 155
Puyung 199, 238

R

Raffles, Sir Stamford 25
Rajas 25, 27, 57, 59, 68, 88, 92, 125, 132, 137, 143, 148, 152, 155, 184, 213, 226, 228
Ramadan 169, 170, 173, 184
Ramayana 22, 31, 40, 41, 60, 83, 87, 217, 223
Rangda, witch 92, 98, 104, 214
Rangdu 132
Rare Kumara, god 46, 47
Rain-forest 16, 17, 21, 133, 189, 191, 193, 194, 196
Reincarnation 40
Religion of Bali 38-45
Religion of Lombok 169-170
Rice-growing 17, 19, 31, 35, 36, 49, 57, 100
  Paddy-field cultivation 19, 21, 75, 88, 125, 156
  Dry cultivation 19, 125
Rendang 151, 154
Rituals 31, 32, 35, 36, 38, 41, **44-45**, 46, 47, 48, 50, 97, 106, 116, 136, 137, 229, 235
Roti, island 15
Rungkang 195

S

Sacrificial gifts 36, 38, 41, 42, 44, 45, 72, 85, 99, 131, 134, 136, 183, 217

Sade/Rambitan 169, 200
Sakah 95
Sakti 104
Salt-panning 19, 68, 149, 188
Sampalan 148
Sangeh 87
  Bukit Sari, temple 87
  Monkey Forest 87
Sanghyang Widhi Wasa 39, 40
Sangsit 130
Sanskrit 22, 223
Sanur 57, 68, **71-73**, 125, 149, 229
  Beach Market 73
  Jalan Tanjung Sari 73
  Museum Le Mayeur 72
  Pura Dalem Kedewatan, temple 72
Saraswati, goddess of wisdom 40
Sarong 45, 49, 50, 62, 75, 92, 96, 128, 146, 200, 216, 232, 239
Sasak 165, 166, 167, 168, 171, 172, 177, 188, 199, 200, 201, 218
Sawan 131
Sea-turtles 73, 199
Sebali 104
Sebatu 104, 228
Sebudi 154
Segara Anak, crater-lake 171, 192
Sekotong 198
Selat 154
Selat Badung, narrows 74
Selong 195
Sembalun Bumbung 193
Sembalun, plateau 193, 195
Sembalun Lawang 193
Sembiran 21, 131, 132
Sempidi 83
Senaru 190, 194
Sendang Gila 190
Senggigi 19, 167, 177, **185-187**
  Batu Bolong, temple 186
  Batu Layar, shrine 186
  Moslem cemetery 186
Sengkol 200
Sepi 165, 198
Serangan, island **73-74**
Seririt 113, 118, 119
Sesaot 184
Seseh 65
Sesong 170
Shadow-plays 31, 45, 88, 94
Shiva-Bhairava cult 100
Shiva, god 40, 61, 86, 91, 98, 118, 131, 133, 134, 152, 181
Sibetan 155
Sidemen 154, 187
Silversmiths 229
Silung Blanak 199
Sindok, King 22, 23
Singapadu 92, 229

Singaraja 26, 83, 119, **125-129**, 130, 131
  Old Port 125
  Chinese cemetery 128
  Chinese temple 128
  Gedong Kertya, library 128
  Colonial Residence 128
  Masjid Agung, mosque 128
  Pasar Anyar, market quarter 128
  Pasar Banyusari, market 128
  Puri Kawan, Rajas' palace 128
  Shiva temple 128
Sira 189
Smit, Arie, artist 101, 103, 228
Society, Balinese **31-37**
Society of Lombok 167-168
Songan 136
Spies, Walter 28, 62, 72, 75, 88, 94, 101, 103, 154, 216, 227, 228
Stick-fighting in Lombok 238-239
Subak association 35-36
Suharto 29, 153
Sukaraja 201
Sukarara 199
Sukarno, Ahmed 29, 72, 152
Sukawana 134
Sukawati 92, 229
  Art Center 94
  Pura Pelinggih Sunya Loka 94
  Pura Penataran Agung, temple 92
Sulawesi 75, 115, 143, 165, 166, 179
Suluban 71
Sumampan 228
Sumbawa, island 179, 15, 22, 24, 165
Sumberkerta 119
Suranadi 184
Surya, sun-god 40, 41, 131
Suwung 73
Sweta 182-183

T

Tabanan 88
  Gedong Marya, town-hall 88
  Puri Tabanan, temple 88
  Subak Museum 88
Tabanan, Regency 83, **88-91**
Taman Nasional Bali Barat see West Bali National Park
Tamblingan 132
Tamblingan, Lake 132
Tampaksiring 105
Tanahlot 65, **89-90**
Tangkas 147
Tanjung 169, 189
Tanjung Aan 201
Tanjung Benoa 71
Tanjung Luar 201
Tanjung Ringgit 201

Dance 31, 41, 45, 60, 70, 88, 96, 100, 101, 229
  Arja-dance 212
  Baris-dance213
  Barong-Ladung-dance 75
  Batek-Baris-dance 218
  Gambuh-dance 94, 214
  Gandrung-dance 218, 219
  Gumbuh-dance 154
  Jauk, mask-dance 214
  Joged-dance215
  Kebyar-Duduk-dance 212, 215
  Kebyar-Legong-dance 215
  Kebyar-Trompong-dance 216
  Kecak-dance 216
  Kris-dance 214
  Legong-dance 212, 217
  Pendet-dance 212, 217
  Rejang-dance 151
  Sanghyang-Dedaridance 216
  Sanghyan-Jaran-dance 216
  Butterfly-Baris 213
  Dances, Balinese 212-217
  Dance in Lombok 218-219
  Tari-Balih-Balihan-dance 213
  Tari-Bebali-dance 213
  Tari-Oncer-dance 219
  Tari-Wali-dance 213
  Topeng-dance217
  Trance-dance 92, 213, 214, 216
  Trompong-Duduk-dance 216
  Trompong-dance 88
Taun 198
Tegalalang 104
Tegalbesar 91, 96
Tegalcangkring 116
Tegaltamu 92
Tegenungan, waterfall 96
Tejakula 132
Temkus 129
Temples 33, 34, 38, **42-43**, 44
Temukus 129
Tenganan 143, **149-150**, 150, 231, 232
Terima Bay 120
Tetebatu 195, 196
Tihingan 147
Tiingan 133
Tirta Empul, springs 106
Tirthagangga, royal baths 143, 156, 157
Tourism 19, 31, 33, 57, 65, 68, 71, 72, 75, 119, 167, 171, 177, 185, 187, 200, 228
Toya Bungkah 135, 136
Trunyan 136, 137
Tulamben 157

U

Ubud 65, 88, 92, 95, 97, 171, 227, 228
  Museum Neka 103

  Pura Gunung Lebah, temple 101
  Puri Lukisan, palace 102
  Saraswati Temple 100, 101
Ubud, region **100-105**
  Monkey Forest 103, 104
  Bird Sanctuary 104
  Campuan 100, 103, 104
  Klatikuning 104
  Nyuhkuning, wood-carvers' village 104
  Penestanan 100, 101, 104
  Pengosekan 100, 102
  Pura Dalem Agung Padang Tegal 103
  Teges 102
  Yeh Ayung, gorge104
Ubung 83, 229
Udayana II, King 23, 98, 135
Udayana University 68, 69
Ujung 156
Ulu Watu 69
Ungasan 69
Underworld 31, 40, 104
Upanishads 41
USA 29, 87

V

Vedas 41
Vishnu, god 40, 61, 86, 87, 133, 134, 152, 181, 185
Village communities 220, 34, 48, 59
Volcanic activity, Bali and Lombok 16

W

Wallace, Sir Alfred Russell 18
Wanasari 90
Wangayagede 90
Wayang 107
Wayang Kulit, shadow-plays 213, **223-225**, 229
Wayang style 94, 103, 146
Weddings, Balinese 47
West Bali National Park 18, 113, 115, **119-120**, 125
Wetu-Telu, religion 169, 170, 171, 184, 185, 186, 190, 200, 218
White Springs 192
Widow-burning 27, 85
World War, First 29
World War, Second 21, 29, 61, 72, 125, 155, 166, 188

Y

Yehembang 118
Yehpanas 90
Yehpulu 99